Off the Cuff
The Lee Briers Autobiography

Lee Briers with Mike Appleton

Off the Cuff
The Lee Briers Autobiography

Lee Briers with Mike Appleton

Vertical Editions
www.verticaleditions.com

First published in the United Kingdom in 2013 by Vertical Editions, Unit 4a, Snaygill Industrial Estate, Skipton, North Yorkshire BD23 2QR

www.verticaleditions.com

ISBN 978-1-904091-78-3

A CIP catalogue record for this book is available from the British Library

Cover design by HBA, York

Printed and bound by Jellyfish Print, Hampshire

'Rugby League's Lionel Messi'

Graeme Swann

For all of my family, especially Vicky, Sophie and Reece

Contents

Thank You

Lee:

I would like to thank my mum and dad for giving me everything and making me the person I am today. Without you I would never have made a success out of my life and I am humbled by your support.

My brothers and sisters: Stephen, Julie, David and Brian, thank you for being the best siblings I could have ever ask for.

Vicky, you've put up with me for the last 17 years whilst I have been playing rugby and I am truly grateful. You have been the rock behind our family and you have done a fantastic job in raising Sophie and Reece, our two awesome kids. I am so very proud of you all. Here's to the next chapter of our lives together.

And finally, I'd like to thank Mike Appleton for his patience, understanding and being a real friend throughout the writing of this book.

Mike:

Helping a rugby league superstar write a book is no mean feat. Lee had to be patient with me, like I was with him at times, and I really believe we will remain friends for life as a result. Thank you Lee for accepting me into your home and giving me access to so much of your life. It's a cliché but I felt your highs and lows too.

On behalf of Lee I would also like to thank Vicky Hall, Clive Griffiths, Bernard Platt, Neil Dowson at the Wolves, Alan Hunte, Ian Lovell for his pictures of Lee in Wales' kit, Rachel Arnett, Chris Baron, Tony Smith, Simon Moran, Graeme Swann, Shaun McRae, Ste Jones at kt8 Photography, Emma Edwards,

Paul Cullen, Andy Wilson, Andrew Johns, Brian Noble, Dave Hutchinson and Karl Waddicor at Vertical Editions.

Special mention should go to Neil Ashurst at P & B Pictures, who was superb in providing most of the pictures of Lee's career. Nothing was ever too much trouble for Neil. His website is at www.pandbpictures.com

Foreword

Lee is one of the most interesting and likeable characters in our sport and one I admire a lot.

Like many people, before I met him I had a perception of what he was like and I think in life we all make judgements before we really get to know someone. The view I have now I have worked with him is certainly different than all the rumours and stories that seem to follow him around.

I have no doubt he's had some chequered times in his playing career and in his adult life. But who hasn't? I've certainly seen nothing but good, and I have really enjoyed coaching him over the last few seasons.

I know rumours get blown out of all proportion and yes, before I joined Warrington, they had affected how I felt towards him. I remember at our first meeting I said I was sure only half the things I had heard were probably true! That broke the ice.

It's true of all of us, when we get to know people they are a whole lot different to what the general consensus is.

I have got to know a very caring person; someone who would do anything for just about anyone, especially if it was for a good cause. That's the side of Lee that most people don't see, know or hear about as he's a very shy person off the field. He finds it very difficult to say no to good causes and he will go out of his way to help if he can. But of course that dedication never gets reported.

I think Vicky and his family have played a huge part in him growing up over the last few years and helped develop his increasing maturity as his playing career progressed. I was fortunate enough to come along when this has been happening and we have all benefited. And he has matured into a very good team member as a result.

Everyone admires his playing ability and the knack he has of turning it on on the big occasion. But what he now has is consistency week in week out and I think that comes down to the consistency he has off the field too. He gets the right mix of being a larrikin and a top class sports person and I'm sure he hasn't always had that balance.

It was difficult not to know about Lee before I joined the Wolves. When I joined Warrington my coaching philosophy was to put an entertaining brand of rugby on the field and with Lee in my side we hit it off. He always was a tricky player to keep an eye on because you never knew what he was going to do next. He can read a play but also act on impulse and intuition. He goes against the grain of things which I think is something to admire.

But it's also something we coaches try and stop. We take some of that spontaneity out of the game sometimes.

Alongside that attacking ability has been more consistency in his defensive efforts too. He's never been known for his tackling ability but he's worked on that side of his game and therefore helps his team-mates out more. And that is all Lee wants to do – help out the team and be successful. Because of that hard work, he's able to take more of a risk and take the chance of catching an interception or putting in a big hit … not that he does many of those of course … hits that is!

It all lends itself to the fact he's in the best form of his life.

He is also very passionate about the Wolves and has been loyal to the club for the majority of his career. He wears his heart on his sleeve and does a lot for the club both on and off the field.

And that clearly manifests in how he plays.

He is passionate about his sport too. Since I have worked with him, he is one of the players who most frequently comes into my office for good reasons – not bad ones – and that may have changed as his career has gone on! He wants to understand why things are done and I have no doubt he has an eye on a coaching career after he retires. He has ambition and I'm sure he will make a great fist of it. He wants to learn about the sport and educate himself on how he can get wiser, smarter and more efficient at what he does. They are all the attributes needed to be a successful coach.

He also has that personality which means people will take on what he says. He wants to understand the game and get better and that is another aspect I wouldn't have expected before we were joined at the Wolves.

Aside from this there is something else I find even more important. He is good fun to have around. He likes to have a laugh and take the mickey out of his team-mates but he doesn't mind it happening to him. He can laugh at himself and others. That's important at a club where team spirit is vital. He enjoys what he is doing and the company of those around him.

That bond has meant we've had a certain amount of success and I feel we are still on that journey. We have a lot of improvement in us as a club and a team.

I was pleased for Lee when we won trophies. He'd competed exceptionally well at times and it was nice for him and the others who had been here for a while to experience those big moments.

And at Wembley he's done just that, turning up with massive performances and winning the Lance Todd Trophy in 2010. It's shown he can compete week in week out and do it on the big stage. When he retires he can look back and be very proud in knowing he has contributed to those occasions.

I know he is hoping to have a few more too before he hangs up his boots. If he doesn't get the chance to do that then he can look back on those big moments and what he has done for his team-mates and his club.

Lee's focus to improve on his game has given him the consistency to be talked in the same circles as the usual Man of Steel candidates. And if you look at the last few seasons as a whole he wouldn't have been far off. He's played well, and competed at the highest level.

How? He's a class act, of course. But that desire to keep on going and not give in to 'age' has a big say. Sometimes we put the age barrier on people and that restricts them moving forward. But he is not showing that. It's a lot to do with his attitude towards training – even that's improved! He would be the first to admit he isn't the greatest trainer but even he is willing to improve in that area and he has shown that on the field.

It's fair to say if we had Great Britain now, in the last few years, it would have been difficult to keep him out. It is well documented he has only one cap and many people think he should have had more.

It's not up to me to give reasons why he wasn't picked. Perhaps it was something to do with his reputation, his lifestyle and his consistency too. All I can say is that may or may not have been the perception of him at that time.

There were facets in his game that were world class but there were some that weren't as strong. People were picked ahead of him because perhaps that was needed at the time. I don't think it was a case of people not liking him. He probably had some deficiencies which let him down and he has now managed to improve those things. He has developed those areas of weakness to a standard and more recently he would have been hard to keep out based on his overall game.

But I don't think Lee would want us to feel sorry for him.

As for the future, I'm sure Lee will play until his body says he can't and it's not saying that at present; it is saying he can keep going and improving. Until then – and it does happen to every athlete – he will continue. He hasn't put a time on it and that is important. If you say one more year will do you, you are usually right. No boundaries and who knows?

What's important is he's taking care of himself better than he has done in the past so who knows how long he can go for?

Finally, I'm not a great story teller but as I have said he is one of the game's true characters. Some of what he contributes … well, his after match celebrations within the sacred sanctity of our dressing room are a sight to behold. Put it this way, it doesn't involve the wearing of much kit. He'll be leading the club song and putting aside all his inhibitions to contribute to his team and the enjoyment of the players around him.

It typifies what he is about; the whole heartedness of getting behind your mates and not worrying if you have the body of an Adonis … or a 40-year-old man. He is able to put that aside and make us all laugh.

That is a great ability to have and it makes him a good bloke, good father, great player and a good friend.

Tony Smith, Head Coach, Warrington Wolves.

The Real Lee Briers?

I've known Lee since he was at Saints and he's still the same person I met all those years ago in August 1996.

He's grown up a lot though and isn't the young kid who used to go out after every game and spend all his time at the Saints club. Nowadays, he'd rather go home and lie on the couch. I don't think he has changed massively though.

When he's lost a match he's awful. He's moody and just wants to be left alone. If it has been on the TV he will avoid it at all costs, so the best thing to do is let him get on with it. If he's won one, he is a different person which you would expect really.

You'll read about a number of things in this book that made Lee look at himself and become the player he is today. But probably the single thing that changed him the most was in 2006 when we split up. I call it his midlife crisis and I know he had a hard time in the four months we weren't together. But things change; we got back together and have been as strong ever since.

On the field 2006 was a massive season for him and he went on tour with GB at the end of it. And it was during that tour he called me and we decided to give it another go. I know in this book he says I saved him and perhaps I did.

So how did we meet? He'll probably tell you something different but he really did woo me! Lee came over to Hull for a birthday night out with some friends. We chatted a lot and he followed me everywhere. I would go to the toilet and he would be stood outside waiting for me and it went from there. Sorry Lee, I had to tell them! At first he was probably more for me than I was for him. But after time we got to know each other better and we'd be speaking on the phone a lot. He didn't have a phone at home so he would go to a neighbour's house to call me.

Lee ended up playing 'on loan' at Carcassonne and his coach at Saints, Nick Halafihi, was going out there with his family to see how he and a couple of other players were getting on. Lee called me and said he'd booked me a flight to go out with Nick. I only meant to go for a couple of days but I ended up being there for three months! Living with four lads in a flat at 18 was interesting. I came back at Christmas and after a few weeks didn't go back to Hull. Lee asked his dad if I could move in and we did. His folks didn't know me from Adam but they said I could stay and that was that. They became like a second mum and dad to me and I'll never forget that. I was over in St Helens away from my family and they looked after me.

I think Sophie was conceived when I was in France and that was pretty hard too. He was only on about thirty quid a week with the Saints Academy and we were very young. But it made us stronger, although Sophie's birth was anything but straightforward as it came on a Mad Monday weekend. You'll read about the eventful birth of Sophie later in this book! We lived with his folks until Sophie was one and then we got our own place. Lee would still go out with his non rugby mates and I suppose, although we had a kid, we were kids too, and he still wanted to do the things his mates did.

I was attracted to him because he was a nice lad. I really don't know how we ended up together – it just happened. When we were just getting started he would get the train up to Hull to see me but my mum wouldn't let us sleep together. He would be in my bed and I would be in with my mum! I suppose we had a strange relationship as there was distance at first and then when I was heavily pregnant with Sophie he was in Australia with Warrington for the World Club Championship. That continues now of course and in 2012 he went over there for three weeks and that was hard. You can cope with one week but three … I suppose there are twenty other girls with kids too and that doesn't make you feel as bad. We are all going through it. And then he loses his phone on these trips – a lot!

I can tell you there's no 'Wag' lifestyle. It's harder than living with someone who has a nine-to-five job because the life of a rugby league player is very irregular. They put in many hours, evenings and weekends and it can be tough. On the flipside Lee has been able to play at Wembley and that was something he really wanted to do before his career ended. It has been nice for us all to be a part of and both families have been there to join in the celebrations. It's been very special.

By the way, Lee is lazy too and has never cooked or cleaned for himself. I reckon his mum spoiled him loads when he was a kid. But the way I see it Lee goes out and trains, plays and pays the bills, so the least I can do is keep a nice house and do things like that. I'd rather clean up myself anyway that way I know where everything is.

You'll see a pic of his kit cupboard in this book … this is why I clean up because that's his attempt at it.

He loves his family and will do anything for us. He coaches Reece and he's so hard on him sometimes. In fact, he's the same as my dad was with my brother Craig. If Reece misses a tackle Lee will shout: 'You miss that again and you're off.' But when he comes off the field he will be 'you've played great, you only did a couple of things wrong.' He wants the best for him and is very much the protective dad. I see that with Sophie every day. Soph is a typical teenager and I know Lee struggles with her attitude sometimes. He'll be constantly phoning her to see where she is and checking up to see if she is ok. But that's because he only wants the best for his kids. I think he forgets when he was a kid he'd walk to school and roam the streets.

Rugby is a massive part of my life and was before I met Lee. Everyone in my family is involved and Craig still plays for Hull KR. Being with Lee is an extension of all that but I have to confess I don't know much about the sport or its rules. It's brought our families together and Lee and Craig are like brothers. They are always talking together and have a strong bond. My dad played for Great Britain and I think Lee looks up to him too. I know they have spoken a lot about their rugby league experiences.

He's always involved me in all stages of his career and when he's been given the chance to move clubs has always spoken to me first. I would never stop him moving to a club but he has always discussed any offers with me. His goal was to always finish his career at Warrington and that is important. I would never say he shouldn't join a club because I wouldn't want to go. If he decided he wanted to then I would back him all the way.

It's scary to think after we've been together for all these years his playing career will shortly be coming to an end. It will be a big change and I've never really thought about the security of it all. He's had a testimonial and invested some of that in property but no doubt we'll be thinking about that as the next season approaches. It's been our life and the kids have never known him do anything different. Beyond that it will be a hard transition for us all.

We know he wants to coach and he has done his badges. Tony Smith has also involved him in the under-19s too. I think he will do well as a coach as he has it upstairs. The game is in his head and he knows what he is doing. The kids will always come to him with their homework so it should be an easy transition to coaching!

Lee has a heart of gold and is fun to be around. I just think he is the type of guy who will do anything for anyone. He is a proper family man and we all love him loads. We wouldn't be without him.

I hope you all enjoy his story because it has been a massive part of my, Sophie and Reece's lives.

Vicky Hall, Lee's Partner

Introduction

I know the perception of me.

I had a meeting with Tony Smith when he took over the Warrington Wolves coaching job and he spelled it out. To him I was someone who liked a drink and who didn't take rugby league too seriously. Funny thing was; people have had that perception of me since I started at Warrington in 1997.

Is it right or is it wrong? Well, I leave that to you. I think I have proven it isn't.

Don't get me wrong, I like a drink as do most people, but I do it at the right time and for the right reasons. But it doesn't define who I am.

The real Lee Briers is a family man. I have a great missus and two kids and they are my life. Apart from those people and my close family and friends then quite frankly I couldn't give a shit.

I am strong minded.

A perception is a perception and it is not always right. I like a laugh and a joke with the best of them … but I can be serious when I want to be.

On the field I have always played hard and to the best of my ability. I was told at an early age that half-backs have to be a little cheeky. So in my earlier days I nagged the refs and did get on their cases. I had fun with them and that gave people the perception that I was arguing and complaining. These days I want the crowd to see I am chatting to the ref and I will have my hands up. But nine times out of ten I will have both hands in the air and be saying something totally different. I did that with Ste Ganson all the time.

It got the crowd going and he always saw the funny side.

I am in the entertainment business after all and like all

good half-backs I like to be an entertainer. I like the craic with the officials, but I have calmed down since Tony has been in charge. With referees though, if you have a laugh with them you can earn more respect – but you shouldn't overstep the mark.

I was born in St Helens and will always be a St Helens lad; yet I consider myself an honorary Warringtonian. I was bitter with Saints when I left, who wouldn't be? All my life I was a supporter of the club and used to climb over the gates with my dad to get in. I never paid a penny to watch so I suppose I got one over them in one way.

To play for Saints was my dream and to leave in the way I did, and not even being in the travelling party to go down to the Challenge Cup Final at Wembley in 1997, hurt. I was bitter and twisted about it for a long time.

If it didn't hurt, then what is the point of playing this sport? You have to have passion for rugby league to be successful. I like a challenge and I'm still very competitive. Leaving was just that – a real challenge. Saints have won a lot of things since I left and I could be sat here today wondering what if. But I'm not. I made the right choice for myself and my family. And over the past few seasons I have certainly seen the fruits of that move.

I know people felt I could have stayed at Knowsley Road because I was young and I could have bided my time. But I was mistreated there and was abused really. They offered me a contract to stay in 1997 but it wasn't much at all, especially considering Super League was bringing new money into the sport. Warrington came in for me and showed interest. The cash was good and they offered me the chance to play first team rugby league. In the end I couldn't turn it down ... and I don't regret making the move.

I am not motivated by money and never will be. I'd just started a new family, had my first daughter and to set my family off on the right course meant the world to me to be able to do.

There's no point in looking back on things and having regrets. Life is too short. I found that out the hard way when my brother died. There's no point moving through life with ifs and buts and the last few years have taught me just that.

Warrington is my home and I am proud to have played for the club. I have had a few offers to move but have always ended up back at the Wolves. I spoke to Ian Millward in 2003 and a deal was all but done – yet Saints signed Jason Hooper who went on to be a great signing for the club and won trophies with them.

I cried when that deal went south – the second time I shed tears for the Saints after 1997. I wouldn't cry for them again.

In 2001, I was very close to going to rugby union and Pontypridd but the deal didn't seem right. It was triple the money I was on at Warrington and that was tempting. But I had just been picked for Great Britain and I thought my future lay in rugby league. Of course, that wasn't to be either – but neither was Pontypridd as they folded the season after. Lucky!

A couple of years back I was on the verge of joining Barrow. I spoke to their chairman about the club and what would happen but it wasn't quite right for both parties in the end. I also had a conversation with Kevin Walters at Catalans in 2009 and the money was very good … as was the tax regime! But I opted to stay.

I love Warrington and I love the fans. You have to be 100 per cent to move and I wasn't.

Rugby league has given me everything and made me the person I am today. From when I was at school all I wanted to do was play the game. I enjoyed PE and that was all. I left school and worked on a farm as a carrot picker. Let's be honest, I wouldn't have progressed much further in that career and as I'm not the cleverest person, finding a job would have been difficult.

I have travelled the world and met the best people. I have gained new friends, played with the best players and got paid for something I love doing. Most people would kill for that. I met my partner Vicky through the sport as well as her mum, dad, stepmum, brother, granddad and nanna … they are all fantastic people.

Quite simply, without rugby league I would have been in jail … or on the road to that.

The future scares me as you never know what is around the corner. It is pointless looking in the past. I am more prepared for the future than I ever was but I take each day as it comes and never ever take my eye off the ball. I hope, well I know, the future will be bright for my kids and if that is the case I will be a happy Lee Briers.

After playing? I'm more prepared for that too. I want to coach and that is what I am now working towards. I know there aren't too many opportunities and I may have to drop down a level and I am realistic about that. I will have to start over again and learn a new path and career. But I will cross that bridge when it comes to it.

Would I do things differently if I had it all over again? Of course I would. Rugby can be a very short career if you get injured. All I wanted to do was play and I never thought about it all ending with a nasty tackle or something similar.

At Warrington we have a player welfare manager who as a player is aware of what can happen on both sides of the fence. He opens a lot of doors for players with college courses and other pathways and that is exactly what all clubs should be doing for their players.

I remember Mark Forster saying to me after I signed that I should save money and buy property. I kept saying I would be ok, I'd do it next year, then the year after that and so on. After a few years I realised I hadn't and that came as a shock. I say that to the young kids now – look after your money as it will look after your family when it is over.

I am the last of the old generation who worked before I signed a professional contract so I knew the real value of money. The kids come straight in now and haven't had that experience of doing a nine to five job. That's something they have to consider so if it does come to an end, they know what may lie ahead.

Some don't realise how lucky they are. When I was struggling for form I went and helped a mate on a building site. It was the real dose of reality I needed. I will use those experiences in my coaching, and hopefully because I have been there it will help.

A few years ago people wouldn't have expected a club like Warrington to be doing things like this. The perception was we were a party club. I think that was because we hadn't won anything for a while and when we did win a game, we went out and hammered it.

For me, my week finished on a Sunday. Most people's ended on a Friday and they went out and had a drink. We couldn't do that until Sunday and if I felt I'd earned a drink then I would go and have one. I would then start my week again on Monday. I know we were no different to other clubs – but they were winning trophies and perhaps earned the beers a little bit more.

Now we're picking up silverware things don't get said as much.

I waited a while to pick up a trophy and it meant the world to me. No one gave us a chance in 2009 as we were awful in Super League. But we prepared so well for the game against Huddersfield that we just knew we would win. And to do it in the style we did was outstanding.

They say winning becomes a habit and we repeated it the year after. You read about the Sinfields, Sculthorpes and Longs of this world saying you get hungrier with the more success you have – that is true. You want more of it because you just can't replicate the feeling of putting in so much effort to win something. You can't buy it.

Yes, I waited a long time … it made me savour it more. I tell the young kids to enjoy it and don't let the moment pass as you don't know when it will come around again.

So here's my story … I hope it was worth the wait.

1

Early Days

What do you want to hear? I was a snotty kid from St Helens who caused bedlam all over the town. Sorry, can't help you there … well, not yet at least. It was pretty hard growing up as the youngest of five children and I had to be a cheeky little git to survive. I was by far and away the youngest too as the next one was about 14 years older than me. My oldest brother recently went past 50 so you get the picture.

I had three brothers and one sister but labelling them as 'siblings' would be wrong. They were more like guardians really. They all used to knock about with each other because they were pretty close in age and then I came along to bugger up their fun on June 14, 1978.

I wasn't planned – I think my mum and dad were trying out condoms and one probably split – and although my 'guardians' looked after me they also made sure I suffered as much as possible. They picked on me a lot and as a result I took great pleasure in annoying them. It made me grow up and toughened me up. I remember once being a real nuisance and my sister Julie came in with my brothers, held me down and put a pillow over my head. I think they were trying to frighten me a little! I still remember those days really well and now it's in print.

I wouldn't say we were a close knit family though, we were

close in some ways but I know families who are a lot closer than ours. That's not to say we don't love each other, we do in our own way and would do anything we could for one another.

We lived in Peet Avenue, a stone's throw away from Knowsley Road, or what is left of it now. My folks still live there. Being close to the ground gave me my love of rugby and me and my mates would bunk over to watch the Saints play – and break in to the ground to have some fun too. I never wanted for anything and even though my folks weren't exactly well off and we lived on a council estate, they always supported me.

My mum worked in the canteen at Triplex and my dad was a plumber on the oil rigs. For most of my young life dad was away for six weeks at a time and then he would come back for a week. It meant I grew up with my mum and she did everything for me. She would drive me everywhere, get up early on the Saturdays and Sundays and take me to training on Tuesdays and Wednesdays. My old fella was out earning the serious money and mum looked after us all.

By the time I was four or five, some of my brothers had moved out. That gave us a bit of room as it was tough when we were all in the house. It was a three-bedroom place and I think I slept in with my mum and dad until the age of about 12. But that was life and we made the best of it. We didn't have a phone until I was 16. We would go to the phone box at the top of Alder Hey Road to use that one or beg the neighbours. I bought my folks one when I signed for Saints. It was like introducing new technology to the place.

It was pretty weird for me having a mum and dad in their 50s when everyone else's were only in their 30s and 40s – you felt a little outcast sometimes. And with them being older, I didn't meet my grandparents as they passed away before I was born. That was pretty massive for me and I would have loved to have met them and enjoyed them being part of my life. That's the difference growing up to other kids who had extended families, but I can have no complaints as my mum and dad looked after me fantastically. Now Vicky's grandparents are a big part of my life and I have known them since I was 18. They are my adopted ones and I love them to bits.

Family holidays saw us pack up the car and head to Rhyl. That was the place to be when I was growing up. All five kids crammed into a small car and my mum headed over on the A-roads as she refused to go on the motorway! We'd stay in a caravan and Rhyl Sun Centre was the centre of our universe for a week. I see pictures of those days and they bring back lots of good memories. But I took my kids there recently and I looked around the place and wondered why the hell we bothered! We went to Rhyl until I was 12 and then off to Palma from there. Every year onwards we went abroad and I suppose you can say we moved with the times.

Holidays were a great time to be with the family and check out the local talent, but you didn't see much in the Sun Centre. I wasn't really into girls anyway as sport was my thing. I went out with one girl in secondary school – from De La Salle – but it didn't last. It never really bothered me until I met Vicky!

Before secondary I went to St Luke's Primary School which was close to Peet Avenue and then Rainford High School which was a good five-mile hike. I would miss the bus on purpose so I wouldn't get to school and other times I would walk so I would only be in for around lunchtime.

I loved the days at St Luke's although they didn't have a rugby league team. They say those days are the best of your life and I would agree. If only you could turn back time and know then what you know now!

Mr Upton was our headmaster and he was big on football. I knew I was going to be into sport from an early age and I think he did too. I wasn't very academic but believe if I wanted to I could have been. Looking back now I wished I had been more studious. I always thought you could be a professional sportsman forever but it doesn't work like that. When I speak to any young kid now who wants to play sport, I always suggest they should have a back-up plan as their careers aren't never ending. Time for me at school was a time to play sport, have a laugh and disrupt lessons. Maybe it should have been more about getting my head down and working hard.

I tell my son and daughter that too. Vicky and I work hard with the kids and hope they do well at school. But I can see a lot of me in my son. All he wants to do is play sport and I was the same when I was younger. So I am trying to get him in to a situation where he enjoys it and works hard at school too.

You'd be shocked to hear that PE was my most enjoyable subject at primary school. No? Then what about pottery in secondary school? A few of us enjoyed that lesson as the teacher would let us smoke. I also liked Spanish and French because the teacher had big tits! She was a good looking woman and we all had teenage crushes. My daughter Sophie goes to that school now and when I went to a parents' evening that teacher was there talking about what a pain in the arse I was.

She told Sophie that she had to lock the windows and doors as we would try and sneak out. That was true too. If there was a window or door open then me and my best mate would be out of it like a flash and we wouldn't be back. Nice of her to tell my girl that!

I played rugby league and football up until around 14 and then I concentrated on league. I would play rugby on a Sunday morning and then football in the afternoon for years. I also had a trial for Liverpool FC but none of the lads at Warrington believe me! Chris Duffy, the coach at Penlake, took me down, but sadly I wasn't quite good enough to make it as I didn't have any real position. At the time I was getting a lot of plaudits for my rugby too so I knocked it on the head.

I looked up to my form teacher, my art teacher and also Mr Calland who looked after my rugby. His son is Matt Calland who played pro rugby and coached at Halifax and Rochdale. He taught me a lot and kept me on the straight and narrow. When I was off ill he would come down and tell me I had to come in as there was a big important rugby match.

Of course I looked up to my mum and dad too – especially

my mum with my dad being away so much. Without her I wouldn't have been playing sport at all. But that goes for all my family too. My brother David was a rugby player but suffered from arthritis and that stopped him going anywhere. Not that it stopped him telling me how good he was! He was quite aggressive and if I'd had that streak then maybe I could have even better. My brother Brian played football for some of the local teams in the town. He was pretty decent too. I played for one of his teams a while back whilst Warrington were in pre-season and scored a hat-trick. The club wouldn't have been too happy if they'd have known.

All my mates were sporty too and everyone played for the St Helens Crusaders – as well as causing lots of bother in the area. Ok, I know earlier I said about not causing mayhem but when you're young …

I remember once that my brother Ste went away and brought Dave back twenty King Edward cigars. I was only around eight or nine – my mates around five years older – and I pinched them and went to give them a go on Piggy Fletcher's farm at the back of Saints. There were around eight of us and we had a couple of puffs, but they were bloody awful so we stamped on them and snapped the rest. When Dave found out what had happened he gave me a right clip but I claimed it wasn't me. Brian ended up taking the blame, which was fair dos of him really. And it saved me a right beating.

Poor Dave got it again shortly afterwards. He had a whiskey bottle and in there was a bundle of change and a £20 note. I'd had my eye on it for a while and managed to fish it out with a wire coat hanger. I bought all my mates a split from the Crispy Cod on Knowsley Road and a fly away football. We had a right laugh, but I didn't want to get caught with the cash so threw the tenner I had left down the grid. This time though none of my brothers would take the flak for it when Dave found out and he battered me. I thought it was funny as the fists rained down … but I wouldn't have got shut of the tenner if I had been thinking straight.

At primary school I would fight every day to prove I was one of the hardest in the year. I would lock horns with Gary Smith and we would knock shit out of each other. We met up after school and hammered away. He went to St Teresa's, a rival school, and that seemed a good enough reason. We were best mates too but it didn't matter as we landed one on each other.

Yes, I was a little sod. When I got to around 14 I would walk the streets all night – after playing Grand National over the neighbours' gardens – and camp out. After a while we would get bored, so regularly we would pop to a farm in Eccleston where we knew there would be some rich pickings. We would climb over an electric fence, past the bleating sheep, past a horse that would always go mental, and jump a hedge to get to a barn where milk, fresh orange and yoghurt would be kept. We would take home all sorts of stuff and I'm sure our parents were made up when there were extra yoghurts and orange juice on the kitchen table in a morning. I have to apologise for that though, it was funny at the time, but not if you owned the farm.

If I was out all night then I would be impossible to get up for school in the morning – not that I wanted to go anyway. My mum would be out around half six in the morning so I could easily miss school and laze all day in bed – provided I was up for about 2pm as my mum would be back for half two. If I got up at the right time I would go out walking in my uniform and come back in later like I'd been in school. Simple.

I'd got away with it a few times but Brian was getting a little pissed off with me throwing away my future. I thought he was a soft touch and he was at first until he cottoned on. One day my alarm went off at eight and I knew I had to be on the bus for around 25 past. I could hear Brian calling me to get up but I was keeping my eyes tight shut in the hope he would go away. He must have told me to get up four times then the next time he came in with a bucket of freezing water and threw it all over me and my bed. I definitely made it to the bus on time that day but there were plenty of times when I used to miss it on purpose. If it was snowing then there was no chance I would make it and I would walk all the way having a laugh with my mates. We did that once and got soaked, only to find the school was shut because the boiler wasn't working. So we had to walk all the way back.

On our walks to school we would reach a bowling green at the top of Crank Hill. One time my mate Kieron Lacey needed a shit and we ended up getting ... well ... breaking into the pavilions. Suddenly, there were police all over place – helicopters, the lot, and they stormed in and arrested us. Kieron was the dumbest of us all but he hid behind a door and got away with it. The rest of us got carted off to school in police cars.

The teachers should have known what to expect really as in my first three weeks of school I got suspended for throwing conkers at the Lollipop Lady. Once again I had my mates in tow and we ended up in the headmaster's office, all eleven of us in his room, waiting for our punishment. We didn't know we would be suspended, but what was good about the situation was the sight of our headmaster, a massive chap, catching his side on the door as he paced around his office. He screamed but we daren't laugh and bit our tongues.

Anyone who knew me when I was a kid would have always seen me with a ball under my arm. I would run and kick with it all the time and yes, it's corny, but it was my best friend really. I would spray it over people's houses and into gardens. I still meet people who say they used to chase me out of their gardens and off their flowers when I was getting my ball back. Golfers say it takes 10,000 swings to be a master and perhaps I put those in when I was a kid booting the ball over telegraph poles and things like that. Also, I don't think I paid for a ball once. When they came over the stands at Saints I was in the car parks snaffling them up. There were plenty of Mitre Multiplexes in my shed. I also managed to rob a full football kit from the old Rivington School. Why, I don't know; the window was open and I just sensed my opportunity.

Continually using a ball I believe put me on the track to being a pro and it's something I tell the young lads: 'Wherever you go, have a ball with you so you get used to the feel of it and its bounce'. My son Reece is exactly the same without me telling him. He's always got a ball and will kick it about. I tucked him in one night and he had the ball with him. He reminds me of me at that age, but he's a lot more polite and a lot less in trouble than I was.

I threw a snowball through someone's window once and should've escaped as I was the fastest. But they caught me as I was laughing so much. I remember my dad gave me a right old battering for that – the belt as well. Like I said earlier, we would break into the Saints ground and play hide and seek, manhunt and things like that. It was like our little home, our own world. It would be like kids breaking into Anfield now – it meant everything to us.

We were all into rugby and I got the bug because my mates were going and it was right on my doorstep. When I first went to see a game at Knowsley Road I was in awe of the place. And when I started carrying a ball I immediately wanted to play for Saints. My mates were also big football fans and supported Liverpool so that was my other true love. I could never understand why someone would support a team that's further away from one that is closer. Seems a little pointless to me.

I learnt a lot from my friends and we had a great time together. They were older than me but treated me like one of their own. They were nine or ten and I was four or five and I could go anywhere. That was what life was all about but society has changed so much these days. I know I did it but I wouldn't allow my kids to go out now for hours on end. The streets were my kingdom. You can't go anywhere now without seeing signs for 'no ball games'. We used to take them down or paint on them. Nowadays kids are into computers and they have no street sense. We could go out for hours and there were no mobiles. I wouldn't let my 16-year-old daughter out without one now.

I was out at 8am and back in at 8pm by the time I was six and we'd go all over town to Eccleston Mere, Leg o' Mutton and Carr Mill Dam and not come back for hours. We'd swim in the Mere and pinch car inner tubes from Mel Preston's tyre shop over the road from Saints. We'd fix up the punctures and then jump on the tyres and float on the Dam over the summer. But the world has gone crazy now I suppose.

*****

It was clear I wasn't going to achieve academically at school because I wanted to concentrate on going out and playing sport. I set a target to play for the Saints, or a least to get picked up by them. I know if I hadn't been chosen I would have stayed an amateur player, or more than likely I would have gone to jail.

The people I knocked about with lived life for life's sake. They were dabbling with things like acid and pot. I started off as a carrot picker when I left school and I doubt I would have got anywhere further from there. I believe if it wasn't for rugby then I would have turned into a burglar or something like that. When I signed for Saints I had to cut my ties with them. I still see them now and again and say hello as you should never forget where you come from. But if you want to make it then you can't be an idiot all your life.

Thinking I could have gone down the wrong tracks frightens me to the core as I detest people like that. The thought I could have been like that fills me with dread. I suppose you play with the cards you get dealt and I got mine. I got lucky, but when opportunity presents itself you have to take it. I think you have to have confidence in yourself because if you lack it then you are in a losing battle. You have to back yourself and back your abilities. Obviously, 60 to 70 per cent of any sportsmen have talent – probably a lot more. Some are a lot more talented than others, but others work harder. But there isn't one person who can turn up and be the best without working hard. You have to put something back and have to keep working at being better. If you don't do that then you get found out. But I guess that is the case in any walk of life anyway. If you have a talent at journalism for example, you can't say you're at your best or are the best; you have to work on it and keep going to evolve with the times.

My first brush with possibly being selected for a 'professional sportsman's' life was my trial with Liverpool. I was at junior school in my final year and playing at Penlake. Our Chairman, Chris Duffy, was a scout for Liverpool at the time and he took me down to Melwood to train with Steve Heighway. He was a good footballer and he brought the likes of Michael Owen through. I played about three or four times there and they were good times. I didn't have a specialist position – I was an aggressive centre half, midfielder and a forward! Wherever I played I was one of the best in that position. But you need to be *the* best and I wasn't. I was an out of towner so didn't really know how much of a big deal it was, but my folks buzzed off it. My brother-in-law Gary is a big Liverpool fan and thought it was great. All I wanted to do was play sport, and if it wasn't going to be football, then it would be something else.

It's scary to think that you could make a decision on a player at 11 or 12, and it's wrong as you can make or break a kid at that age. I know I wouldn't ever put my son in that position. My nephew got picked up by Blackpool, and my brother Dave took him over there back and forth. But once he was playing for them, he couldn't play for Bold Miners and missed out on his youth and a lot of friends too. It's sad when that happens.

I was four when I made my under-nine debut for St Helens Crusaders – seriously. I used to head up to Taylor Park with my mates, watch them train and don the kit too! I played in their first ever game against Ince St Williams and coach Danny Rylance said: 'Go on Lee, get on the wing.' I think we got beat 94-0 – I certainly didn't touch the ball or make a tackle! It was thirteen-a-side, full length pitch with kicks at goal, and I can still remember the smell of Wintergreen ointment on the field.

I stayed in the under-nines until I caught up!

When I turned nine I moved up a year, played a level above, and then came back down to play my normal age. We didn't win anything but that wasn't the point really. It was all about having fun and getting me out of the house.

I got picked for South Lancashire at under-11s and played at hooker, full-back and scrum-half too. I think the coaches saw how good I was with the ball in hand and I could kick and pass. I was also a gobby little git too which meant I could bully people around the field.

I first went to Wembley in 1987, and I'd love to be able to tell you that it stoked the rugby league passions, but it didn't. I went with the Crusaders on a bus and it broke down on the M6. My mate saw a magpie and announced we would get beat as a result. He was right. Saints lost 19-18 and I still hate fucking magpies to this day.

At under-15s I got picked for the North West Counties and went to Australia on tour. Before the trip we had to raise around £1,600, so the six of us chosen from St Helens got together and did all sorts of things, including bag packing at local supermarkets. It was hard work. We trained with our clubs and every two weeks we would come together to train as a team.

Thankfully, I had a passport because of my folks' European excursions to Palma (and Rhyl), but I do remember having issues finding mine when I went to Lanzarote with Warrington a few years back! We were leaving at five in the morning and 9pm the night before I couldn't find my passport. I got so worked up I ended ripping the stitching on a chair in anger – and it was actually inside the settee! Nightmare.

Anyway, the excitement of the trip built up for 18 months and the tour saw us start in America for a few days, then move on to Fiji, New Zealand and finally to Australia. I wasn't the first choice half-back on tour, but after the team lost our first two games, Hayden Walker threw me in for the match against Rockhampton. We were drawing 18-18 and as the siren went I got the ball from dummy half and booted a drop goal from 30 yards. I didn't lose my spot after that.

It was great fun because we all loved the game and enjoyed each other's company. I'd only ever been to Spain with my folks, so to venture further was amazing. It was superbly organised and we had a right laugh. Most of the time we were billeted out with other families and that did make you feel a little homesick. I stayed with Tony Martin – who played for Melbourne, New Zealand Warriors and the Celtic Crusaders – and he still remembers it too. One thing about billeting is that you realise you don't get treated as well if you're in a pair. If you stay somewhere on your own then you really get looked after by the families.

During the trip we spent four days on the Gold Coast between matches, and a few of us went out and made the best of it. Afterwards Hayden came into our rooms and asked what was going on as we were giggling and being a pain. It was probably my first drink, believe it or not. We also stayed in a Surf Club in Mackay and we would sneak out of the rooms, open the fridge, pinch the beer and have a few at night. Good times.

That tour kicked me on as a player but I was worried that I hadn't been picked up by a club. Thirty-six lads went on the trip and I reckon around 14 had been signed. A lot had been chosen by Wigan and Warrington, and I was becoming concerned. I knew I had to keep plugging on but I didn't know if the opportunity would come.

It did though and it came after a fantastic local derby between St Helens Crusaders and Wigan. Even at under-16s and through the amateur scene, those matches were always keenly fought and fierce. It was a Lancashire Cup Final and we beat them up on the field and on the scoreboard too. Wigan had a top team back then but we were too physical for them and I won man of the match.

After the game Kevin Creance came up to me and said he wanted to chat to my parents. He was a scout and told me

Saints were interested and asked me to come up to the club a week later. I hadn't spotted him before the game, but you never knew if there were scouts at matches anyway as they would turn up, do their thing and stay in the background. To be honest, whatever they offered me in that meeting I would have taken it. They could have thrown a tracksuit over the table at me and I would have grabbed a pen there and then. In the end it wasn't much more than that anyway! To celebrate I played another match afterwards on the local bowling greens with my mates.

The week leading up to my meeting at the club was exciting, and the thought of me being a Saints player by the end of it was even more. By the time it came, I was signing no matter what, as all I ever wanted to do was play for them. Before long I was sat in the chairman's office and signing a contract for a grand every birthday and a few bonuses such as making my GB debut. But the add-ons were bullshit really as I was only 16 and had no chance of playing for my country before the time my contract ran out after my 19th birthday. I became a Saints player on July 1, 1994.

These days you are signed to a club much earlier and work your way through an academy system. Everything you do builds you to becoming a really good player if you work hard. You get whatever you want; you have dieticians, better training facilities, kit and better coaches. You are given the best life possible to become a success and I wish I could be 16 now and get what these guys have! I don't think the kids these days realise what they have got. We were lucky if we got a pair of boots, now you have full kit and boots given to you!

Things have changed so much. Some coaches tell kids they aren't allowed to spin pass a ball. Why are we trying to coach a great skill out of our players of the future? If someone has talent you have to keep it. We can't be too robotic in the way we coach with our kids. There's too much coaching people into a particular position too – we should be encouraging kids to play rugby league not pigeon-holing them. We need to keep on evolving, and that means leading the way as we have done in the past.

One thing I am pleased to see change is the move to summer rugby. If you watch under-12s playing in August you'll see them pass the ball for fun, get it wide and score some brilliant tries. Come November and December they pass 20 per cent less than they would do. You can see that on amateur pitches – there's no mud on the outside! And that's why GB will always match Australia in the forwards but not on the wings! We haven't got the skills, but now we have the chance to nurture them in a summer environment.

I've stood on the touchline long enough watching my son playing and seeing kids crying because it's that cold. I wouldn't let my lad play in the street in winter in a t-shirt if it's snowing! What's the point in that? Now we've moved to summer we can attract the kids who would otherwise play football in the winter.

Coaches now have more tools to work with, but these days down the age groups, you're likely to have someone who hasn't played the game before. I'm trying to stop that cycle by helping to mentor at Thatto Heath Amateur Rugby League Club. But the be all and end all for me is that move to summer. I know there was opposition and I don't want to criticize the British Amateur Rugby League Association (BARLA) as without them I wouldn't be here today. But you don't see them on the sidelines when it's pissing down and snowing. The Aussies have athletes who have honed their skills in the summer, and even the pros prefer it too. I firmly believe that more kids would play rugby league in summer and we would find the athletes. We now need to wait and be patient to see the results of the move, but it will take a number of years.

Look at me talking about athletes. I wouldn't class myself as an athlete! I have never been an Adonis, but I have always done enough to make sure I am ready to play the game. I get the piss taken out of me as I don't lift many weights – and when I do they aren't the big ones. I always say though, it's no point looking good in your underpants if you can't play rugby league! I have seen players with the best bodies lift everything in the gym then get on to the rugby field and can't play.

Maybe I should have worked harder in the past, but my main priority was to play well. Perhaps I should have done more work in the gym, but I was always practising passing and kicking and the odd bit of defensive work hence my 'Axe' nickname. That came from Mike Wainwright after I put a big hit on someone in a game against Widnes and it's stuck ever since. It's based on Trevor Gillmeister who would knock them over for fun in Australia.

I've also been pretty lucky with injury too although I have done a cartilage whilst at Saints and my left hand has more plates than we have in the kitchen cupboard. I have four screws in my finger and plates in my hand and wrist. I've also had the odd hamstring pull, hurt my shoulder in 2010 and did my neck in 2012.

One time the ligaments in my back were playing up and I had to go to London every Monday to have needles. I would be in Euston for 1.30pm and then get on three tube rides to be at the doctors. When I got there they would have to give me five numbing injections so I could have the big one, and that would mean getting back to Euston gone five. I couldn't be bothered with that one time as there was an extra train running which I could catch at 3pm, so told them to fuck the other needles and get the big one shoved in. It was about five inches long and I have never felt pain like it. I couldn't move, and to make matters worse as I got to the station I saw the train pull away … and then had the pleasure of sitting in agony for the best part of two-and-a-half hours for the next one. I didn't return for the next batch of needles.

Would a 16-year-old Lee Briers get picked up by a club now? I'd like think he would. When I signed for Saints I went straight into the Saints Academy. Now there is a scholarship team for each year and kids are signed by pro clubs earlier. I was signed late and perhaps that made me a better player as I'd matured in the amateur system.

But maybe they wouldn't have liked what they saw! That one chance, that one scout, on another day might not have been there.

2

Debut and Heartbreak

Anyone who signs for their hometown team will tell you straightaway, they want to play first team in front of a full house in their stadium. I was no different. St Helens was my club and I'd taken my first step in making that dream become a reality. But I'll lay off the clichés and just tell you my St Helens story and how much of a whirlwind it really was.

And yes I do realise that is a cliché …

Ok, I'll admit I was lucky. I moved straight into the youth set up at 16 and captained a successful academy side which had great players and great coaches. Nick Halafihi, Graham Liptrot (Lippy) and Jon Myler were rugby people and were awesome in what they taught us. Graham in particular used to treat us like his own kids and we were all one big happy family. We played and trained hard and were rewarded with a shot at Wigan in the Academy Grand Final at Old Trafford.

In the lead up to that game, John McAtee dropped down from the Alliance team to play with us and came down to training on the Tuesday night before. He was late by about half an hour and Lippy asked him where he'd been. Macca responded in the broadest Mancunian accent ever: 'What's it gotta do with you, you fat git?' That resulted in banter and wisecracks flying all around the team and the coaches. That's the way we were. We were close and it paid dividends.

I remember one time we were running up and down the terracing in Knowsley Road. After about five minutes Lippy said: 'Ah fuck this, I wouldn't enjoy this either, let's go and have a game of tick and pass.' That's the way it was, we didn't do that much in training, but the coaches got the best out of us – and it worked as we turned Wigan over at Old Trafford. From there I won man of the match on my Great Britain Academy debut and a lot of the side moved up to the A team and I was named captain too.

I also travelled over to France to play for Carcassonne for three months as part of my rugby league development. When I signed for them, they thought I was the next big star coming out of Saints, when in reality I hadn't even played a first team game. I received a king's welcome and on the first night enjoyed a big dinner. We were sat at a long table and were allowed to drink and smoke. I'd never been far out of England before and was really excited to be there. I got steadily drunk and started swearing, so I took myself off to go and lie down in a car they'd let me use. It was a Volvo and you had to bump start it, but it was stuck in the middle of a farmer's field.

They told me not to start it and drive, but of course I did. I got outside and within about five minutes of finding it in pitch black I'd given it a go. I was running along the car with my foot on the clutch, in second gear, and seconds later it had tipped over in a ditch and I was upside down. Everyone came out of the dinner to see what was going on and I was the other way round with the car on its roof. My new team-mates had to tip it over to get me upright. A great start to life in France.

I actually learnt how to drive in France, but after a few crashes the police got in contact with the club chairman and instructed him to 'tell Mr Briers to stop driving as he is causing problems in the village'.

Back in England, as well as playing rugby I was working part-time on Cooks Farm, and they were great with me. I would train on a Tuesday and play on a Thursday and they would let me have time off. When I was 17, I trained to be a chef but didn't last more than a week! It was too bloody hot and clearly not my bag! I also worked for director Eric Lathom's company, Kerr's Minerals in St Helens and stayed there for a year before I then went full-time as a player. Back then it was pretty normal to leave school at 16 and work when you weren't playing. But things are different now. At Warrington when you sign as a kid it is compulsory to carry on some sort of academic career. Sometimes I wish I'd had that kind of support when I turned pro. It is frightening to think about how you can survive if the game just spits you out. You can earn a good living from rugby, but you can't retire on it; you have to have some kind of back up or profession. When you retire from playing, you aren't retired as such, you just can't play anymore. You are not even halfway through your life and almost need to start again.

We have a player welfare manager at Warrington, and if you want to do any sort of course, he will sort it out. That is big for the kids coming through at the club. They are made aware they need to have something in the future – advice I didn't heed, like with Mark Forster telling me to invest my money and to look into property. You need to look after the money you make because that way it will look after you. Cheesy, yes, and in some ways it also goes against what I believe in. Since I lost my brother Brian to cancer, I believe in living your days like they are your last. I think life is too short to worry beyond a few weeks, but I also make sure my kids are looked after and my family is ok.

Anyway, when I was promoted to the Alliance team, I realised that people were starting to take notice of my performances on the field. I was called up to play for the first team in the Norweb Challenge on Boxing Day 1996 at Wigan and scored a try and a goal in a 32-22 loss – although we wiped out the deficit in the second leg a couple of weeks later. I then played against Leeds at Knowsley Road in another friendly on January 24 – and we lost again. I never expected anything to come of these games and just wanted to get my head down in the Alliance and do well for them. I never actually thought

I would, or even could make my debut for the first team at 18 as there were people in the Alliance in front of me – my mate John McAtee for example – I thought I was lower down the pecking order.

In those two friendlies I was welcomed in and treated like a member of the first team. I knew Alan Hunte from training camps and things like that as well as Bernard Dwyer. He worked at the ground with Paul Loughlin and used to chase me round Mulberry Avenue when I was younger – after I had thrown stones at them. Bernard would see me on Taylor Park with a bottle of cider and would go mad at me. I also knew Bobby Goulding as he would take me out to do a lot of 'one on one' training, then when I moved up to the Alliance team I was his understudy and he looked after me. Everyone who knew Bobby knew he had an aura on the pitch, but he was followed by a lot of rumour, conjecture and controversy off it. That's what made him what he was and still is. It probably made him that off the cuff player who dominated the position at Saints and led them to the League and Challenge Cup double. For me I can only say good things about him. He was a top player and a top bloke and he'd give up his days off to come in and help me with my kicking game and skills. And if I ever needed to talk he was always on the other end of the phone.

On February 8, 1997, Saints took on Wigan in the Challenge Cup fourth round and towards the end of the first half in a typically fantastic and physical game, the transfer-listed Bobby smacked Neil Cowie late and high to spark a massive brawl and a red card. I was watching the game from the stands and I never thought about what was going to come. I was more interested in the result as Saints turned in a superb performance in front of a massive crowd to get into the next round. In the week following the game Bobby was suspended for eight weeks, reduced to six on appeal, and withdrew a transfer request he'd put in earlier in the season. If I knew what was going to come I would have asked the disciplinary to give him 20 games instead of eight! I didn't think about it but I suppose it was the start of my career.

Saints were due to take on Hull in the next round a couple of weeks later, and in the build-up I was given the nod to play. To be honest, I can't remember how I was told but I was totally chuffed to bits with being chosen. I had been playing the game for 14 years and it was everything I had worked towards and everything I wanted to do. To play for your hometown club is something else and I couldn't wait. All my family were getting tickets and they were really proud of me. Talk about pressure!

I remember walking up to the ground in the same way I would normally for any match, and not really feeling that pressure, but how proud I was at what was about to happen. I walked into the dressing room and wasn't allowed to get changed in the first team one as you had to be a regular to get in there! There were no special words from Shaun McRae or anything like that, I just needed to get the ball to the forwards and kick when I needed to and I did that. I was always a cocky sod anyway and that helped because I was in a pivotal position in the halves. The players had confidence in me and that gave me the confidence to do well. It was daunting but I scored a try and kicked five goals in a 54-8 win.

There's two things that stick out in that game – the roar when the Saints ran out on to the field and the fact Hull had Tevita Vaikona who was about 18 stone and he kept running at me.

From there I played against Keighley and kicked two goals to get us through to the Challenge Cup semi-finals, then away at London Broncos (28-24), kicked six goals to beat Salford 50-20 in the semi-final and won man of the match in a 22-10 win over Wigan at Central Park. I then made, what would be my final St Helens appearance, in a 32-12 victory over Sheffield.

That Salford semi-final really stuck out for me as it was a great occasion to experience so young. It was a glorious day and to make the Final at the home of our enemy – Central Park in Wigan – was even sweeter. Everything we did came off and we rubbed a little bit of salt into the Wiganers too! I never expected the run to continue and knew that when Bobby came back I could be back in the Alliance – who I hadn't yet played for – or on the bench. And when I was chosen as 18th man for our trip to Paris, I wasn't concerned but accepted that the run may have come to an end. Bobby was one of the best in the world; I knew that I could play off the bench, but the coach was in an awkward position to pick another half in the 17.

McRae was a good coach but you heard plenty of stories that the directors were picking the side and he didn't have much control in it. But I never expected it to turn sour as quickly as it did.

The first I knew I wasn't going to Wembley was a few weeks before. There was a meeting about what suits we were going to wear and who would be going down to the team hotel on the Thursday before the match against Bradford. They said they were going to take so many people down and it dawned on me when I was sat listening that I might not be going with the first team. Chris Joynt stood up in the meeting and told everyone that it would be a joke if I wasn't on that trip. He backed me and I knew a few of the players agreed with him too. But it made no difference and I wasn't selected in the team or to travel down with them.

People say I got Saints to the final and yes, I probably played a massive part in their progression. I accepted when Bobby came back from suspension chances would be limited. But to be told I wouldn't even be going, nevermind playing, really pissed me off. I was washed to the side, pushed out and treated like shit. You shouldn't get treated like that and as a young kid it knocked my confidence too. I could've packed the game in. I loved St Helens, they had been my life since I was born, but to be put aside like that was a joke. At the same time I was offered eight grand to go pro too and, although I'm not good at maths, I didn't think that was enough either. Vicky was expecting that year and I realised that sort of money wasn't going to get me far.

It all left a sour taste. I realised I could hack it in Super League and I was good enough to make the starting 17 of any side. But it was simply not being included in our Wembley experience that finished me off. So as Bobby and the Saints were turning over Bradford 32-22, I was in Paddington getting pissed with my mates. It was a great trip! We booked into a hotel that cost £25 for three nights, so I reckon you can guess what kind of quality establishment that was. As soon as we got our keys, we ran upstairs and crashed to the door fighting each other for prime position. Whenever my mates roomed together it was always a shit fight for the best beds, so if you were at the back of the scrum, you were knackered.

I got in first and noticed the room had a normal bed, a double and a pull-out. I picked mine, dropped my kecks and pissed over it. I turned round and said: 'That'll do for me.' Danny Whittle had bagged the little one and Adam Cotham and Paul Gartland were going to get cosy in the double. Pissed off, Danny grabbed my bed and threw it in the shower so I couldn't sleep in it anyway.

We got pretty drunk that evening and the next day I was first up with a banging head. Danny was at the end of his bed and about six foot away Adam was snoring with his mouth open. Whittle then squirted a loop of piss out of himself and its perfect fountain trajectory landed in Adam's gaping mouth. He jumped up choking and gasping and went ballistic. You had to be there, but it was very, very funny.

I was hiding away the pain really as I knew I should have been on the pitch at Wembley … or at least on the bench … or part of the party at least. But I'd signed for Warrington before then anyway. They had approached Saints on the off chance they were prepared to off-load me, and with everything that happened I thought why not. They offered me a lot of money and the chance to play first team rugby at half-back. I could have bided my time of course and waited – nobody knew what was going to happen with Bobby and in hindsight I could have stayed, but the opportunity at Warrington was too good to turn down. I signed for £36,000 and that was a real head turner.

When you're offered that much at 18 then you are going to at least be interested. And I was. I was never planning to leave but when Saints came to me and insulted me with their offer – I earned more in three games in the cup that year – then my mind was elsewhere. I felt like there was no way they were going to do me again like they did when I first joined them.

*****

Saints made me grow up. I was bitter and upset over the way I was treated for a long time but it made me stronger. I know the fans were pissed off and I was too. But the Saints board got what they wanted – around £65k with additional cash if I played 10 and 20 games and so on. They did the same with Gary Connolly who moved to Wigan while they tried to retain other local lads on the cheap. But I don't regret moving to Warrington. I have had a good life with the club and I love the place. It's my home.

I signed on the Friday and had a bundle of cash in my pocket. I'd never seen more than about a grand and my plan was to go out and get royally pissed. But my new coach, Darryl van der Velde, turned round to me and said he had some boots and a kit for me to try on. I'd be playing on Sunday and I'd be up against, yes, the Saints. It was all a bit weird and we lost by about 50. Beforehand I think I trained in Les Boyd's old gear and the kit was massive on me! The week after the match I bought a house and invested my money that way.

Once I'd made the decision to move to Warrington, I did worry a bit, wondering if I'd made the right choice, but not to the point where I'd say 'fuck, I've made a big mistake here.' The only thing that pissed me off with the situation was that Saints then went into a period where they won everything and I missed out on that. But in recent years I've experienced a little bit of that with the Wolves and it feels good. Hopefully there is more to come.

Did I ever wonder if the success would come with Warrington? My expectations at first were totally different. We were never challenging for honours and were in the middle to bottom of the Super League. We had three semi-final losses in the cup too, which were hard to take, but we were patient and in recent years it's come good. Moving to the Halliwell Jones Stadium was the catalyst and with the board we have at the Wolves there is plenty of scope for more success. Back in 1997, I signed a three-year deal with Warrington and extended it by a year after I won the Young Player of the Year award in the same year. I never asked for an upgrade, they just came and did it. Warrington have always been good to me.

Ok, so what am I, a Saint or Wolf? I will always be a St Helens lad as I will never forget where I am from. That's where my roots are. But I am an adopted Warringtonian. I love it as much as St Helens. I won't lie, I support Saints and I have no doubt I will take a bit of stick for that. If it was Saints taking on anyone else, I would want them to win. If we are playing on a Sunday and Saints are playing on a Friday I will go and stand in the crowd. I like to watch good rugby and Saints have been successful for a long time. I know people behind the scenes at the club and when I go back I will always say hello.

But if you ask me to choose Warrington or Saints, then Warrington are my team.

In 1997, I joined Warrington late on in the season and travelled Down Under as part of the team in our World Club Challenge matches. They were the best three weeks of my life. We had lost to Cronulla, Penrith and Auckland at home and before we went on the tour, Darryl van der Velde said we were probably not going to win any games, but to use it as a learning curve. Basically, he'd given carte blanche for 25 rugby players to fill their boots for three weeks. We had some fantastic times, including snowboarding in the mountains near Auckland and some fun in Kings Cross, one of Sydney's more 'lively' areas! I roomed with Scully (Paul Sculthorpe) and we had a right laugh. It was a paid-for holiday really because we didn't crown ourselves in glory on the field!

We lost 12-48 to Penrith, 0-44 to Cronulla and 4-16 to

Auckland. The Super League was stronger over there and we got our backsides kicked. And we weren't that good anyway! The game against Auckland which was played in Christchurch sticks out as it was freezing. George Mann ripped them to bits but Mark Forster got hypothermia which was no surprise considering it snowed then hailed! But it was a good experience and introduced me to my team-mates in the best way possible.

It was the start of the new future.

3

Reality Bites

My first season of professional rugby league had been pretty eventful. I'm sure there aren't many players who have made their debut for two clubs as well as appearing in Challenge Cup semi-final and World Club Challenge matches in the same season. I'd also won the Young Player of the Year and my partner had given birth to our first child. Not exactly the quietest 12 months of my life.

Warrington finished ninth in 1997 and we wanted to make sure we improved on that the following year. As a full professional, I wanted to make sure I was fit enough for my first real season in Super League. I'd never done a pre-season before and it was tough. I was small and fragile and they wanted me to bulk out so I could stand the rigours of the game. I was getting into weights for the first time and everyone had the jump on me. But I just couldn't pile on the pounds at all and the other players were lifting more than me.

I realised then what I needed to do to become a first team regular. All the work goes in in pre-season and that's where the dark days really are. I had a lot of catching up to do and had to put in the hours. I was young and we had an older squad so I had to try and get up to their level.

You hear all sorts of stories about professionals taking all sorts of things to get their weight up. I'm not talking about cheating – that's not in the make-up of proper sportspeople. Nothing was ever mentioned to me in that respect but I know one thing that will make your weight increase – Guinness! I could never drink it until about four years ago and you have to have 'black' in there. It does work too, but all the weight goes around the stomach. These days there are supplements coming out of your ears but I have never really taken an interest in them. I believe in eating right and I have the odd protein shake now and again, but other stuff is not for me. It's a case of being disciplined with what you eat. Ha, ha, who am I trying to kid with my body!

I have seen people who are religiously into building their physique, but as I have said before, it's no good looking good in your underpants if you can't play rugby league! You have to do weights and look after yourself, but I think people can go over the top. The kids coming through the system now have all this drummed into them because of sports scientists and things like that. When I was growing up, Vince Fawcett was massive and probably the first player I knew who was into supplements. He was ripped to the bone … and played one season for the club. He trained like Tarzan and played like Jane!

In 1998, we signed a number of good players to help us make that next step. Michael Eager, Danny Farrar, Danny Nutley, Steve McCurrie and Brendon Tuuta were all quality additions to the side. We signed Danny Whittle too who was and still is my best mate. He's a St Helens lad and I ribbed him saying they only signed him to drive me about. I couldn't drive – legally anyway – he never did take that too well.

We had a rock solid pack that season but we couldn't get it together and make a real good crack of it. We faded during the season and never really got going, finishing tenth. Although we didn't have much success, we always celebrated like we did. We had a rule that it was compulsory to go for a drink on a Monday. You didn't have to drink, but you had to come out with the rest of the team and enjoy each other's company. I didn't need asking twice and Mondays turned into lengthy card nights and a 2am getting home session. One time I lost more than a grand, McCurrie lost two grand and Peachey did the same too. Whittle took it all home with him! Lucky sod. I would drive home after these sessions which was stupid as I had no licence either. I did later on although I lost it when I got done for drink-driving.

Tuesday would come and some of us would turn up still pissed, train hard and then go for a few pints knowing we had Wednesday off. Nowadays, if you have one drink every two weeks you are doing well, but that's the way it was back then. We were slow in changing our ways and culture at Warrington, but it certainly doesn't help when they make it compulsory! I was 18 so what else would I do? It was a frequent thing after a game too. When we played in Yorkshire we'd hit the Corn Mill in Huddersfield and the directors would buy us drinks and stay for a while.

Could we have done better in that season? We always aimed high but only won seven games. Saints were changing their culture and were on the cusp of winning things. We were happy to avoid relegation.

There were several dark times that season too. There were times when we weren't getting paid or getting paid late. We were very close to going under, but at the end of the year the board resigned and Greenalls took over. The council bought Wilderspool too and we rented it off them. We sold Scully to Saints to pay off the debt. I was gutted about that as one of my reasons for signing was because he was at Warrington.

I never had much money back then, and not being paid didn't really register much. I had just got into the side and won the Young Player of the Year and therefore thought I would be ok for a contract. That's not me being big headed but I have never really worried about anything like that. Maybe I wasn't so smart to not think about administration and all that would have come from it. If it had suddenly happened one day and I didn't have a job then that would have been different, but it never came to that. I always thought I would get paid tomorrow and that was it. That's life I guess, but don't worry, you might be dead tomorrow.

I can't remember too much of my first full season with Warrington as I think I might have had too many pints. We played Castleford at Cardiff Arms Park and lost by seven points. It was great to play in front of a good crowd and be in Wales too. I also remember a match at London Broncos which involved Brendon Tuuta. Toots used to wear an arm guard and when the touch judges came in to check us, he never had it on. When he went out he would put a shin pad on his arm and wrap strapping around it. Half way through the match he cleaned out Glen Air with a massive forearm tackle. It hit him flush in the chin and I have never seen anyone knocked out like that. Before the match Broncos' Mark Carroll had been telling everyone how soft we were in this country, so Toots hammered him all over the field which was very enjoyable to see.

Speaking of hammerings, we played Saints and Vila Matautia came through on a drop off ball and Danny Whittle tried to tackle him. Vila smashed him backwards about 10 yards and to this day he still blames Steve McCurrie!

There were a number of changes off the field in 1998 too. It was the first year of the play-off system where winning the league didn't mean winning the competition. It was weird when it came in as I had grown up with first past the post. It was a top five system similar to the Aussie one, but it was fantastic and made the game what it is today. The winners are the ones that win at Old Trafford now and that's all that counts. It stops teams running away with the league and leaves the door open for every side to make the play-offs. It didn't make much difference to us though as we were on holiday by the time those games kicked off.

The salary cap also came in to stop clubs spending too much on players. I had grown up with Wigan winning everything by being fully professional and the other sides trying to play catch-up. This system made it fairer. It's been very good for the game

I think. If you look at the table, Warrington, Huddersfield and Hull are all competing, not just Saints, Wigan and Leeds. But we need to be able to adapt. The Aussies have increased their cap level. We have been watching average Aussie players in our league since 1998 and there has been a few in Warrington too who have been paid well. You can't argue with the players as they are the ones who have been offered the money.

One thing the cap has done though is widen the gap between Super League and the Championship. The days when a team in a lower division would beat a Wigan, Saints or Warrington are long gone. You might get one every five or six years possibly, but because we are playing in the summer era, the weather can't even it out now. Wind, hail and snow are all levellers! In 2011, we hammered Swinton 112-0 and they couldn't live with us. The pace we played at was too quick. Home season ticket holders also got in for free, and that meant Swinton didn't even earn from it. In the past they would have taken about £30,000 home, even more if corporate was doing well. I know the authorities want to increase the numbers watching the cup, but we should be doing as much as we can to help these clubs.

When we hammered Swinton I felt sorry for them and I never want to see another team going through that. Warrington players were speaking to Swinton's lads on the pitch encouraging them to keep going. I am friends with the likes of Ian Watson and Phil Joseph and we were helping them out on the field. Joel Monaghan was telling the winger where to position himself so that when he went through, the guy would have a chance to tackle him. I have never seen that on the field before and it just showed the respect he had for a fellow rugby league player.

I suppose that is the way it is now in professional sport. I have no doubt that Swinton and the likes of Featherstone want to win the Championship and the Challenge Cup isn't high on their list of priorities, but the gap between rich and poor has made it nigh on impossible to compete.

I broke some records in that Swinton game – kicking 16

goals and scoring a hat-trick for 44 points – a club record. I also passed Steve Hesford's points scoring record of 2,416 too for Warrington. I knew that record was on, but also knew I didn't have to go out to try and break it in one game. It is surprising to think I have scored all those points since I joined the club. Other than in the last five years, we haven't been anything like a top team. Other than that we have been looking at eighth to fourth. We were never top scorers yet I have broken the record. It's superb and I couldn't have imagined it in my wildest dreams.

2011 was a real breakout season for me. I became better as a rugby player and scored more tries for the season than I had done before. I don't know why it clicked so late in my career but I just kept on learning, worked hard and had a great squad around me too. The medical team were fantastic and everything just came together for me. The challenge of never knowing when my last game would be also made me play and train harder. But there was a lot of learning too. Early on in the year, I got pulled off the field during our 24-22 win over Hull KR. I was playing pretty poorly and Tony Smith dragged me off. In the past I wouldn't have come off, I would have tried to change things on the field. But I had a chance to see things from the stands and it was great. Beating Saints was the biggest thing though … finally after a million times of trying!

As in 2011, 13 years previous we had great team spirit, but unlike the modern version of Warrington it was because we drank a lot for team bonding! We built our team on that and we worked hard. When I joined the club, Darryl van der Velde gave me a sound footing in the game. He was way ahead of his time in the way he worked and how to play the game but his man-management let him down.

I remember in 2000 that he would have all the English players and Toa Kohe-Love in at 7am getting flogged whilst the Aussies were allowed to have a bit more time in bed. They'd come in at 8am, do their weights and then join us and we'd have to do the same again. Alfie Langar didn't like that but couldn't do anything about it. When that happens I don't think a team can be successful as you have two separate teams. If I could go back now I would have made a stance and said something. But thankfully a lot has changed since then.

Despite that, team spirit was good, we always had a laugh and played a lot of practical jokes. Mike Wainwright and Gary Chambers used to share a car and after training we had a couple of hours to kill before our afternoon session. On one occasion in the down time, we went to Morrison's, bought a kipper and I put it as far under Wainwright's back seat as I could. We had a horrific summer, it was roasting and the car was foul. After a week or two they couldn't cope with the smell so Mike came into training and demanded we show them where it was. They had torn the car to pieces to find it. I took on the task and managed to pull it out of a one inch gap on the back seat. It was heaving with maggots and stunk. It was awful, all the guys were wretching!

Another time, while Adam Doyle was in the gym we took the two back wheels off his car and hid them, but Danny Nutley got his own back, taking the rubbers off my windscreen wipers. He did it on a day it poured down and I had to put my head out of the window to see down the road … not good, I had no licence. I drove without one for a while – and I know another guy who did it for more than 10 years. (Hey Ben).

A personal favourite is prawns in air vents, you can't shift the smell!

On our World Club Challenge tour in 1997, Paul Cullen and our conditioner Phil Chadwick went for a meal with Les Boyd. We broke into their room, took all the light bulbs out, robbed the quilts and put water on top of the doors. We turned the air con up to maximum cold so they were freezing and placed ironing boards on the floor. So when they came in they got covered in water, tripped over and almost froze to death. We left them a flannel to dry themselves!

On the same tour we broke into Chaddy's room and he looked like he was asleep. But he leapt up like a bear and attacked us. We put shoes in pillow cases to give him a good hiding but he decided to take us all on and wrestle six of us on the floor. He was crazy! Last one now – George Mann – we once put matches between his toes and lit them whilst he was asleep. I have never heard a bloke scream as loud as that!

George was a great bloke who used to pick me up for training. But in 2000, I got a phone call from him asking if I could lend him £1,500 and he would give it me back in a couple of days. Like I said, he was a good fella so I had no hesitation in doing so. What an error that was because as soon as I transferred the money to this bank it was the last time I heard from him. I'm not motivated by money and if he was to ring me up and say he was struggling to pay it back, but would do eventually, I would be fine with that. I later found out he'd also done it to other people too. It was bad news he did this because he was a super person.

*****

Although I didn't have the greatest season with Warrington, in 1998, I was offered the chance to play for Wales. It came totally out of the blue and wasn't something I was considering until I got a call from Clive Griffiths. He'd heard I had Welsh in me, either through Iestyn Harris or perhaps Keiron Cunningham when I was at Saints. Clive asked if I wanted to represent Wales and I thought I would give it a go and I have enjoyed every minute. Every time we went to camp it was like going away with a club and your mates rather than a rep team. Everyone was close and there were no agendas, we always had a brilliant time.

Would I have picked Wales if England had come forward? In hindsight I may have chosen England with how the international game has changed with the splitting up of Great Britain. But I wanted to choose Wales as it was 'my' country and my opportunity to play international matches. And I never regretted choosing them at all.

Later in my career I was asked if I would consider switching back to England, but I couldn't do that. I can't for the life of me understand how you can play for one country and then play for another. It doesn't sit right with me; you're either one or the other and people do bend the rules. There is a loophole that allows 'switching' and that means players have a right to do it I suppose. But for me the international committee should close the loophole. It all started in Australia and they exploited the passport loophole to its full capacity.

I'm not from Wales and people said I shouldn't be playing for them, but I had chosen them as my country and I think you should stick with your first choice. People move from one country to another to perhaps play against bigger teams. They move from a smaller nation to a bigger one to do it. But I also think it is for money too – you get more money when you play for the bigger nations against the bigger sides. It's hard to argue against that as you have a short career, but lesser countries don't get treated as well as the other ones. My Welsh ancestry comes from my grandmother on my mum's side. Sadly I never got to meet her as all my grandparents died before I got the chance.

And of course I did spend a lot of time in Rhyl as a kid!

My debut was against Emerging England at Widnes and then we played at Vetch Field in Swansea where we lost 24-17 to Ireland. I can't remember much about the game but I did hit a drop goal and Richie Eyres was sent off very early in the match. A week later we travelled up to Scotland and lost 36-16 although I scored a try and kicked two goals. I think it was a triangular tournament and Ireland won it. But it was a good experience to start off my international career.

I have spoken to players who have represented England and the difference from them to Wales is unreal. There have been times we have phoned around before a game to try and get a team together in the week building up to a match. We played England at the Racecourse one time and we were calling players on the day to see if they had any Welsh blood in them. I think Keith Mason came and played for us as a result of a call like that. We certainly aren't scraping around for a team now, it has been totally transformed. We have junior sides, 18s and 23s all competing well. The work people have done in Wales is amazing and they need commending on that. It is brilliant.

And, I know the Welsh anthem too. I may struggle with it, but I still know the gist! In 2000, we had the Welsh National Choir to teach us. We had a few sessions with them before our first match of the World Cup. It is so much better than the boring English one – *God Save the Queen* and all that. The thrill of when you sing the Welsh anthem is something special. It's something you are duty bound to do if you play for Wales, and we all like a good singsong don't we? Being Welsh and all …

I always enjoyed playing for my country and we had a good laugh on and off the field. There is always pressure when you pull on a shirt as you want to represent whoever you are playing for in the best way you can. At Wales we had little resources in my early international career, and until the Crusaders came in it was all pretty amateurish. That changed when the professional Welsh club moved through the leagues as we had more players available and of a better quality. It also meant we could have a full-time training camp as we had more full-time professional players. You only have to look at Scotland and Ireland for example. Most of their lads are from the Championship and that means they work for a living and can train now and again. I've been there, it's hard, but until a professional side comes in then it won't change.

We all know what happened to the Crusaders in 2011 and I was gutted about it. Without knowing all the ins and outs I thought the move up to Wrexham was the right one at the time. The sport took off in North Wales and I firmly believed that it needed the time to grow. Wales is a rugby country, whatever the code, and has plenty of talent to tap into. London's had years to get bedded in so the least we could have done was do the same. Crusaders had good foundations in South Wales and went into administration for the right reasons. I firmly believed that over the next four to five years, the sport in Wales was going to be stronger – especially with the semi pro South Wales Scorpions.

So when Crusaders pulled out of the licence process I was shocked and perhaps the doubters got their wish. My reaction when I heard it on the TV was quite simply, what the fuck, as I always thought it was strong. I think the only people who knew what was going to happen were perhaps the owners and maybe the Rugby Football League. The players hadn't had any inkling and head coach Iestyn Harris was the same. The first they heard of it was about 20 minutes before Richard Lewis announced it live on Sky Sports News and the Crusaders' owners weren't even in the country apparently.

You have to say that it stunk massively. We all thought unfortunately Wakefield were probably the team to lose out, and some of the players at Crusaders had signed three-year contracts and weren't looking for another club. The lads at Wakefield were looking for other clubs as they expected not to be in Super League in 2012. I spoke to Ben Flower and Lloyd White and they couldn't believe what had happened. It was bad enough they didn't get a franchise but the fact they weren't told about it – that's their livelihoods and careers gone in a second. How could we allow players to sign a three-year contract when a club was going to pull out of the process, and then only tell them 20 minutes before the announcement?

What made this all worse was the unbelievable decision to allow all the overseas players at the Crusaders a special exemption. It meant any player who had signed for Crusaders could effectively be classed as 'English' and therefore not count on quota. That is bullshit of the highest order. A club who has, say a young English centre, who is due a full-time contract can replace him with an experienced overseas player and save a quota spot! And you have another young player lost to the game. In effect you could sign a player from the Crusaders for five years and they are home grown. That cannot be right; we should be looking after our own rather than those on quota. To their credit the GMB said they didn't want this to happen, but the RFL agreed it and you can't blame the Aussie players who got caught up in it. At the same time the league was losing Engage as its main sponsor and it's hard to think this wasn't having a negative effect on finding another.

In the build-up to the announcement, we played Wigan in the quarter final of the Challenge Cup and it was a superb spectacle. Both sides went for each other and it was end to end on national TV. THAT should have been what the press were writing about but instead they were focused on the Crusaders and that shouldn't have happened.

There are a lot of people who want the licensing system, but if they genuinely thought this put rugby league in a positive light that day then they are obviously coming from a different angle than all rugby league players and 95 per cent of fans … excluding Wakey's of course! It was great they got in as a founder club, but the way the whole thing was done stinks big time.

Maybe I'm wrong, but I can't honestly believe that the RFL only knew the day before that Crusaders were struggling. I knew they were struggling! I knew of seven players at least that were owed more than £400,000 and their pensions were affected. There were people in that club who were out of pocket. We all knew they were struggling but it was kept quiet and secret. And what happens? The fans and players have been stitched up again.

It's frightening to think what will happen to Welsh rugby league without a pro club. In this book it will come across that I am blaming people for what's happened – and perhaps that's true. Wales have come from virtually nothing to challenge in the World Cup in '95 and 2000, and then go backwards and struggle. Then, we finally get the team, the Crusaders, to build us up into being professional once again and be a force. But now I can only see it going one way and it really upsets me. It is wrong as I don't think enough has been done. I love London Broncos and what they stand for but they struggled and we helped them out. We can't pump money in to help these teams out but you have to help them to get going.

Thankfully, there are dedicated people who are working hard to make sure the good work of the last decade doesn't go to waste. The national body has got a strong academy system on the go and the new clubs in the country are a big step forward. Phil Davies and Mark Rowley are good people down there and I hope it goes well. But it isn't a Super League club and we need that. There are thousands of kids in schools playing our game, it will still go strong, but you need that Super League professional team to be a beacon and a pathway for those kids.

We do have one weapon that can help us and we need to get him on board. Gareth 'Alfie' Thomas is a legend in both codes of rugby and he is all over the world teaching people about our great game. He is a champion too; our sport can only benefit from someone like him and we should use him to promote our game. I also want to be involved and will continue to be for a long time. I always enjoyed playing for Wales. I did retire from the team in 2006 because it was becoming almost too amateur though, and this is why I am passionate about it now. We have come too far to let it go back to those pre 2006 days. We were playing Papua New Guinea at Brewery Field and we didn't have enough shorts to put on the lads. When they were coming off we were changing shorts! I'd had enough of it then really. I had been putting my body on line for them and it wasn't in the best state anyway! I needed a shoulder operation too and I suppose all that, as well as 'shortgate', finished it off. It wasn't easy and that was probably one of the main reasons. It wasn't easy to turn my back on it after 10 years of service, but perhaps the time was right. It meant I could spend more time with my family too, and that was very important. But I did return a couple of years later as the professionalism returned …

*****

1999 was my third season at Warrington and we were beginning to show signs of improvement. We were maturing, and having someone like Peter Deakin on board behind the scenes meant we were growing there too. Deaks, God rest his soul, was a great bloke. He could sell anything to you which was handy as we brought him in as chief executive. His enthusiasm was superb and we all buzzed off it. He was the man behind 'Bullmania' at Bradford and he brought that to the club and moved us forward. Not everyone liked him but what he did was fantastic.

On the field I felt more experienced, and at 20, more settled too. We brought in quality players like Danny Farrar, Simon Gillies, Alan Hunte and Dean Hangar and they improved the squad. We all enjoyed playing together and it makes it a lot easier when off the field the club is settled too. We finished seventh after getting off to a good start but ran out of steam as the season ended, losing our last five matches.

We still had some of the usual characters like Lee Penny who we loved to wind up. Penny was a nutter. If we had to meet at half-one for a 3pm kick off he'd be there for 12.45pm, in full kit, rubbed, strapped and ready to go. He'd ask our kitman 'Ocker' or one of the players if his shorts were too tight. We'd tell him they were and they would be changed – two or three times this would go on and of course the first pair he threw off would be the ones that would be perfect. He'd pick players up in Wigan to bring them over to training and if we started at say 8am, we'd want picking up about 7.15ish. But he would be there at six in the morning beeping his horn and the lads wouldn't know what was going on! He was a strange and awesome lad but thick as shite to say the least.

I always remember going to a gentlemen's evening that was part of Chris Rudd and Gary Chambers' double testimonial celebrations. It was around 1998 and was held at the club at Wilderspool. They had organised strippers and a comedian. We weren't into women taking their clothes off to be honest but one decided to jump on Penny. She was sat in his lap and rubbing her tits in his face. He thought he was the coolest person on the planet having all this done but what he couldn't see was that she was squirting all sorts of cream all over his crotch. When he realised he launched her straight off. He didn't have the longest fuse at the best of times and he fired her some distance and we thought he was going to snap big time. Thankfully he didn't. The comedian was piss poor too and one of the lads decided to abuse him senseless until he was forced off the stage. To great applause he exited stage left and Dean Busby took over. Anyone who knows Dean will know that before he has a drink he stutters. But he'd had a few that night and with the stutter gone he entertained us all with a fantastic hour's worth of his best gags!

About that time we lost to Bradford in the cup. I remember us kicking off to Lesley Vainikolo and he came off his line and went the full length of the field! Scott Wilson said: 'If I thought Eric Grothe was playing I would have brought my autograph book.' A few minutes later Simon Gillies was brought off and as he left the field he said: 'Good luck fellas' to us all. Suffice to say it wasn't to be and we were something like 36-0 down after about 30 minutes!

Bradford scared teams to death as they were massive. If our forwards were as big as their wingers we would have been happy. They had Graeme Bradley, Jimmy Lowes and were a nasty side who bullied teams. Paul Anderson, Stuart Fielden and Jamie Peacock were the pack and once you'd dealt with them they would bring two other fuckers on. They were called the awesome foursome or something like that anyway, but it made no difference as they were trampling over us at the time. Going to Odsal was bad enough without facing those fellas and the only view I ever had was behind the posts as they slotted over another conversion.

There were a few rule changes that season and one that really benefited my game. That was the 40-20 rule where if you kicked from inside your own 40 metre line to the opposition's 20 you would get the ball back. That was great for me as I loved kicking and the balls flew. I think I must have kicked 20-odd that season. Wilderspool's pitch was small and so I could use that to perfection to gain field position. It was easily the best rule ever! It would be great if they could come up with another rule that rewards attacking play as much as that. Something where the attacking side gets a bonus for trying something out of the ordinary.

Another rule that was changed in 1999 was when you scored, you kicked the ball back to the opposition – a bit like in the NFL. It seemed a little weird to me really as it wasn't worth having a crack at drop goals and things like that. It was brought in to stop the big scores but it didn't work of course!

One of the rules I would think of changing would be reducing the number of subs to say eight. At present we have guys who play 10 minutes, have a rest and then come back on fresh. Those subs would have to be used better and be tougher and that has to be a good thing. I'd also like the scrums to go back to a good push and striking for the ball too. That's only because I am not involved in them – the forwards only pack down for a rest anyway! Ha.

Is there a rule that frustrates me? I think we have it pretty much bang on but it does piss me off that we are rugby league and have two sets of rules! Our set and the Aussie set. What is all that about? It's stupid. Football doesn't have it, rugby union doesn't so why us? If we want to attract sponsors to our game then it needs to be marketable and on a level playing field. We need to play by the same rules and look after each other. And that means playing to the same set of rules which means international teams are on a level when they face each other. You only have to see the recent World Club Challenge games. British referees let the Aussies lie on, but will hammer us in the regular season for doing that. Our sport is so dictated by Australians that it winds me and a lot of other people up in the game.

Inconsistency with referees is frustrating and in the past I used to have a go at them a lot. Everything that went against me, I would have a go and let them know about it. I don't do that as much these days as Tony Smith has helped me in that respect. Now it's more about having a laugh and trying to get them to bite too ... it is a hard job so I like guiding them now and again! Touchies wind me up though as they seem to be watching the game as a spectator. Only kidding, I love them really. The game is too quick for the referees to see everything all the time and the judges should be helping. I have seen them put their flags to their chest for a forward pass, but because the referee doesn't see them doing it, the game has continued and teams have scored. You're watching the players celebrate and then turning to the touchies. They have seen it but won't get their flag in the air to signal no try and that's a joke.

I also know for a fact – and you can ask refs and they'll say they don't – but they are influenced by the fans. At most home grounds, if the fans shout for offside and forward passes then at some point that will get to the referee. And it does happen; it's a big influencer.

I've always got on well with Steve Ganson and we had a good laugh on the field. We have known each other for years and have shared a fair number of beers too. He knows who I am and vice versa and I loved to wind him up. When he reffed, he called what he saw and was straight down the middle – and that is the way it should always be. Sometimes it must have looked like I was complaining to him but I would have been talking about what's on the telly or something!

I don't think referees are biased as such, but they can make a few mistakes. There have been a few dodgy decisions in the past and a few that stick in the memory. One in particular was in the Challenge Cup semi-final against Bradford. We were leading 20-8, something like that, and Nikau scored under the posts. Stuart Cummings didn't go to the video screen and disallowed it for some reason or another, and yep, Bradford went up the other end of the field and scored on the next set. From there we were on the rack and the Bulls came back. There's no doubt the video referee would have given it though – even though they make mistakes sometimes too! I don't know how though as they have slo-mo's and plenty of time, then sometimes they give 'benefit of the doubt'. If there's a doubt, don't give it! Who would be ref? Not me!

You know, I'm three chapters into my book and I haven't mentioned Vicky yet and I'm feeling her intense glare on the back of my neck! We met in 1996 when I went over to Hull with Dave and Dale Holdstock. We were playing against Castleford's A-team on the Friday and we went out in the city. She was Dave and Dale's cousin and we clicked really. At the end of the year I played for Carcassonne and she came over to see me for a week but ended up staying three months. She then moved over 'my way' from Hull and that was it really. It was love at first sight and she fell pregnant about six months into our relationship so that was it! It was tough when she moved over from Hull as she didn't know anyone other than her cousins. She had to find her own friends and get around the area too – but she succumbed to old Briers' patter and the rest is history. People get together young and split up all the time but we have always been strong. Having Sophie helped us too – she was born in September 1997 – and we were, and still are, very happy. Since then Recce joined us and we are a close-knit family.

I can't say Sophie's birth went well for us; well, it certainly didn't go well for me but Vicky did a cracking job! It was at the end of our season and therefore Mad Monday was in order. We went out on the Saturday and Sophie was due on the Sunday. We both had a chat and agreed that it was unlikely it would happen on that day – it never does, does it? So I went out. Of course, at one in the morning Vicky went into labour and I was blind drunk. I managed to get to the hospital and at one stage I tried to get into bed with Vicky because I needed a lie down. I ended up sitting in a chair pissed out of my face whilst the love of my life was in agony. Things were taking a bit of time so the midwife said to Vicky she had run her a hot bath as that was supposed to help. I thought she meant me so I got undressed and jumped into the bath. It didn't do me much good. In the end they sent me home at around 6am to sober up and within a few hours I was back at the hospital and my little girl was born.

Vicky has always been there for me. She knows the ins and outs of rugby as her dad, Dave Hall, played for Hull KR and GB too. Her uncle, Roy Holdstock, also played the game and Craig Hall plays for KR too. Rugby league is in her blood. If I have to make a decision I go to her first, well most of the time, and we agree on most things. I don't agree on the amount of money she spends though – but I guess that's a woman thing really!

Warrington have had a history of signing big name players and in 2000 we brought in Alfie Langar, Andrew Gee and Tawera Nikau. These signings signalled to the rest of the league we were serious about winning things. Of course, many people, and probably some of our fans too, thought they were past their best, but what they did for the club was something else. They were probably the last people of their generation to come over to England and by that I mean world class players. I learnt a hell of a lot from Alfie, whilst Nikau was a monster who would look after us on the field and be prepared to fly in with a few fists when needed. Gee was the same too.

All three were different types of player but Langar was special. He was one of the best ever to play the game and we were great mates. He liked to drink and I think we became closer because of that – Gee and Nikau were the same too. It wasn't long before the compulsory Monday drinks had more members! We went warm weather training in Lanzarote in pre-season and after the very first session at 4.30pm, Alfie was telling everyone it was happy hour at half five. We'd hit the Buds and the idea was get to dinner at seven and then have a meeting with Darryl van der Velde. Of course we missed dinner and when Darryl came down and saw the tables full of beer and all of us playing drinking games the meeting was cancelled. Alfie made sure that we were all there at half five for Happy Hour for the rest of the week.

It was a good trip until we went into town and things went a bit wrong. Paul Wood was arm-wrestling with a local and he beat him without much of an effort. Next thing it was like the Wild West and people were fighting everywhere. Steve McCurrie was smashed with a steel chair across his head – and needed 50 stitches – whilst Andrew Gee and Dave Highton got knuckle-dusted. Later on Gee was mugged at knifepoint and had his Visa card and ring stolen. Looking back it was funny how it all started – Woody winning a wrestle – but it wasn't then!

On the field Alfie was one hell of a player. He could take on the line, pass, kick and put players through. He was only 5' 4" but was so good; head and shoulders above everyone else … and I'm not pardoning the pun. He was calm and loved a joke and that's what made him so good. He wasn't so serious most of the time but when he hit the field he was.

We had a lot of good times that season but annoyingly, we didn't hit the heights we should have done and finished sixth, missing out on the play-offs again. We got beat by Bradford in the cup semi-final. We probably did drink too much but we were no different to other clubs – the only thing was we weren't winning anything. People questioned why we should drink so much and they could have been right. But my views on having a pint haven't changed since earlier in this book! Those players didn't bring a drinking culture to Warrington – it was alive and well back then, but maybe we all responded and took it to the next level.

There were highlights in 2000 though for me and I was learning all the time, especially from Alfie. We drew 30-30 with Saints at Wilderspool and totally blew the chance to win. I hit the post from around 50 metres out with a drop goal attempt and 'if only' that would have gone through then we would have ended all that stupid run that followed. I remember Alfie ripping the ball from Tommy Martyn in Saints' in-goal area to give us a chance and Sean Long on the pitch with a pair of earphones because Ian Millward was going mental in the stands. We nearly got them that time and it's one I am forcing out of my memory.

The cup game against York earlier in the season sticks out too. I scored loads of points – 40 – kicking 14 from 14 in the pissing rain in an 84-1 win. There was three or four inches of shit on the field and I started at stand-off. Steve Blakeley was on the wing and we'd signed him as a half-back. After a few minutes of the second half Darryl swopped us, and I ended up scoring a hat-trick and sticking it to the wingers afterwards about how easy it was! Kicking always came natural to me and in that match I honestly didn't think I would kick them all. But as the first few flew over I became confident and it went from there.

I have always practised my kicking and because I played football as a kid I had a natural strike which I have gone back to in the last couple of seasons. At the moment I am hitting the ball as well as I have ever done. When I was a kid I would draw an imaginary line in between two lampposts and kick over that. I've always had that round the corner soccer style of smashing the ball but I don't think about it too much as it messes with my mind. I did have a kicking coach at one point, and he wanted me to focus but it was playing with my head. I didn't kick for two years after his coaching. Great!

A lot of my game then was off the cuff, but with modern coaching it is difficult to play like that as you have to fit within a system. With me it's still in the locker as sometimes you need something a little different to break defences. You need to be able to surprise. If I don't know what I am doing then the defence certainly doesn't know either. Sadly, kids are being taught not to play off the cuff these days. It is ok to play to a system and break teams down that way, but sometimes you need that off the cuff style to change a match. The game has become too regimented. Players are playing in set positions, playing robotic and do not have any flexibility. You can see that in the NRL too. Rugby league in Australia has become five drives, a kick and wait for a mistake. Thankfully, we're encouraged to 'play' and I wouldn't want to change that as we have a duty to entertain the speccies too. But we are in danger of becoming too regimented and if kids are taught not to play, then there is no going back.

I always said to Toa Kohe-Love that I was an entertainer, he was a defender and we'd have a laugh about that. Of course you'd take a win, and take it any way you could too, but we have to entertain and remember what people come to our sport for. I would hate for us to copy the Aussies and go the same way. Wigan did that in 2010 to some extent and their game was very stereotypical of that. But they played some good rugby in their own half too and brought that 'English' style to their play. I would hate it if we all went down the same route though.

But, it will happen as we have a number of Aussie coaches in our league and the frightening thing is some see it as a stepping stone to getting somewhere in the NRL. If a club accepts that, then I suppose there is nothing you can do, but it does seem to stop the English coaches coming through as no one will give them a chance.

There are two career coaches in this country in John Kear and Brian Noble who have managed to keep a job and be wanted when others appear. Aussies come over and then go back. There's one exception and that is Tony Smith. He's never had an interest in going back home and he's probably had offers. He is a naturalised Brit and it's his home. When he goes back to Oz he calls that his holiday, so fair play to him. There are a lot of assistant coaches getting overlooked for the bigger jobs but hopefully that will change as I will be in that position one day. It's a shame if they do all the hard yards and then don't get the rewards at the end of it. English coaches are good enough for the jobs but need to be backed. Does that worry me in the future? Not really as I'm confident in my abilities like I have been as a player, and when the time comes I hope I have the expertise to step up. That's probably not for 15 years I suppose, but I hope that I can back myself to do what is needed when the chance does come up.

Anyway, another memory of that season was heading down to Newport to take on London Broncos. As we came off the motorway we pulled up at Celtic Manor which was the best hotel in the UK at the time and we were buzzing. We drove under the roof outside to be dropped off and Deaks grabbed his bags and jumped off. The coach door immediately slammed behind him and we pulled away. He was staying in a five star hotel at God knows how much a night and we stayed at a dive around the corner. Shithole does not describe how bad it was and it's lucky we pulled off a 28-18 win after an appalling night's kip! But it was good to play in Wales and we were glad to show the fans at Newport what we could do.

Ironically, a year later I got offered a contract to go and play rugby union at Pontypridd. It was massive money and I have to admit it turned my head for around ten seconds. It was more money than I have ever been offered and was something like £150,000 with bonuses of £50,000 starting in 2001. But I turned it down. Why? I was close to playing for Great Britain and I was determined to do that. And I did play for GB … once … so it was a good choice wasn't it? If I'd have known would I have gone? No, probably not. I have won the Challenge Cup and have done nearly everything I have dreamed of. I've had a testimonial too so in hindsight it was the right choice.

Rugby union has become more of a threat to our sport because of the increase in their salary cap, and these days it is more tempting for league players to make the jump. I spoke to someone who moved over recently and the average salary was about £100,000. If you offer that to a young kid, then it is more than likely they are going to take it. Being a professional sportsman carries a short lifespan and if you're motivated by making money then it is daft to turn it down. I was never motivated by money – I just wanted to play. Money does help though but what's the point of being the richest person in the graveyard?

Something will need to change or we will lose players to union and the NRL. Perhaps kids who have been in the system since 13 shouldn't count on the cap? But then there aren't many clubs in profit, so if rugby league upped its cap would it work anyway? Until we have money it's unlikely we'll see a union guy coming here. You can't take a punt on a player that's earning 100k in union and put them on the bench – that's not far off our sport's top earners. And let's be honest, they aren't going to take a cut. NRL clubs can now take a punt at our players too with their massive cap increase. Their minimum wage is something like £62,000 and some of our kids are running around for £5,000. There's plenty that our administrators could do, but I'm not clever enough to say what and I'm sure they are working hard at it. The world continues to evolve and we have to evolve with it or we will get left behind. The cap has done wonders but we have had it for too long and there needs to be a change. So it's over to the RFL now.

If a player came to me after they'd been approached by union I would be very positive and explain the reasons for staying. Then it all depends on whether they think they can go all the way in the sport. You can make a good living out of rugby league so if it's your sport you don't have to move. But I understand that cash is king in most people's lives. I made my choices for different reasons and who's to know what I would have been offered if I'd had a chat with the Welsh Rugby Union. But I turned it down flat and I am sat here with three Challenge Cups, a Lance Todd and a successful testimonial too.

I have no regrets and I'm enjoying it as much today as I always have.

4

On Top Of the World ...
Nearly

At the end of the 2000 season, the Rugby League World Cup came to these shores – and Ireland – and I was picked to play for Wales. We had a strong squad with Keiron Cunningham and Iestyn Harris probably playing some of the best rugby of their careers and we had genuine hopes of doing well. Our main goal was to reach the quarterfinal and depending who we got, kick on from there. I suppose no one expected us to do as well as we did as we ended up being the surprise team of the competition and very nearly pulled off a win over Australia in the semi-finals.

I was playing well and felt very settled in the life of a professional player. The World Cup and the Wales squad was probably the best time of my life. We came together as a group and became very close knit. In our build-up for the tournament, we travelled over to South Africa for a week's preparation which was an unbelievable time. And we played a game too whilst over there, but that was a bonus really.

South Africa was a very scary place and we travelled everywhere by bus and tried to keep ourselves to ourselves. One time we went up to Sun City in two mini buses and the South Africans just filled them up with beer and told us to enjoy it. It was a four hour trip and we made the best of it. Our conditioner, Edgar Curtis, was driving one bus and there were bottles flying out of the windows. We had a pick-up truck with us too and Dean Busby was in that with our Doctor Scott. It was about 40 degrees heat and by the time we got there, Doc was that red he slept for six hours. Chris Morley leant out of the window, picked up a traffic cone and launched it at the other bus. It ended up underneath it and caused it to skid. Stupid thing to do but we thought it was brilliant.

At Sun City we had a great time in the whirlpools and casino, but at the end of the day we had another four hour trip to cope with. And to make matters worse it was throwing it down all the way back. We stopped at some lights and, bored out of his head, Chris Smith jumped off the bus with some oil, which was in the back of the bus, and threw it over the windscreen of our team-mates. They couldn't get it off and it took them an extra hour to get home as they had to clean it. Happy days!

We stayed in Pretoria before the match and were playing Shoot, a card game. I ended up winning about £3,200 in one pot. Our hooker Mick Jenkins lost about £1,200 in one pot and he owed me £800 but I let him off. It was great though as I didn't need to go to the bank for the rest of the tour. As I say, a great trip!

We did have a game to play though and we beat South Africa comfortably 40-8. It was red hot on the field and I got sun stroke. I was laid up for a couple of days afterwards, but it was a fantastic bonding trip all round. We felt we were ready to give the World Cup our best shot.

Our first match was down in Wrexham at the end of October against the Cook Islands and we knew we needed a good start for the bigger games to follow. It lobbed it down all through the game – it did the whole World Cup to be honest – and we won 38-6 in front of a decent crowd. It was one of the most physical games I have played in as they were tough and just kept on coming at us. They were huge human beings and Kevin Iro pulled the strings. Dave Whittle got under their skin though, and every time he got the ball they knocked him to pieces. He never stopped going and ended up with his nose all over his face.

We played well at Wrexham but four days later we faced Lebanon knowing a win would more than likely put us in the quarterfinals. We played at Stradey Park in Llanelli and hardly anyone turned up to watch. They missed a really tough game and at one point we were 18-10 down and struggling. It was a horrible game against a horrible team. They spat at you, gouged, bit and took your head off given half a chance. It was sad really as they were a good footballing side. If they'd have taken that dirty shit out of their game they would have been good. Thankfully, Iestyn was on fire and turned around the deficit to hand us a 24-22 win.

It was good to get four points from our opening two matches as we got mullered by New Zealand in our final group match. It was Bonfire Night and to use a cliché we failed to sparkle on the field! Don't shout at me for that one. The Kiwis were simply too clinical for us and we got spanked 58-18 at the Welsh National Stadium as it was called then. We rested a few players as we knew we had qualified and they were just too good. David Solomona played in that match and chased me around the stadium – he still talked about that when were together at Warrington! Facing the Haka was awesome though. You have to front it up but as my career has progressed, I have understood it more. A few of our boys at Warrington have done it to players who are leaving and it's an unbelievable experience in front of you in a small changing room.

It was good to have three games in Wales, represent the country and show the people that came out to see us that we could play a bit. The fans were great and really got behind us and despite the weather it was a good craic. We got treated like superstars wherever we went too and our team boss, Mike Nicholas, would have sponsors for us which meant free food and free beer! He got the pub Brannigan's to sponsor us and we used to walk in after hours and he'd sort out tables for us full of beer. I think that's why we were so close and did so well as we bonded after hours. We took advantage of the free kegs, but didn't go too far. But I can't stress what a good time it was. We got fired up before matches, especially singing the national anthem after the Welsh National Choir came in to give us singing lessons.

A week after our defeat to New Zealand, we played Papua New Guinea at Widnes and won 22-8. Once again the weather was absolute shite but we got stuck in. The scoreline flattered us a little but it was a tight match. They were as tough as Lebanon and as big – and again they would fly into you and try and knock your head off. I remember us forcing them to drop out early on in the game and they began to chant. I couldn't quite make out what was being sung but it was like a war cry. Thing is, I was due to catch that drop out too. It was very strange and unnerving!

Getting to the semi-finals was a remarkable achievement for a small country and matched our performance in 1995 too. We were to face Australia who were red hot favourites, but we weren't fazed and went about our preparation in exactly the same way as our other games. We went out in Warrington a few days before the game and the day after we jumped on the bus ready to head to training. When we sat down everyone had a squad number and we had to call them out in order so everyone knew who was present. We got to about 16 and – I won't mention who it was – one of the lads shouted '16' knowing the player wasn't there. So when we got to training we started doing a few reps and drills and things like that. We pretty much got to the end of the session and Neil Kelly asked Clive Griffiths where X was. Iestyn, me and Kez (Keiron Cunningham) were covering for him but were rumbled by that point. He was at home pissed in bed. It would have been amazing if he'd have got away with it but he got severely disciplined!

The match itself was one of the all-time classics. We were led out into the McAlpine Stadium and you could see Welsh flags dotted around, and no doubt mostly English people waving them. The anthems were belted out and we got stuck into the Aussies from the off. Everything we did seemed to stick and we led 20-8 at half-time. Kriss Tassell's try put us ahead in the first half – luckily I suppose as my pass had gone wayward – and then I chased a massive bomb and outjumped Darren Lockyer to score. Then I slotted two drop goals – one from 30 yards – to rock the Aussies.

Everyone always points to how well I played in that first half and it is almost like I am the only person on the field. I have watched that first half on the video a few times and yeah, I played well, but I didn't play that well. Yes, I dropped the goals and caught the ball over Lockyer, but Kez and Iestyn were world class in that half, whilst Chris Morley and Anthony Farrell smashed them to pieces.

Anyone who says the Aussies were off their game in that half and didn't show us respect, well I would say that is bollocks. We played a wicked 40 minutes to lead in a match no one gave us a cat in hell's chance of winning. To be honest, we didn't think we would do as well either! You don't go into a game expecting to get beat, but up against the Aussies ... We were pretty much a part-time team, so common sense would indicate we didn't have much chance. My try to take it out to 16-8, when I went up over Lockyer, is one of the highlights of my career. I was giving him at least a foot over me, but the timing of the kick and my run on to it was perfection. I was more surprised than him!

At half-time we were confident and not overawed at what we had done. We believed we could repeat the performance and pull off a remarkable win. We wanted to play our game, but play safe too. In the second half we had a chance to further extend our lead. Iestyn passed to Anthony Sullivan and Brad Fittler came in and knocked it down. If that pass had stuck we would have been three scores up. I'm not saying we would have gone on to win, but we would have had a great platform.

But the game started to turn and the penalties flowed too.

Russell Smith was the referee and he begun to give us a hard time. We didn't seem to get the crack of the whip in that half and if we had, well, we would possibly have been in with a shout. I am a big believer in making your own luck and we tried to do that. But Smith took that away from us. He might have seen what we were doing wrong and we conceded a lot of penalties. We were trying to slow the game down but we weren't a dirty team. Giving so many to Australia wasn't something we wanted to do. It meant they played a lot of the game in our half and the pressure told in the end.

The record books show we lost 46-22 but the performance said something different. The first half and our courage as the Aussies came back epitomised everything about Wales, what we stood for, and believed in. There was no point dying wondering. You either win or go home, so we took the game to them and entertained. We also had some quality players in our team. Keiron was the best hooker in the world. Iestyn was probably one of the best halves in the world and we all went along with those two. They were great leaders and they nearly got us all the way.

It was a shame there weren't more people in the ground that night to see a home nation put on a performance like that. Wales v Australia in England seemed ridiculous and you have to blame the organisers for not having some flexibility to take the game to Wales when the fixture came out. If we had played at the Racecourse in Wrexham then perhaps more people would have come to see it. Who knows? That night though, the people who stayed away nearly missed something very special indeed. There were 8,000 people in and they were all cheering for Wales. It was a great contest and we raised our game for them.

It was also satisfying in the back of my mind that England got thumped the week after against New Zealand. They'd had a poor World Cup which had been set up for them to excel in. They weren't as good as they thought.

Ok, we were miles apart from Australia but on any given

day underdogs can win. We were so close to being right on it but they came back and showed what a world class side they were. We were upset at the end of the match because we knew we were close but all we had to show for it was pride.

After the match, we went back to our hotel in Runcorn and got heavily pissed. It was a free bar and we had a good drink. I got naked a few times too and as well as a massive hangover I had a few other surprises when I surfaced the morning after. I had no eyebrows, half my head was Bic shaven and, to put it bluntly, I had a massive dollop of shit in my ear.

It turns out that Chris Morley had followed me to my room, picked a turd up out of the toilet and put it in my ear. I was asleep blind drunk so there's no way I could have stopped him. But you have to question what goes on in people's minds to do that! It was everywhere ... on the pillow, bed sheets and I had no eyebrows and half a head of hair. To make matters worse, I was going to an ex-Hull KR players' sportsman's dinner three days later so had to go looking like Uncle Fester. Vicky wasn't very happy either. I have got Chris back since but I will tell you about that later in the book!

Sadly Wales didn't move on from this match and fell away massively. We had a springboard to get bigger and better and we didn't take it. I say we, I mean the RFL. I wasn't part of 1995 when Wales got to the semi-finals and I've been told that the RFL missed a trick with not fast-tracking a team in Wales into the top flight on the back of that. To not do that again in 2000 was fucking scandalous really and we declined as a result. The lesser countries got left behind as the powers that be focussed on England, Australia and the usual suspects. We had a base in 2000 to grow and that wasn't taken advantage of. A successful Wales was a gimmie for the RFL and they ignored it. It was appalling that Wales didn't make the 2008 World Cup after being in the semi-finals in the past two tournaments. We had to qualify and didn't make it. PNG went straight in and we beat them in 2000. That can't be right?

The authorities have come up with a number of good ideas,

but the number of bad ones outweigh them. The latest one was to split up Great Britain after bringing it back together following the tournament. History has been taken away from our sport as a result. You could play the Four Nations once every three or four years and the other nations could play when necessary but you need a proper Lions tour that could tour Australia and New Zealand every four years. People go on about playing too many games on tours but this is what you play rugby league for – to take on the best with the best. Tours seems to be a thing of the past and therefore that representative level of league is removed. The Aussies could come here and play Yorkshire, Lancashire and then GB. Or, they could face Wales, Ireland and then GB. Surely that strengthens our game and helps develop the so called 'lesser' nations?

Super League players want that but we aren't being listened too. Players want to play for GB and also represent their nations too. Without that top level of representative rugby we force players to choose to play for another country instead of their own. That isn't right and one of the reasons I haven't moved from Wales to England.

I was asked if I would play for England but I turned it down, and it annoys me that there is a loophole that allows you to do it. Once you choose who you play for you shouldn't be able to change. I can't blame players for doing it though as the loophole is there and we all want to better ourselves. And, if someone is dangling a carrot for you to switch then that makes the decision even more tempting. Bring back GB and you remove the loophole and stop this. If you only get to face the big nations once every four years then players will automatically choose England as they face those countries nearly every year. That devalues your smaller nations and they get smaller. Fans want to see Wales, Ireland and Scotland play the best with the best players but they can't.

I probably earned more in that deck of cards in South Africa than playing for Wales. That isn't the point though as it is a privilege and honour to play for your country. I know some of our players have taken time off to play for us and others who have travelled from overseas to pull on the jersey. That is superb commitment to your team-mates and the country. But it can't be right. When we beat Ireland in the 2005 European Cup, I asked everyone to meet at the bar at 9am the next morning as we were flying out later on. I put my card behind the bar and made sure everything was free for the lads all day. It was a treat for our performance and to show my appreciation for all they had done.

Playing for your country shouldn't be about finance, or rules, or loopholes. It should be about pulling on that jersey and running your blood to water. But we make it easy for players to switch countries and make our sport a laughing stock. Internationally our game is struggling and we need to make it stronger. We need to look after our players and it's no wonder some are getting their heads turned by rugby union. That will continue until we look at doing something different.

A year later I realised a massive dream by pulling on a Great Britain shirt in a pre-Ashes game in France. We won 42-12 and I scored a try and kicked a goal. When you become a professional and make your debut for your club you want to progress to the next stage and make international honours. It's in the blood of all professional rugby league players and I was no different. I didn't know if it was possible; I was ambitious enough to hope but I never took it for granted. I'd made my debut for Wales at a young age and was pleased to represent them and put in good performances. But I knew I'd only get to play the 'top' sides once in a blue moon and therefore gaining full honours with GB was a real goal.

So when I got the call up it was surreal really. I had recently played against England and did well. We'd lost a tight match and I think David Waite, who was coach of GB as well as England, was impressed with what he had seen. It was brilliant to go into camp for the upcoming Ashes Tests with the 'superstars' and I really enjoyed it. We trained hard and I was picked to play against France in Agen. I can't remember a whole deal of the match but I know I was nervous beforehand. I scored a try and kicked a goal and I thought I had done enough to put myself in the shop window for the upcoming series against Australia.

As I mentioned earlier, at this time I turned down a contract to sign for rugby union as I was on the verge of breaking into the GB side and I wanted to do that. I made the cut down squad for the Ashes alongside other halves Paul Deacon and Paul Sculthorpe. But throughout the whole tournament I didn't get a game and I was at a loss as to why.

Brian Noble was the GB assistant at the time and I'm not saying that had anything to do with it, but he obviously knew Deacs better than he knew me as he was his coach at Bradford. He knew Paul on a day to day basis and I have no doubt that went in his favour. Plus he was a top player.

After one of the Tests, a few of us went into Chester on a Monday and had a few beers. I drove back and got back to my hotel about half past eleven and went to bed. I woke up the next day, and after getting ready I heard a knock on the door. It was Barrie McDermott who told me I owed Brian Noble an apology. I asked Barrie why and he said I had knocked on his door bollock-naked in the night. I know you won't believe me but I do sleep walk now and again after a few beers. I'd only had about five pints though and I explained this to Brian. He told me he understood, said it wasn't a problem, was one of those things and it wouldn't go any further.

I was aware of how it might have come across but I trained really well during the week and I gave it everything until the Thursday when David Waite was to make his selection. If you got a call from him at around 8am on the Thursday morning you knew you wouldn't be in the team. He would ask you to come down and meet him and that would be it. But I had trained well all week and all the senior players were telling me I was going to get the nod. Even though I hadn't had the go ahead from David, I started to believe it too and started to get excited. But in the morning I got the dreaded phone call.

When I got downstairs he told me the news and I asked him why I wouldn't be given a shout. He just turned round and said: 'I think you know why – for what happened on Monday'.

So I was training as a GB player for three weeks and not getting a look in – and I turned down a move to rugby union too! I'd been training for a long time and gambling in casinos to fill the time knowing I wasn't going to get picked. It must be hard for players who go on tour to Oz and don't get a look in. That is one of the reasons I think the proper tours should come back so everyone can at least get a game against other teams rather than the country.

There's no point having players going out there for six weeks, getting flogged and not getting on the field. I did that in 2006 for two weeks and played against Newcastle as part of the GB squad for the Tri-Nations. It was funny how it came about. Hull were playing Bradford in the play-off semi-final and if the Bulls had won, I wouldn't have been on the flight as Richard Horne would have been in in front of me. So when Hull beat Bradford to set up a Grand Final with St Helens I was celebrating. I put a couple of quid on Bradford to win too, so whatever the result I would have been a winner!

The result went the right way and I got a call from Abi Ekoku to get my bags packed as I had made the squad to play against Newcastle and a country side. I was gutted in a way though as I thought I should have been in the squad anyway without having to wait for a match result for my ticket. Warrington had beaten Leeds in the play-offs before losing to Bradford and I thought I deserved the chance to show everyone what I could do. Sky commentator Eddie Hemmings was starting his 'Briers for Britain' campaign at the time and that was also pretty humbling to be honest. But once again I didn't get to play in a full Test and I was gutted – especially after kicking five goals and winning man of the match against a Newcastle XIII at the Energy Australia Stadium.

It was a good trip and a great experience ... well almost. One training session saw us get flogged in 34 degrees heat in Manly and I was spewing from one end and shitting from the other. It makes me wince thinking about that session – but that's what the lads who didn't play for the full tour did all the time. You can see why some players become disillusioned with it after that. I remember we trained for a week solid, and coming up to the Saturday, the GB staff said we could have a drink in the evening. We had been flogged big time and we were looking forward to it. We were in Manly and next thing there were riots in Cronulla and Penrith. Those places were more than an hour away but the bosses decided we couldn't go out and had to stay in the hotel.

I was 28 at the time and I spoke my mind. Perhaps that's why I never got picked because I was outspoken. I do think there are players that won't say anything and go along with it. If you have something to say then say it and that's what I did. When someone says you can't go out of your hotel because there's a riot two hours away – that's like banning us going out in Warrington because it is kicking off in Hull. That's ridiculous!

It was agreed we could have a few in the hotel and we accepted that in the end. We were allowed three bottles each, which was stupid. They disappeared pretty quickly so I went up to the bar but the tab was closed. As I turned around to tell the boys it was closed I overheard someone from the RFL putting their beers on a tab. They were still using another tab but the players weren't allowed to. I thought that stank so I said to the lads if they were ordering to get it put on their tab, and that's what we did. We hit them for about 1,000 bucks! It's petty that they had stopped the lads going out when they were away from families and then stopped the tab but were using one themselves. The Aussies are allowed to be men when they come over but we go six weeks across the world and aren't allowed out because of a riot two hours away!

It was frustrating waiting for another chance after my cap in 2001. I suppose a reputation goes a long way, and until you get to know a person then it can stand in your way. I saw that when Tony Smith came to Warrington and his perception of me. It is probably different now to what he thought. But if I am being honest, half-back has to be a dominant part of the team and if you look at Warrington's record over those years we weren't exactly ripping it up were we? We weren't consistent enough.

You can't argue with the people that went before me; they were the guys who were playing in the top four and making finals. Sometimes you have to go outside the box though and I always believed I would have been more than good enough for Great Britain. Yes we were playing players from the top four but it wasn't getting us anywhere and surely that should have seen us trying something new? For instance, I would have loved to have played with Sean Long. We would have been great together and would have rubbed off on each other. We both play off the cuff and kick from different sides but we didn't get the chance. Other people outside the RFL were saying it was worth a chance, but it didn't happen and that is a shame.

I could probably turn round and say in hindsight they were right as we won Tests and beat the Kiwis in a 'drawn' Test series. But mainly we only beat France, so perhaps it was worth a shot. I'm confident in knowing I would have been good enough and I would still back myself to play for GB now if they had a side. Is it satisfying to know they couldn't pull it off? Sure, but it isn't nice to see them lose. I am a proud Brit and there's no point me dwelling on it but I'm sure I could have offered them something different.

I never asked Tony Smith why he wouldn't pick me, although he did ask me to play against the All Golds at Warrington in 2007, which was decent of him. I turned it down though as I'd had a few injuries that year and my body was struggling a bit. I didn't think I would have been worthy of it in the state I was in.

I know there won't be many players who have scored more than 2,700 points and not made regular appearances at the highest level. I can't explain why; that is for other people to answer. I can only say I am proud of what I have done. To represent Great Britain more times would have been great as I did my utmost to get into the squad and show people what I could do. But it is disappointing when you see the likes of Kevin Sinfield and Paul Sculthorpe playing in my position. If we can't beat the Aussies with people playing in their best position then how can we beat them playing out of position? That's never made sense to me, although Sinny and Scully are class acts. It has also been a shame that GB coaches have always been club coaches too as they need to be independent. Those coaches are always going to favour their own players as was my experience.

There is also a train of thought to select players on reputation, although it is changing. It should always be who is in form at the time. You will always get three or four players in the side for reputation, you need that for stability, but in the past it has been far more. You need to give people a chance, especially if they are playing well. But in the past we have picked the same people who have been in the side for the past six years. What have we won with them? There are some great club players, but there are some very average international players.

Take the 2011 England v Exiles match for example. Sinny is a great loose forward but not a stand-off. We have good stand-offs in the competition so why not give them a try? Jonny Lomax at Saints was on fire that season and although he was pulled into the set-up, he never got to play. As I found to my cost, you shouldn't bring players into the squad if you aren't going to play them. All this 'experience' bullshit about being in camp – unless you play it's a waste of time being there.

That's the same with 'train on' squads. It's just filling spaces for me and that's pointless. Obviously they have to have people in there, but there are players you know won't play and will be disappointed. You know when you aren't going to get picked even if you are in the train on squad. I would love it if one year people said: 'Wow, I didn't see that coming,' but we could probably pick the team about six months before a tournament because we know the script.

What I have noticed in GB camps is there is a lot of focus on fitness work. For me I can't understand why you have the best players in the comp and all you want them to do is fitness work and wrestling. All a coach has to do is make that team gel and get defensive and attacking combinations right. These players are at the top of their game and should be fit enough. If they aren't at that point in the season then they shouldn't be playing rugby league. As you can read I think I'm the next Wayne Bennett!

But I feel they treat you like kids in camps: 'You can't do this, you can't do that, go out ...' and most players won't stand up to that. I would and always have. If you're abroad, six weeks is a long time to be away from home and you need something to break it up. You don't need to be school teachers with players as the vast majority know the boundaries.

Are there cliques in camp? I haven't experienced any and there wasn't in 2001. I have always been approachable and not in that bubble. That year I had my own clique – a group of one Warrington lad – so I had to get on with everybody. In the lead up to the Ashes Tests we stayed at Neil Harmon's house and had a good blast in Leeds. I suppose that's in the past as now you wouldn't get players from another club staying in another city at another player's house. But that's the way it was back then. If you were Saints, Leeds or Warrington you all went out.

I will take all these experiences for when I am coaching. In Wales, camps can't be as intense as we aren't full-time and players are losing money when they are with us – unless they have booked a holiday! We do work hard and in camp we enjoy each other's company. We talk about our camps during the year and email and text each other all excited about it. That doesn't happen in any other camp, trust me. We have a laugh with the coaching staff and team manager and everyone is approachable. Ten years ago you could go out two nights a week, but as the game has got faster you can't do that. It is more of a club atmosphere than international and if that was lost, Wales would struggle. Our team spirit is brilliant and when I was away for a couple of years and returned, that hadn't changed.

We keep winning the European Nations and that puts pressure on the authorities to let us have a crack at New Zealand and Australia. Would we want to play them every year? Not really, as we are unlikely to win, but we would give it our best. But we do need that experience to make sure we can compete. The only way is to somehow make our way back to Great Britain and then everyone can benefit.

The 2011 Exiles match is a case in point. We had a Super League team in Wales and none of our players could play for England or the Exiles. Pat Richards played for them and he played for Ireland a while back. I put my name forward for the Exiles and heard nothing back. Yet, you keep hearing how the League talks to the players and understands their side.

The Lancashire v Yorkshire experiment was a brilliant experience but fell by the wayside when the clubs took over and wouldn't let players play because of injury – but they made miraculous recoveries at the weekend for Super League! I played a couple of times for Lancashire and really enjoyed it. Ian Millward was our coach and he was fantastic – very different to what I was used to. I liked his style of play and his success with Saints shows how well it worked. Saints still play to his blueprint; being fast around the ruck and being able to blow you away. He took the concept on board and tried to make it as close to the State of Origin series as he could. We would meet up at a camp, have a beer, train, have another one, and try and get some spirit in the camp. It worked too, as we won the series.

I remember we were practising drop goals and I was the man to do it. I nailed one from distance and he stopped us and said: 'Right, what happens if it comes on the other side or they come to charge down?' I was cocky and so instead of running and passing it to another player, I set up for a shot; I stepped and banged it over with my other foot. 'That'll do,' he said.

Internationally, it's all about England, Australia and New Zealand because they draw the crowds and the money. Does rugby union think like that? They have internationals all over the world and look after each other. The RFL has made a profit for the last few seasons and where is the money going? It isn't going to the lesser nations, so the fat people get fatter.

I moan about it, yes, but we all know something needs to change. We've lost a professional club in Wales and the future will be hard for us. Meanwhile, unless you win the European Nations Cup you aren't going to get into the Four Nations. If you do make it to the finals then a lack of big match experiences is likely to see you finish bottom of the comp.

So, magic wand time. I would bring GB back. Kept that quiet, didn't I? I would take GB on a tour to Australia every two or four years and then the next year the Four Nations would get together. After that I would make sure New Zealand or Australia came to us and played proper matches – taking on the Super League Champions and things like that. They would also play perhaps a mix of Wales, Ireland, Scotland, Lancashire and Yorkshire as well as a Test match series against England. That would give people a chance to see matches mid-week in-between Tests and give players an incentive to stick with their countries. There needs to be a lot of work for that to happen and we need to be less club focused. Clubs hold the power and perhaps that isn't right, but we moan when we don't win internationals.

I know it's probably not on the same high list as winning the Ashes or anything like that but I am so glad I have won something with Wales. Those coaches who didn't pick me for GB? Well, they haven't. A medal is a medal and we were European Champions in 2009 and 2010. I love saying that to Moz (Adrian Morley). I joke that his loss-win rate is about 80 to 20 and most of the wins are against France. Mine is better. I know we are on a different level and we don't play the big nations, but you can only beat what is in front of you.

5

Changing Coaches ... and Times

In the year I got the nod to play for Great Britain, I experienced yet another indifferent and under-achieving season with Warrington. We once again finished outside the play-off places and lost our second Challenge Cup semi-final in a row to Bradford. This time Paul Anderson came off the bench and the big bugger tore us to shreds. But we were growing as team and I think, looking back, the foundations of the success we would have later in the decade was being formed.

Pre-season was one of the toughest ever as Darryl took us to Plymouth to train with the 29 Commando Regiment. We didn't get off to the best start as there was a crash on the M6 and it took us 10 hours to get there. When we were stuck in traffic, Danny Nutley got out and had a pee on the central reservation. As he was finishing the traffic moved so we decided to lock all the doors – which saw him running down the motorway doing up his flies. We weren't going fast, but every time he got close we would move on and I reckon he ran a mile at least.

The camp was a real shock to the system and was on a nuclear base which meant we couldn't go offsite without being in two mini buses and only when they told us we could. We were plotting to escape for most of the trip!

It was ridiculously hard. On that first day, because we got there late, they said we could go out for a drink or go round Plymouth. The mini buses would be leaving at around 3am so it was unlikely we would just have some food and go for a walk. All but a few of us went out on the piss and we got back to the base at around half three. I'd just put my head on a nice cold pillow when they burst in and told us to get dressed and get outside. We hadn't been asleep more than half an hour and were still pissed and they had us doing stress positions and other tests. Dean Busby was in floods of tears and laughing at the same time because he was in so much pain.

One freezing day we went swimming too. We came into a courtyard and they broke the ice in what looked to be a small trench. We had to jump in with our full clothes on and carry a log. It was so deep you couldn't touch the floor. Lee Penny couldn't swim so was thrashing about, but every time you clashed logs you would have to stay in another minute. He kept on doing it and we were screaming at him to keep on treading water and keep going! His lips went blue.

Another memorable trip was to Dartmoor. We had to walk seven miles one way to meet an instructor who would tell us a story out of a newspaper cutting. The plan was then to navigate back and recount the tale. That was really hard. Andrew Gee was hallucinating he'd been so flogged ... then we couldn't remember the fucking story either. Good times!

We kept talking about our escape route and me and Toa Kohe-Love planned to steal the bus keys and drive back to Warrington in the middle of the night. But it never happened.

That was Martin Masella and Steve Georgallis's first look at their new team-mates too. They had travelled from Sydney to Warrington to get there just in time for our 10-hour drive to Plymouth. They'd been up for 36 hours when we hit the town for that first session. They were in rounds together and Martin was drinking Caffrey's and shots. He would get two beers and a shot of water for himself and then a shot of Tequila for Ste. They had battered their respective rounds for five hours and I have to say Georgallis is still, to this day, the drunkest person I have ever seen. So that was a great start to the season and it went from there! It was an enjoyable season really.

Speaking of pre-season fun, one of the best was in 1998 when we went to Aberdovey to do all sorts of team-building stuff and mountaineering. One day we had to build a raft, get in the sea, go round a buoy and then come back. But the current was so strong it took us out to sea. Some of the lads couldn't swim and were bricking it. On another day there was an assault course where you had to run up to the rope, jump on and then propel yourself on to a net. Underneath it was the foulest mud that must have been there for more than 100 years. Warren Stevens missed the net and went straight in and I have never smelt anything as bad as that, it was horrible. Adam Fogerty, aka Gorgeous George out of *Snatch*, had to climb logs that got higher and higher like the rest of us. When he got to the third one that was about 16ft up he clung on and froze. He refused to move!

On that trip I had to leave after a couple of days as I was in court for affray after an altercation with some of lads at the Saints club. It had happened a year previous and we ended up going there about 13 or 14 times before we got off not guilty but obviously we were. I was due back on the site after the court appearance but when I got to the camp, there was no food for miles. Mike Wainwright was out on the piss with the boys and he brought me back a vindaloo with some crackers. The curry was awful but I crunched up the crackers and put them in my mate Danny Whittle's bed. But when I had to go back to court I stupidly left my stuff on site. When I came back it looked like a dog had got it. All my gear had been ripped and cut – served me right I suppose.

Another signing that season was Kevin Walters who Vicky and I got really close to along with his wife Norrelle and their three boys. I was worried when he came in as I was the club's stand-off and he was one too. That would have meant Kevin and Alfie Langar being the half-back partnership as that was their positions at Brisbane. It meant I got shunted to full back, which was never my best position. But Kevin didn't settle and went back home. I learnt a lot off him in that short time and he probably made me a better player. Thinking about it, Alfie and Kevin at half-backs and me at full-back – that's much like the modern day game in a way. The full-back position is very much like an extra half when attacking. I caught up with Kevin when he was coach at Catalans and he tried to sign me. But that's for another chapter.

Like I say, it was an enjoyable season and we put in a lot of effort, but towards the back end we struggled a little bit and started to drift away from the play-offs. I broke my thumb in the 'State of Origin' Lancs v Yorks games and Alfie Langar was called up by Wayne Bennett to play State of Origin for Queensland and became the first player not based in Australia to do so. He ripped New South Wales apart too – silencing the doubters who said he couldn't compete as he was in Super League. We were delighted for him as he showed what a class act he was. It was great to watch our team-mate do so well. There's only special people and players who can do that.

Alfie is easily one of the top three players ever to come into Super League from overseas, if not the best, and it was sad when he decided to stay over in Australia. In the same month, Darryl van der Velde went back home too and Steve Anderson came in for the last few weeks of the season.

If I'm truthful – and I'll apologise now if I offend him – Steve was the worst coach I have ever played for. His ethics were totally different from what they should have been and I think the day he came out in a press conference and said we weren't going to be peaking for the Challenge Cup was the day I thought he was a load of bollocks.

We played Barrow in the first round and we won something like 10-0. Anderson told the press he wasn't bothered as we would be at our best around the 12th round of Super League That was a shocking comment as the cup is a massive part of our tradition and the British game. Before then we'd fallen out after I came back from playing for GB.

Although I only played one game, I was in camp for six weeks and then went on holiday after the tournament with a few of the GB lads for a couple of days. I got back on the Monday and noticed a load of missed calls on my phone. It was Steve and I called him to ask what was up. He said he'd been after me, gave me a lot of abuse for being unavailable and told me I had to report for training on the Tuesday. He said I'd missed the Monday session and that wasn't good enough.

I told him I'd been in camp and was due a holiday and also allowed six weeks off at the end of a season. But he didn't agree, even though it was in my contract, and threw a written warning at me for missing training. He said I could sit at home on my wage and have a think about it. I thought if that's what he wants to do then fuck him, I would do it. He backed down but we'd got off to a bad start.

2002 didn't exactly start the best way and with the players he was bringing in as, with all due respect, they weren't Super League calibre. We'd lost Alan Hunte, Toa Kohe-Love and Alfie Langar and needed to sign experience. But we didn't. There were rumours he had to keep the budget down to get his wage up but they simply weren't good enough. It wasn't the fault of those lads though, they tried their best, and they weren't going to turn down a Super League spot.

You could also tell that something wasn't quite right with his methods. We did no real pre-season, no fitness work, no hard training and no tackling of any sort for the first couple of weeks. Some people might say that was ideal for me! We had to come out on to the field together. We weren't allowed to cross the whitewash until he said so, and we would stand along the touchline with our own ball. If we forgot our ball it was a £50 fine. He also opted to take us to Lilleshall in the winter and, shock horror, it snowed so we couldn't train!

Early in January, we went to Blackpool to have a team bonding drink and were well into a good session when Steve got us into a huddle. It was about 9pm and he told us we'd be in at half seven in the morning and be hitting the hills to see how mentally tough we were. That's not mentally tough, that's just fucking stupid and asking for injuries and trouble. I'm not saying I have never been drunk at a training session, because I have, but after encouraging the session, to do that was stupid.

As we moved into the season he put Tommy O'Reilly at half-back and moved me to full-back which wasn't the right move for the balance of the team. It isn't my best position but I went with it for the good of the side. We were missing quality and it seemed a strange move to shift around the team and I was always going to find it hard at the back. And it was no surprise when we struggled as a result.

He had a five-year plan and isn't that typical of a coach that may struggle? Good coaches have a plan for now but his was not to peak for the Challenge Cup.

Ironically, he turned to me when his days were numbered. The board wanted to meet the players as we continued to show poor form. Before we met them, Steve pulled me to one side and pleaded with me to tell them it wasn't his fault but the players. I told him to get stuffed and not long later he'd gone – 10 months into that five-year plan – and David Plange, his assistant, had taken over. Perhaps Steve was out of his depth in Super League with the way he went about his business and how he tried to get players on board.

Warrington have been amazing over the years I have been there. Everyone makes mistakes and maybe they misjudged the appointment. You have just got to put it down to bad judgement. But Anderson left the club in a bad state and with the wrong sort of players to get us out of it. Plange knew what he was on about and got the team to go with him, but he had the same players and he struggled. Then, later in the season, Paul Cullen took over and he had the same problem.

*****

We were lucky not to go down in 2002, beating Salford in the dying stages of the season to stay up. We might make light of it, but I did think we were on the brink of dropping out of the league for the majority of the season. It was that scary. Even though the lads were trying, and you can't knock them for that, they were out of their depth. Thankfully, the work of Plange and Cullen kept us up by the skin of our teeth. Cull came in with around five or six games to go and signed Nathan Wood and Ben Westwood. It's fair to say they turned us around and were massive in raising our confidence.

Wood was a real character and we became very close friends. I think he is probably the toughest bloke, pound for pound, I have played with. He could fight anything and was a real prankster. He would go round to one of the Aussie's houses at night, break in and run into the living room to jump on them with a devil's mask on. Some of the tales about him are unreal. We roomed together in London and one night I got up to go the toilet at 3am. It was pitch black and as I headed back to my bed, all I heard was a dog biting at my ankles. He'd woken up to do that and I shit myself. It takes a special – or mental – type of bloke to do that.

Cull was a Warrington legend and knew what the club was about and what was needed to stay up. He had passion, and although that can only get you so far, it was what was needed at the time. We needed someone who knew the history of the club and the people of the town and what it meant to them. And that is what got us out of the shit. He was very brave as it was a massive gamble for him to take it on with only a few games to go. Had we lost those games then he effectively was the coach that would have taken us down. I'm glad it paid off.

We had a lot of fun with Cull. He would give us video sessions and sit there with a remote control winding an old VHS back and forward. I bought a little laser thing that would block infrared, so when he tried to pause, I would turn it on and fast forward it … then rewind it back. He would scream at Paul Darbyshire, his assistant, to get him some new batteries and he would be smashing the remote and smacking the video to get it working. They were the best video sessions ever. He must have gone through ten sets of batteries and three remotes before he called Martin Dawes to get it fixed. A great scam for something that cost me a quid!

Steve made Matt Rodwell captain, but by the time Cull came in I had been given the title. It was a great honour for me and a real privilege. I had been captain at junior and academy level but it wasn't something I had thought about as a pro. I was young too and therefore it wasn't a goal of mine. But I loved every minute of it until I decided to let someone else do it.

I enjoyed being a leader on the field but what I did struggle with was pulling myself away from being one of the boys. I needed to calm down and lead more. If I had my time again I would probably do that. I always thought I was a team player and thought I had to be part of the team and not focus on individual accolades. Perhaps that's where I slipped up a little and now I'm not captain I have gone on to have more success. At the same time I was captaining Wales too and that was a big honour. It was different because I was a leader in the Welsh squad in other ways. It was a very proud time for me, that's for sure.

There are two kinds of captain; you can lead by your actions or you can lead in what you say and do. It is definitely a proud thing to be. I always tried to lead by my actions on the field, but maybe not enough off the field. At the time I was probably drinking too much and giving it some hammer. Being a rugby league player and captain is a lot to deal with when you are younger, and maybe I needed some guidance. I should have stayed at home instead of going out I suppose. Those days are gone now and I don't regret them. They are part of my history and part of my life. I know other players who drank a lot more than me. I wasn't winning anything though so people could complain.

Anyway, that season was a real close call and the result over Salford was our only real highlight. We finished one win clear of Wakefield with a points difference of minus 395. If we had gone down it would have been tough. We were struggling for money and with a new stadium on the horizon it may not have worked heading in there as a Championship club. It's all 'what ifs'. Perhaps if it had worked out differently I wouldn't be sat here writing this book.

In 2002, Saints tried to sign me. Ian Millward was really keen on bringing me in and I was very close to agreeing a deal. But he turned round and brought in Jason Hooper who did a belting job for them. That was the second time I had cried over them and I promised I wouldn't do it again.

It was very close to happening but I'm glad it didn't.

6

Brian

For all the highs and lows of rugby league, winning trophies and representing your country, nothing can prepare you for the shock of losing someone you love. In April 2001, we lost Brian to cancer.

Brian was a cracking brother and friend and was taken from us at the age of 34. It happened very suddenly. It was a massive shock to be told he had the disease as you hear about it but never think it will happen to one of your family. I remember the day he took ill like it was yesterday. I came home from the pub and he was a greeny-yellow colour. We took him to Whiston Hospital and just seemed to be sat in the waiting room for hours. When they called him in for tests you could just tell by the doctors' faces they knew what it was. It was testicular cancer.

The news blew us away, but when we began to think about it, we knew the recovery rate was good and we were all positive. We had to stay positive for Brian.

But, after a couple of chemo treatments at Clatterbridge, he just passed away. It had been five weeks since his diagnosis. How the fuck did that happen? I couldn't get my head around it at all. People walk on the moon and things like that and here was my brother who had just died from cancer.

The phone rang at 5.15am and you just know, don't you,

that something is wrong. My stomach lurched and the nurse told me I had to get to the hospital as quickly as possible. Unfortunately, he had passed away before we got there.

You know what? A song was on the radio as I headed to the hospital. It was Nelly Furtado's *Like A Bird*. I knew then he was flying away, but I wasn't prepared for what would happen at the hospital or to me as the days went on. Stephen, my eldest brother, was there first and broke the news to me. It was surreal. I will always remember mum and dad going in to Brian's room and the sight was so sad to see. Being a parent you never want to see your kids going before you. He was asleep in his bed, still there and smiling, but there was no life left in him. His organs had given in to the chemo and his loss was devastating for the whole family.

For the five weeks he'd been really positive. The chemo knocked him a little as expected. I spoke to him and said we would get the best treatment but he didn't want to do that. He didn't want us to spend the money and he would fight it in his own way. I believe he was probably hiding something. It was more than testicular cancer I think. He was the type of person who wouldn't tell us as he wouldn't have wanted to put my folks through it. I always remember the doctors saying he had shadows on his lungs and I think that's where the cancer had gone too. He was bedridden and weak after the chemo, but I don't picture him being in that bed. I picture him with his great smile, cracking a gag, and smacking me about a bit.

He was a happy-go-lucky type of guy and still lived at home with my folks, even though he was getting on, the old git! He would go to the pub every night and smoked no more than five a day when he had a beer. He loved being in the Black Bull on Knowsley Road and I think there's a plaque in there for him now. He'd go to work, come home, go to the pub, and mum would have his tea on when he got back. We had the craic together and it is just a shame really that he didn't meet my son Reece. I take him to the grave now and again though.

For Sophie my eldest, Brian was much more than an uncle

to her. He looked after her all the time and doted on her. He was just a great brother and a top mate as well.

I would take a few bollockings off my other two brothers and would rob stuff from the house. He would take the rap for it and would watch for me wherever I went. He was big into sport too and he would come to see all my amateur rugby and football games. I played for his football team in the off season too and always told him I was the better player! I never saw him with a girl and I kept teasing him about that! He was just one of us though and would never harm a fly although I wouldn't have wanted to get on the wrong side of him.

He'd do the *St Helens Star* paper round when he was a kid. At our folks we could go behind next door's garage. One time I was hiding behind there and my dad went looking for me. When he went around the back, he must have found around six weeks' worth of papers. There must have been 2,000 mouldering away. He was taking the money and running! At the back there were hedges that split the gardens and we would vault over them doing the Grand National. He would chase us all over it … good times.

Masses of people turned out at the funeral and St Helens Crematorium was packed. There were people outside and all my team-mates came down to support us. The fans were fantastic with me too, as were other teams in the league, and I am truly grateful for that.

I did reflect on my life a lot back then and decided not to take anything for granted. I tried not to let things worry me as much. I had smoked from about the age of 10 and was going through about 15 a day. From the day he died I packed in and never touched another. It just woke me up and I thought there's no way I am going to kill myself, it's hard enough staying alive as it is. I live life to the full because you never know when your last days are going to be.

When we got to Wembley in 2009, the semi-final was on Brian's birthday. I still get chills thinking about that and he was watching over us as we beat Wigan. I am not religious in anyway and by any stretch; I believe in God, but I'm not a churchgoer. I just believe that day was meant to be.

The following year it was his birthday the day before and I scored in exactly the same spot. When you reflect on that you have to think there is another life somewhere. He would have loved the trip to Wembley and would have given his mates stick after the match as they're all Saints fans.

He was there though, as he always will be, but not in person. I miss him lots.

Here's to you Brian. Son, brother, uncle and best mate.

7

Goodbye Wilderspool

A massive part in the life of the town and the game ended in 2003 when Wilderspool finally closed for business. We all knew the stadium had seen better days, and for the club to move on we needed to move out.

We all wanted to give the place a big send-off, especially with the history of the stadium and the great names that had played there. And looking back, we made the play-offs and did what we wanted to. But I was injured for the back end of the season and missed out on so much of the party. Every game was a carnival atmosphere because we were one game closer to leaving the stadium and becoming a bigger club.

No one liked Wilderspool – except Wire players. I think I can vouch for others when I say that. To be a Warrington player on the field though was something else, and it really gave us the advantage. The fans would be on top of you in the Fletcher and Railway Ends, creating a tight and tense atmosphere, but the facilities were awful.

As the home side, we would play about with the heating in the away dressing room to get an advantage. If it was baking hot, we'd turn up the heating, and if it was cold, it would be switched off. The showers were a nightmare too, there was never enough hot water – unless you were in the home dressing room of course! That was the way it was in those days, you'd take any advantage you could.

The worst dressing room I've been in is Salford's old Willows ground by a country mile. It was ok for me as I'm short, but for big lads their heads would be touching the ceiling, and the showers were in the corridor with members of the public walking past. Basically, you'd get a massage, piss and get washed in the shower – and the toilets leaked too. I'm sure it was a ploy of theirs.

As I've said before, we nearly went down in 2002 and it would have been a very difficult season if that had happened. Spending our final year in our ground as a Championship team, on the verge of a new stadium, would have been difficult to pull off, but maybe a promotion run might have given it a fitting end. Fortunately, that didn't happen and we went into the season as a Super League team. As well as Paul Cullen bringing in the calibre of players that we needed in Benny Westwood and Nat Wood, he also got rid of the shite we had the year before. The likes of Brett Grose, Graham Appo, Darren Burns and Sic Domic were better, more solid players, and they strengthened our team. It meant we moved from a close season of worry to one of optimism and hope.

Once again we were blessed with the usual mix of nutters and characters. Number one was Nick Fozzard. Absolute top bloke but an utter barmpot. He could moan for Great Britain. His mandatory statement every morning was: 'Is everyone else tired? I'm tired,' and that would go on. He would do naked chin-ups and bench presses – which wasn't a pretty sight. He is also one of the tightest guys I have ever met and plays up to being thick.

Mark Hilton was an absolute beast and the hardest trainer I have ever played with. He would abuse his body physically and after training finished he would still be going with 20 kg plates on his head to strengthen his neck. He never drank either, and when he came back after injury I told him to relax and have a pint and he did. He loosened off and did really well. I'm not saying drink is good for you, but he was outstanding after he started!

Warren Stevens was absolutely puddled – when Saints had offered £350,000 cash and two players for Paul Sculthorpe a few years previously he'd turned round and said he knew who Ian Pickavance and Chris Morley were but didn't know this Cash bloke!

Lee Penny wasn't much brighter either. I don't think I have ever met anyone who was more puddled than Penny. In fact, I don't think I have ever met a sane person from Wigan either. Nat Wood continued his 'barking' credentials too. After training he would come out of the blue and tick you. Next thing you'd have 25 grown men running all over the pitch trying not to be tagged. You'd be flogged at training, but find a new lease of life. It continued when we hit Lanzarote for pre-season too. Someone would be ticked and we would all be flying about, jumping in the pool not to be caught. I'm sure the families on their hols there loved it.

We had some great golfers. Darren Burns was a shark. His handicap was 16 and he ended up leaving us on three – with a lot of our money in his pocket too.

*****

With the new stadium on the horizon and our last year at Wilderspool, the mentality was to hit the play-offs. That was no different to any other season, but we thought this time it was realistic. We didn't want to head into a relegation fight once again as that wasn't a nice experience so we focussed on reaching the top six.

Perhaps the threat of relegation in 2002 woke the club up because we never looked like going down from that point again. It was in the back of our minds throughout the year and it was an added motivation. The squad for 2003 was too strong to get us into that mess again and I genuinely believed we could make the play-offs with it.

All that said, I didn't play much that season, making about 15 appearances in total. I broke my wrist against London and managed to score two tries as well – hard as nails me! We were winning and they tried a short kick off. I dived at the ball, caught it expertly with my right hand but my left broke my fall. It got more and more painful during the game but I didn't think anything of it and thought it was a strain at most. I got it strapped up and got on with it. I played another 50 minutes, scored twice and we won the game.

That night I went to Old Trafford Cricket Club to watch REM and smashed in about 10 pints of wine and lemonade so didn't feel any pain at all. But when I got up, my wrist and hand had ballooned and looked a right mess. We got it scanned and I had broken my scaphoid. Apparently, it's the only bone in your body that can die when you're living and you don't really need it. Well, if that's so, why was it hurting so much? After the X-ray they said it was a 12-week injury and I couldn't do anything. It would either repair or I would need an operation.

So I was sat out for the rest of the season and missed the final game at the ground against Wakefield and the play-off with Wigan too. Appo was at full back, and with me out of the side came into stand-off and ripped it up. Anytime he would make a break he was scoring and he kicked goals too, but it's a pity he couldn't do that in his second year. After looking at the 2004 season review DVD, Mark Hilton said he knew we would struggle when one of our players came back as an 'overweight hamster'. Appo piled on the timber in the offseason and didn't back up his great year.

I was sat in the stands watching us play and missing being out there. It was at that time I got seriously into looking at coaching. With so much time on my hands I was analysing the coaches and taking a really good look into what they do and how they operate.

Injuries are part and parcel of the game and all those other clichés. You are devastated you can't play but I am a big believer in the team so you can't sulk and moan as that can bring your team-mates down. You've got to help as much as you can and that is what I did – as much as it hurts and you get down. It is also hard for your partner and kids as when you get home you are low, because you don't want to show your team-mates you are struggling.

Of course I was training really hard at the time ... ok, I did a little bit! I love having a ball in my hand but hate running, so it was always going to be a tough time. It had to be done I suppose but I didn't do a lot.

The hardest part was that final game at Wilderspool against Wakefield. I was captain at the time but was more helping and analysing what Cull was doing. We thrashed them – as we had to do – and at the end of the game everyone got carried around the ground to give the place a really good send-off. But I didn't feel part of it because I hadn't played. I just blended in at the back, and if you look at photos of that day, you can see I wasn't really part of the celebrations. I hadn't been out there so couldn't earn and didn't deserve the plaudits.

The players wore a special kit that represented the first one the club wore many moons ago. It was like a t-shirt though, so by half-time it was ripped and we went back to the usual kit. Not the brightest idea the marketing bods have ever had!

Thinking back, there's no way I could have been ready for that game as my wrist still hadn't healed, as when I did try to come back it still wasn't right. After nine weeks I started to do some press-ups as I was really keen on playing for Wales against Australia. But it just hadn't healed properly. In the end I had a bone graft from my hip to my wrist and was out for another 12 weeks. It ended up being a six-month injury.

It was sad to see Wilderspool go, and even sadder I wasn't a big part of that final year. I was honoured to captain Warrington and the chance to lead the side out to its final game at the venue would have been etched in history. But it wasn't to be.

Wilderspool is still up now and we used it for three or four years to train on before we moved to the University of Chester campus in Padgate. It was a nice set up for us and the gym was superb. We liked training there even though it was a complete shithole. I grew up with 'poor' grounds such as Knowsley

Road and Wilderspool and they were fantastic experiences.

New stadiums are all well and good and are what rugby league needs but I do miss the nostalgia of the old ones. Knowsley Road will always be remembered, even though it is flat, because of the road names on the old site. Wilderspool still hosts Academy rugby, but Salford? I won't remember that. Knock it down and keep it as rubble! You'd walk through the tunnel and 'fans' would be spitting on you and throwing beer. I wouldn't mind, but half of them were only 16! Salford has always been a tough ground to play at and your entrance to the field would be intimidating enough. Then you would face David Hulme. He was one of the toughest but dirtiest players I have ever faced. He would gouge, bite, stamp and get in your face. That was what it was like. The supporter make-up of clubs has changed over the years and on the whole they are great people. If you go and watch football there are some real weirdoes who go over the top. In the end it's a game and no one is going to die.

I enjoy the banter with fans as long as it doesn't get stupid. I've been called fatty and the GB reference has come up a few times but I take it as a compliment. It means they're worried about me, doesn't it? I've always had 'you used to play for a big club' via the Saints but that stopped in 2011 for some reason!

The best ground I've played at has to be Wembley. I'd love to play at the Millennium Stadium when it is full, but a full Wembley was special. The old Salford was the worst ground easily, but had a decent pitch! The worst pitch was the Watersheddings in Oldham or at Bradford maybe. It's always cold at Odsal and I don't like that. I was glad when we went to summer because it meant I could only be semi cold in Bradford instead of freezing.

Our new stadium kicked off our revival. We'd all been looking forward to it and then that final game against Wakefield came and went and it hit us. The stadium was a stepping stone to us moving on as a team. We hadn't gone backwards as such, just plateaued and we needed the change.

One of the main people behind the scheme was Andy Gatcliffe who took over from Deaks in 2000. I can't tell you how much good work he has done for the club. I have heard players who have been at Warrington and left call him, but Andy couldn't do enough for the players, coaches, directors, fans and the back office. He's had good backing, but he's been the man to steer the ship. He's always been there for me and listens to what I have to say. Whenever I have asked for things as our player rep or captain, he has given me a fair crack and I can't thank him enough. He's made us what we are today and we should be thankful.

As good as 2003 was for the club, with my injury it was a pretty poor time for me, and I made it worse by being done for drink-driving in March. We'd beaten London 29-8 at Brentford and the coach was full of beer on the way back. I remember giving my keys to Mike Wainwright, who was there with his wife, and Ian Sibbit and his wife who'd had a crash on the way down to London. I ended up having a skinful but stopping an hour-and-a-half before we got home as I thought that would give me time to sober up before I got off the coach.

I got the keys back and jumped in my new Z3, but when I came through Great Sankey I saw blue lights in the rear view mirror. I knew straightaway I was in trouble. I thought though, I might be ok as I had my Wolves training gear on and they might know me and send me on my way. But when I got out of the car I was covered in beer and one of the police officers was from Newcastle and the other was a Scouser. I blew into the bag and blew well over. I felt a right prick but hoped the desk sergeant might know me and let me off. Deep down I knew there was no chance and when I got to the nick it was confirmed.

That was the start of an 18-month ban, a big fine and something I regret big style. I don't regret much but this I do. I had to take taxis, and travelling from St Helens to Warrington didn't help. Vicky had a new born baby and I had let her and the club down too. It was in the papers and on the radio and I felt ashamed when I woke up. I had this knot in my stomach and I knew I had to phone Cull and tell him. I have so much respect for Paul and I had let him down and misplaced his trust. The club looked after me but I knew I had made a mistake and wanted to repay them.

It had a big influence on me growing up as I realised I couldn't keep acting the way I was and be in the public eye. I thought I was a normal guy, but I had responsibilities with being a professional rugby league player. I have always been one of the lads and that needed to stop. My friends won't like me saying that as I have never been Lee Briers the rugby league star around them, but I needed to face up to what I had done.

In his foreword to this book, Tony Smith says I have matured over the last few years and he is right. Apart from a bad time in 2006, that drink-driving case was the turning point where I looked at my life and decided I needed to grow up. Sophie was getting older and our son Reece had come into our lives so I had to change – particularly for Sophie so I could give her the right example and show her the right path. I suppose you do that the more you get older and when your kids grow up too. I had to get right for them to show them the right paths in life and the right habits. I consider myself to be a grounded and normal person, so it was pretty easy to make that change. My mum and dad did the same with me when I grew up and it made sense to do that at the time.

Having a few beers after a match has always been part of being a rugby league player. It counted towards being a professional and it wasn't something people batted an eyelid to in the past. We played hard on the Friday or Sunday and then gave it some hammer afterwards. We'd go out and have a drink and it was the way we were. Times have changed though and I have had to change with them, as has every other player who started at the same time as me.

For players who come into the first team set up now, it's not the norm to go out drinking all the time. I have spoken to those young lads and I wish I'd had the knowledge in 1996, or 1997 that I do now, then perhaps I might have gone on a different path. I'm not jealous of the kids now; I have had my time, that's the way it was back then and I have no regrets. It would have been nice to experience what they are going through now but that was then and this is now.

On the field, I have always wanted to improve and continue to learn. I've always lived by that – to keep learning. And even if I might not think something is right, I still try to take it on board. If I stop learning or want to stop learning then I will pack it in. If it comes to a morning when I wake up and I think I can't be arsed learning, and I'm not enjoying it, then I'll pack it in because there is no point. You are never too experienced, you've never played too many games and therefore you are never old enough to stop. There is always something new to learn. For instance, the perception of me is that my defence isn't very good. I have now learnt a way of how to defend and that came at 30 years of age and onwards. It is something I continue to develop and am comfortable with. I haven't got it off to a tee but I'll keep working on it.

I'm always excited to learn new things and get on the field. I'm not excited when it comes to pre-season though, but then again that is a challenge I have to face, and I like challenges. I like moaning and sticking it to the lads, but most of it is to wind the coaches up. The money has been great, but the enjoyment has been a lot better and success has come as I have improved further. It's exactly how it played out in my amateur career. At St Helens Crusaders I only won stuff at 14s, 15s and 16s and then I went pro. Now it's happening again!

When I wrote this chapter I had signed on at Warrington for the 2012 season and at the back end of the year signed for 2013 too. I love the club and made it clear I want to finish with them. I have always said you are a long time retired but I wouldn't want to go around another year if my body wasn't right. I need to be contributing to the team. And I am not one for just saying 'another year' because I will get X amount of pounds, I need to be fully committed.

It would be nice to finish on my terms of course, with my body intact and with the rest of my life to lead and coach my son and look after my daughter. You have a long life to go after rugby and I don't want to face it with both shoulders being fucked and with shit knees. When I finish I want to say I have had a good playing career and I am happy and content with what I have done.

Would I move clubs to go into coaching or anything like that? You can never say never, but the perfect scenario would be to finish intact and coach at Warrington. Perfect scenarios don't play out as they should of course, but you never know. I was very close to joining Barrow before I signed my last deal with the Wolves, and in hindsight I have been lucky with what happened over there at the back end of 2011. I was also offered a contract at Crusaders for this year too, and we all know what happened there!

All this talk was with other clubs before I had spoken to Warrington without knowing what they wanted. Thankfully, the Wolves have always wanted me. When they come on board, that is where talks finish with other clubs. I am loyal to Warrington and it works both ways. All the way through my life I have been loyal – I live and die by that – and I have been a part of the club since 1997. You don't get that with only one side being loyal. I could have left, but it felt right to stay. I could have chased the coin and gone to rugby union in the past, or more recently Catalans and lived a good life over there. I'm not saying Barrow wouldn't have been better compared to the Med mind you.

Certain people fit into a place and I believe that is me at Warrington. My family are treated excellently and it is like a second home. We are adopted Warringtonians and it has been a good relationship.

*****

In 2004, we finally moved into our new home and it was an

exciting time for all. We played Wakefield in our first match at the Halliwell Jones Stadium and it was my first match for a while too. I came back about three stone heavier and Nat Wood scored the first try. He had a few bob on himself to score too. Now, I'm not saying he could have passed … but he could have passed all the time. The atmosphere was electric and 14,000 turned up to watch us, including the taxi-full from Wakefield. We had played in front of 6,000 at Wilderspool and to turn out in front of so many was unreal. Although I had missed out on the experience in our last game at Wilderspool, I had the honour of leading the team out this time around.

I wasn't the oldest at the time at just 25 but I was one of the more experienced lads there and it was good to do it. It was a great experience and something I will never forget. As I have said before, captaining my club was very important and I still reflect on moments like that since it ended in 2007. I continued to captain my country but I still look back on my captaincy at Warrington and what I did right and wrong. When you are younger you think less about things and it can pass you by.

In the modern game these days, you think even less when you're young. Coaching and the off field side of the game means you are told what to eat, what supplements you need to take, your position on the field, where you need to be, the defensive structure, and more. I was the opposite – I never took notice of what to eat, I went anywhere on the field, I wasn't robotic and I was more natural.

I have learnt as the years have gone on to be more of a team player though, but that isn't to a point where I can't go off and do my own thing and be off the cuff. I was like that when I was younger and instinctive but I think more about the game now and have a better reading of it. I know when I have to be part of the discplined team structure, and also when it's time to to let my instincts run free and do different stuff. Kids will have to do that the opposite way round now and I think that is a shame. You can still give them the right diet and things like that, but when it gets to a field, you should never be coached to have instinct and natural flair taken away from you.

I think up to a certain age, maybe up to 14 or 15, you should get the chance to play in every position to get to know the game and be more versatile. Of course, you know some kids will never be a half-back, but they can play in other positions. We seem to be too eager to put some players in one position and that is that. It comes down to coaching and I think there are too many average ones in our game. Without being big headed I mentor coaches at Thatto Heath and I think most amateur clubs should do that. All pro clubs should send players down to local amatuer clubs and link with them to talk once a month to the coaches. We should be talking about the fun aspects of the game and getting the basics right. I don't want to hammer these coaches as most are parents who have volunteered to help. But if as a nation we are going to want better players at first grade, we have to start at with the seven-year-olds to give them good skills. The coaches need to have these basics and should be qualified, as let's be honest, you wouldn't let a non-qualified dentist hack away at your teeth, would you? Pro clubs should also look after the Championship clubs who in turn should also link with the amateurs. You can't have a 'Super League' and stop there. If we're serious about getting better then we need to do that.

I go to Thatto Heath off my own back. Without St Helens Crusaders, I wouldn't have been in the position to write this book – or have won three Challenge Cups and a Lance Todd. It means everything to me to be able to put something back. It isn't much; an hour twice a month. It doesn't take much time and that is what our sport needs. Yes, focus on the top clubs but don't be afraid to look below the top league.

Whilst 2004 was a massive year for the Wolves with a new venue, that didn't really translate to performances on the field. We missed out on the play-offs by nine points so it wasn't the best of seasons. But I suppose it was all about the stadium and having a venue that meant we could compete. We had some great wins that season and the squad was a lot stronger from the one that got a play-off spot the year before. Our attack was strong too but we couldn't defend for shite and let in far too many points. We were a new team really and were bringing in quality, so perhaps the season was a settling in year for that. Any team will experience it when they move, but we may have had a little bit of 'new stadiumitis'. We had to learn to play on a different pitch which was bigger than Wilderspool. The crowd were also set further back so maybe it took some time to get used to it.

We won ten games but couldn't quite beat the big teams and we played Saints three times too – we couldn't beat Saints at any time, let alone three matches in a season! Whenever Warrington play Wigan and Saints, it's a derby, and it takes a lot out of the team. A lot of energy and effort is put into it and the team struggles for the next week and the week after. So to make us and other clubs play the same teams three times, I never understood it. It should be home and away, end of. It makes no sense to the players or the competition. I feel sorry for teams who have to play us or Wigan or Saints as I know how I felt in 2004 knowing we had to face our biggest rivals three times – now teams are doing the same with us. It doesn't add up and it is something we need to get rid of.

They tried to do it in football with the 39th game and there was a load of uproar and it was done away with. We have done it since 2004! It's time now, especially when times are tough and the country is in recession, that we make our sport as simple as possible. That means not facing a team three times in league fixtures.

So what about the Magic Weekend? I'm either way on that at present as it is a third game we don't need. I wouldn't be bothered if it wasn't there, but if it is I would like it to be done right. There's only one way you can do it, one team would have to give up a home game for me and then it would alternate. One team would get the money one year, and the other the next. Let's not get this wrong though, I am not against playing more games as long as it is fair. If the competition goes to 15 or

16 teams then there are more fixtures and the sport can make more money. But it is a fair way of doing it and doesn't put a slant on the table.

When we moved into the new stadium, the club became more attractive and it wasn't a shock when we were bought by Simon Moran. He's a big Wolves fan and has certainly put his money where his mouth is, and backed us to succeed. I have nothing but admiration for the bloke – he saved Warrington. What we went through to where we are now is a million miles apart and that is through Simon's vision. He bought into the concept of the new stadium and splashed out for Martin Gleeson (for the 2005 season) with his own cash. We also bought New Zealand internationals Henry Fa'afili and Logan Swann.

Simon is perceived to be a very wealthy man but he is so down to earth it is untrue. I have always kept my feet on the ground and I think that is why we get on. He is the same. If he can do anything for you he will help you out. He was also realistic when he came in. You can't expect to spend a fortune and start to win things; it has taken the best part of eight years to get to where we are today. Winning the Challenge Cup was unbelievable for us all and I have no doubt fantastic for Simon. He's not like other directors and chairmen as he stands in the South Stand with the fans and sings with them. He has never wanted fame and if he walked in here you wouldn't recognise him. He is a normal guy who has been supportive of everything I have done. Hopefully, I have repaid him.

His vision is important. He put in his own money and has bought players and that's something not many clubs do these days. He only wants one thing and that is success for Warrington. He is willing to pay for it and try to bring in new players – but it is down to hard work too and it has done wonders for us. When you work for someone like that, it makes you want to succeed even more and helps you win stuff. It is like that in any employment I suppose. If you respect your boss, you will work harder and you can repay their faith in you.

It's not just about the players though, it is also about the staff behind the scenes. The offices compared to Wilderspool are something else. There simply is no comparison. Simon is big on marketing and making sure the brand of Warrington is as big as it can be too. In 2012, we took that brand to Australia to take on South Sydney, which shows how far we have moved on. It isn't just about rugby league, but our brand, which is hard for an old timer like me! But it's the way sport is these days and is what is going to happen in the future. You see it in football with Man United in Japan and Liverpool in America – if you want to be the top dog you need to get your brand out there and work hard. Other teams have to follow that now.

We also have a reputation to uphold and the players have to buy into that. It's important we reflect the correct image of Warrington so perceptions of our club change too. Community visits are important to achieve this and a rota makes sure everyone is involved. It is very enjoyable to do as well. Seeing kids at Christmas in hospital and seeing their faces when we come in is a privilege not a sacrifice. It cheers them up at a time of need and it's great that we and the club can do that.

I've been a little harsh on our performances in the 2004 season but there were a couple of stand-out memories. We made our third Challenge Cup semi-final in five years and lost to Wigan. We'd lost to the Bulls in the last two so I thought it would be our year at last. We were also playing well at that time and our form was good, but Wigan were too good for us. They had been in the big games and Brett Dallas was unbelievable. He skinned me for one of his tries – I thought I had him and he kicked and was away. We were gutted after that game as the semi-final is the hardest place to lose. It's horrible knowing you are so close to a massive day out and it would have been at the Millennium Stadium too. That wasn't necessarily another incentive as I wanted to play at Wembley – the cup only belongs there for me. All dreams come true I suppose!

When we played London away that season I was on my bed in the hotel flicking through the paper. As I turned over the page, I did a double take as I noticed a story about our conditioner Tony O'Brian. It was a story about a woman running a brothel from an apartment and it turned out to be Tony's missus Sharon! Weirdly, the night before that our wives were in that apartment as they went down with Sharon to have a night out in London. I remember getting a phone call as they had gone to a club and seen somebody get dragged out, pasted and dumped in the back of a car. The women were pretty worried to stay in the place.

So to read that story a day later was a real shock. It turns out an undercover reporter had gone in and found it all. I got Tony in my room and asked him what it was all about and he wasn't worried at all. But someone had gone and shown it to Cull and we expected the worst. Cull just said: 'Fucking hell, what's that all about, that's my old fucking couch in that picture!' That was all he was worried about, not his conditioner!

Actually, come to think of it, the year I was banned for drink-driving I sold my car to Sharon and she paid me in £50 notes. I kept thinking where is she getting them from and she told me it was a council job ... now I know where it really came from!

Anyway, the Challenge Cup is a real worry for me as it is getting pushed out. It is all about the Super League season as that is where the money is alongside Sky's coverage. It will never be totally pushed out of course, but it is a prestigious cup to win and is known all over the world. It is also a very hard one to win as we all know. It has the history and the big day out at Wembley and has always been my favourite to win. Although I haven't won the Grand Final, I haven't been disappointed with the cup. It's been everything I have dreamt of and more.

It upsets me to see how it is going and I'm not sure if it will change any time soon. The BBC try hard but they don't give it the coverage it really deserves. I don't understand how you can have a classic final with 90,000 fans and there isn't every sports channel fighting for it. Someone up high isn't doing their job properly if they can't see what a fantastic spectacle it is.

I know it's hard for TV companies to get interested in the earlier rounds so maybe we need a handicap system. It's hard for Championship teams to beat Super League teams, so do you give them a 20 point start or do the Champ teams play off to get through to face the Super League sides? Those Champ sides would be at home of course. We need to keep the early rounds attractive and I have no doubt if Sky had it permanently they would make a massive deal of it.

Over to them …

8

Joey Johns

The first I heard of Andrew Johns joining Warrington I was knee deep in shit with the kids wandering round a damp Sherdley Park. I was squelching around the St Helens Show – the town's annual extravaganza of rubbish and funfair – and Cull was on the phone telling me we had signed the best player in the world on a short term deal.

Trying not to swear in front of the kids I said yeah, sure we have, and he told me we'd signed Joey Johns. I thought the whole thing was a wind-up. But sure enough he turned up on a cold Tuesday night and we all met up in a restaurant in Stockton Heath. Glees, Cull, Jon Clarke and Logan Swann were the official welcoming committee and we chatted over a meal about Warrington and had a good laugh. He was buzzing about being here, jet-lagged of course, but he couldn't wait to get started.

It was unbelievable that the club could pull off a deal like that and showed the rest of the League how far we had come. I was excited too as everyone knew what a class player he was and I would be training and playing alongside him. What I didn't realise was how much of a good mate he would be and the impact he'd have on us all.

I always thought I knew the game and how it worked but on our first training session he showed us what the game really was about. I stood in awe of the guy with some of the things he did. He was telling players what he was going to do three plays on and we'd still be on the first. He'd be moving players around the field, getting them ready for a move in four tackles time. His kicking game was awesome and he was fitter and stronger than most. More importantly he was a great bloke with it all too. He could have come over and been an absolute twat and thought he was the best thing ever. But he was down to earth and I think that is why we really got on.

Playing with him was different too – it was ridiculous. He ripped Leeds apart in his first game and went on record afterwards saying it was probably the best atmosphere he'd played in and it certainly was a cracking day. I remember being on the field and looking at the walls in the corners of the ground and people were standing on them. I'd never experienced that before. You couldn't hear anything from the first minute and when Chris Leikvoll smashed Rob Burrow, we knew it was going to be our day. Poor Rob, Chris was 6'. 5" and he cleaned him out. From the scrum Joey hit me and I hit Martin Gleeson with a long ball and then Henry Fa'afili and we were up. Joey ended up with five goals and a drop goal in a 33-16 win.

Glees was a big signing for Warrington and he just clicked with Johns too. He's definitely in the top three players I have played alongside. He was in the mould of Toa Kohe-Love. I just knew where he would be on the field – Toa that is – and he would do his stuff. Glees was the same and we took it to a whole new level. I remember Joey mentioning it and saying that Darren Lockyer was the only other player he'd seen who had that skill – the ability to throw a huge cut out pass into space. Me and Glees were telepathic with that really. He had the ability to get on the outside of the opposition and would let the ball do the work. The ball would create the space for him and he'd go to the place it was going.

I think the mentality of the club changed on that day. There was no more 'we can win this game' or 'we can give them a game' in the changing rooms, it was more 'we'll smoke these and we will do it'. It's probably why we are being successful now to be honest.

Yes, his short-term signing was controversial. We were the first club to do it and Adrian Morley was the next heading to Bradford. I wind him up saying he took Andy Lynch's Grand Final ring! My view was this really: the rules allowed it so why not. If Joey had gone to Wigan or Saints I would have been very jealous. I know he was paid well, but it didn't matter to me, he could have got a million. I got to experience training and playing and became a friend for life with one of the true greats of the game. And I'm sure the club made the best of it and got it all back on shirts! The only thing that really pissed me off was he had a brand new Merc and I had a total shit heap! That came with the territory. His Merc was covered in his name though and that all had to be taken off as he had people following him.

After a decent first year in the stadium, our second year was a bit up and down. We didn't start very well but put a real run together at the back end of the season and that win over Leeds was big for us. We won twice in our first eight games and then put a good run together to finish fourth in the league. It was the most success we had in terms of winning games and the club was a good place to be around. We were knocking off some of the top teams – although we were suffering to some of the lower teams – but Halliwell Jones was feeling more like home and something like a fortress.

It was pretty strange early on in that season. We had a good team but couldn't turn sides over. We were up against London early on and they came back and won. They got a feed against the head in a scrum, which was very unusual, and they scored off it. We then played Leigh at home and it was a tough game where we only just nipped it. The crowd booed us and that was hard too.

We were prepared for the season but perhaps didn't play the conditions well early on. We'd had a good camp in

Lanzarote, training three times a day. We'd be up at half seven doing 10 lengths of the 50 metre pool to get us ready for the day. After a while I cottoned on that the coaching staff would get there late on so when they opened the door to the pool I would get in at the other end, do a length, jump out and shout 10. Then I'd be off to bed. It was a hard camp though and we got through a lot of work which we couldn't have done back home at that time of the year. So it was strange at the start as we never got going.

That season we had two cracking games with Saints. Longy kicked a drop goal to beat us 31-30 at Knowsley Road and we almost had them at the Halliwell Jones only for us to blow a 16-4 lead in the last seven minutes. I was ill after those games for sure. In some ways I preferred the games when we lost by 50 or 60 to them as we could identify the problem and where we went wrong. We'd bridged the gap and got closer but were still losing. We also lost to Leeds in the cup too. When we were mid-table and in the bottom half we'd get Leeds, Saints and Bradford in the cup. Now we're doing well, we're getting the easier teams! People say it's fixed, hot and cold balls and all that, but it isn't. I've done the draw!

Johns coming in and that win over Leeds gave us a good chance to finish in the top four for the first time in ages. And we did that by thrashing Hull to set up a tie with the same team in the play-offs. We were on fire at that point and there was a lot of talk about hitting the Grand Final. We may have started to believe that and got a touch ahead of ourselves as we got snotted at home to Hull. There was a party atmosphere around the club and I think the worst thing we could have done is to have gone to Hull and mashed them. We would have been better playing another team other than them, and it showed as we just didn't turn up on the night. Fair credit to Hull, they did their homework and they tore us to bits. It was disappointing to lose in the play-offs like that considering we were in good form.

It was hard not to get caught up in the euphoria and we

probably let ourselves believe we could do it. We hadn't experienced it before and we had a superstar in the team. The press were talking us up too and we got caught out. We would do it differently if it happened again of course. But it was a masterstroke of Cull and Simon to get Joey over and it very nearly paid off for us.

Joey's legacy continues at the club to this day. We're signing good players in Australia and being linked with the big names because of him. Top players talk to Joey about the club and he tells them what we're like. This wasn't about three games in the end, it was the beginning of a massive culture change at the club. Now, he still comes over and has a few weeks holiday on us, he trains with us on our pre-season tours and brings Brian Carney – aka Potato – too. It's a good relationship and we're all the better for it.

Off the field there was a controversial aspect to Joey's character but I can't say enough good things about him. We didn't know about his bipolar illness and ecstasy issue, that's not for me to comment on, but off the field with us, he was just a great bloke and a true friend. He liked a pint, but he did it at the right times. He trained hard and played hard and we had some good times. We had a good social session at the end of the season for sure!

We were in Wigan on the second day of Mad Monday and were round at Glees' house having a few beers. I was going back to play for Wales and I called Martin Hall, our coach, to tell him I'd found him a world class player to play for Wales. He came to the house and walked in and there must have been 60 Buds on the table. He asked where this player was and Joey walked out from behind the door. Hall turned around and his face dropped. Thing is though, if he hadn't played for Australia, he could have played for Wales. He has family from there. One that got away! I'd definitely rank him at number one with the players I have played with. Alfie Langar comes close of course, but I think if I'd played with Joey for a season or two more we would have blown everything out of the water. He was going to sign for a season at the end of his career, but a neck injury forced him to retire.

*****

After I'd recovered from a superb Mad Monday it was on to Wales who were playing for the first time in a while. It was the European Nations Cup and definitely one of the highlights of my Welsh career. No one gave us a chance as Ireland had a great team, and Scotland and France were pretty decent too. We beat Scotland in a horrible match, knee deep in shit on a rugby union field.

Then we went over to Ireland and weren't expected to do much. They had a great team with Barrie Mac and Terry O'Connor leading their pack and it was going to be a tough game for us. We got changed in a clubhouse before the game – it was like a poor amateur club – and there was not much more than one man and his dog there. It pissed it down too but when the Welsh anthem came you could hear someone singing it really loud in the crowd and it warmed us. I'm sure it was the chap with his dog. We ended up smashing them 31-10 but it was how well we controlled the game that was most impressive.

I will always remember later too, the night I managed to get back Chris Morley for THAT incident in the 2000 World Cup. Afterwards we got shitfaced beyond recognition and as Morley was rooming with me, I seized the chance. I got a couple of lads in the room who videoed it. We got his kit bag, moved half of his stuff and I fired off a perfect turd in his gear. His clothes were then shoved back on top and rummaged up for extra bonus points. In the morning he woke up and began putting on his gear. I kept one eye open and I could see him retching all over the place and a rank smell filled the room. He was stood there covered in shite, and I can remember clearly to this day Chris looking somewhat green and saying in his Mancunian accent: 'I feel queasy.' That still lives with me, and I think that's one-all Chris?

I also asked all the lads to meet up for breakfast at 11 and once we'd had our meeting at 12, I put my card behind the bar for them all to have a good drink. Our flight was later on in the day so we spent about six hours in the hotel knocking them back, singing, games and having fun. I got hit for about £1,400 mind you, but I didn't worry about it. The lads had given so much and I wanted to give them something back. Most were part-time and it was great for them to let their hair down and relax after a fantastic trip.

When we got to the airport we had fun there too. We were slightly intoxicated and Damien Gibson and me did the bowling ball where I would lie on the floor, he would be over me, I would grab his ankles and he would do the same to mine. We lined up a few of the lads and he dived forward and propelled us, scattering the lads as skittles. A few fell over and there was one at the back wobbling until he fell over – to raucous applause. Yep, it was a little mad really and now we are a little older we do it less and less. On that trip we also had our own chartered plane and they were handing out the drinks. You had a surreal situation; we were throwing cans at each other and the stewardesses weren't bothered.

The final was against France and whilst I never blame refs, this chap fucking mugged us. He was a New Zealander and he caned us. He gave everything to France but we gave it our best shot and had a right dig. There was a big fight and one of their players smashed Anthony Blackwood in the face. He split him big style and Blacky got sinbinned. As captain I questioned the ref and he did me too! I was very polite and just asked him why he did that ... and I was off the field. We ended up losing 38-16. There were players crying in the changing rooms afterwards and I was one of them. We'd put a lot of effort into that tournament and to lose the way we did was really hard. It was hard to console the lads, but we tried to make the best of it and went out round Carcassonne and painted the town red.

It was a bad night for two of the lads as they ended up being locked up and we didn't know whether they'd get back

Baby face. Here's me with my mum

With my mates celebrating my
first trophy win

Summertime blues? On holiday with my folks. I
look a little unimpressed here!

The face of an angel – you
would think butter wouldn't
melt in my mouth

Playing snooker on the floor

Off we go. On my way abroad with Brian. I would have driven him mad on the plane

Posing for holiday snaps with my dad in Spain

Friends reunited. All my mates together on our first holiday in Spain

Can you see me? The North West Counties Under 15s squad pose for a team photograph before our tour of Australia

Keeping my concentration. Kicking for Saints under the watchful eye of kitman Stan Wall

Homegrown. I made my debut for Saints in 1997

Early days with Warrington

Breaking records with 40 points against York in 2000. 12 years later I recorded 44 points in a match against Swinton

Coaching at Portico Vine in 2003

Don't ask ...

One of the drop goals that beat Leeds in 2006. Great times on the pitch but I was suffering off the field in that season

G'day mate! Andrew Johns was a great fella who came over to Warrington in 2006 and is still a good mate

Bit of a shocker this ... I have worked on my defence though. I am the Axe!

Pointed out by my mate Stu Fielden. He doesn't look happy with me

Never a fan of pre-season, or sand dunes, or hills, or running. At least this camp in 2012 was in Australia

Poser ... not sure about my mullet on this one

Giving Stacey Jones the tongue!

Semi final at Widnes in 2009. I score against Wigan to help us to Wembley. A year later I did the same against Catalans and crossed in exactly the same spot

Bang it over. A drop goal against Wigan in the 2009 Challenge Cup semi final

Wembley ahead. Celebrating with my dad after our victory over Wigan in the semi final

Leading the Wolves out at Wembley in 2009. I'm fine but Reece seems worried

The nerves have gone for Reece at the line up and we are just taking in the moment

Emotional scenes with Vicky after winning the cup in 2009

Done it! What a legend Moz was that day to let me do this – to lift the cup

Pride. My family
with the Challenge
Cup in 2009

Welsh pride.
Celebrating our
win over Scotland
in 2010

Just announced over the PA
at Wembley ... I'm a Lance
Todd winner

Wembley celebrations in 2010 after back to back Challenge Cup wins

Are we good enough for the X Factor? Singing the Welsh anthem at Leigh before we took on England in 2011

Setting up for a promo. It's hard to believe but this was for a picture on the back of a truck

Make mine a triple! Challenge Cup winner again in 2012

All smiles. Having a laugh with Phil Bentham, James Child and Sam Tomkins

Family affair. With Vicky's brother Craig

With my parents and siblings. David, me, Stephen, Dad, Mum and Julie

With my partner, Vicky, and our children, Sophie and Reece

Toned and ready to play. I hope to be on a beach like this in 30 years time

My kit cupboard. Vicky reckons I'm untidy

Grand Final 2013. Here I'm putting a kick in as we keep Wigan under pressure

It wasn't to be. Wigan lift the Grand Final trophy but Tony Smith tries to keep our spirits up at the end

Gutted. But the least I can do is applaud our brilliant fans

in time for the flight. It was Bonfire Night and two lads in a car fired a firework in their direction. Chris Morley ran straight at them and put his foot through the back window. There was an altercation and he and David Mills got locked up. They spent the night in prison whilst we had a session! That continued the day after too and I had a bet with Gibbo (Damien Gibson) that he couldn't swim the Carcassonne river. It was 3pm and about 40 metres across, but he stripped down to his undies and swam it. The current was pretty strong and he struggled a bit but he was alright! A great end to a pretty decent season!

The following year was big for me too as it was my best in terms of points production and improvement in my overall game. But it came during a period of my life when everything was falling apart. As a club we made the top six ahead of Wigan who had a poor season and nearly went down until Stuart Fielden came in and saved them. I was playing with freedom, and when I think that I got 277 points that year, I was probably in the form of my life. My family life wasn't as good though. During the season I went through a difficult time with Vicky and we broke up. I moved over to Warrington and spiralled down into a bad time.

I wasn't as fully focussed as I should have been and I probably was drinking too much. Everything was about training, coming back to the flat, and then getting as blitzed as I could. How I produced the figures I did when I wasn't treating my body in the right way I don't know. Looking back, I was pretty depressed and it led me to drink, and I have to say I was drinking more than I had ever done in my career. I was single and filling in the time by looking at the bottom of a pint glass every night. I didn't know how to handle being away from my family – especially my two kids at the home I had left. I had been with Vicky for nearly 10 years and she did everything for me. So to cope I turned to drink and I'm not proud of the state I was getting myself in.

Perhaps with everything that was going on I tried to make those 80 minutes I was on the field the best I could. It held me together. Rugby was a release from the pressure and pain I was feeling at home. I played with enjoyment and off the cuff as a way of getting away from it all. Although I was living in Warrington and it's only a few miles away, it might as well have been 100 when I was away from my family. Reece was three and Sophie had just turned nine and I couldn't cope. So I'd play like a superstar and then go to the pub to forget it.

At one point I pulled my hamstring and was coming in to do my rehab. I knew there was a stag do going to Benidorm, but there was no chance I was ever going to be allowed to go. So I cooked up a story and asked Paul Cullen if I could go out there and see a friend of mine, Adam Fogerty. He agreed and I went over there for three days, with 36 mates, and had a great time. As often happens I lost my phone on the way there and didn't turn into training until the Monday. Cull had been trying to get hold of me and it turned out that someone had seen me over there and grassed me up. He fined me a month's wage but I fully deserved it.

I don't think I have been fined that many times, perhaps twice. When I first signed for Warrington I had already booked to go to Wembley with my mates to watch Saints. I missed the Monday session and got fined. A great start to my Warrington career.

Me and Vicky eventually worked it out and I am glad we did. I guess I didn't know what I'd got until it was gone. Just before I went on tour with GB we met up and said we should have another go when I came back. We did, and I have to say we are as strong as we have ever been.

Anyone going through a break-up, well, you know the feeling. It may be for the right reasons, but whatever the reason it affects everything you do until time becomes that great healer. It's worse when you are in the limelight too. As a professional sportsperson, people think you only have the sport side to you. Some people don't realise you have family and kids and you can be going through a tough time. People thought I was just on the piss and being Lee. But that wasn't the case. I was in a dark, dark place and I'm so glad I came through it.

It wasn't the reason I went back but if we hadn't got back together than I shudder to think what might have happened to me. I think serious things could have happened for sure. Vicky has always kept my feet on the ground and without her I was spiralling out of control. She has been a rock and was the level-headed one. Without her I was drinking and had it gone on another month or two, then maybe it could have got a whole lot more serious.

I reckon rugby kept me out of prison when I was younger and getting back with Vicky kept me … well, I don't want to say it as I don't want to think about how bad it nearly got. Perhaps someone up there really likes me and wanted me to be alive. Thankfully it didn't happen and we are together. The club also backed me and that helped. They knew I was having a tough time and Cull was excellent. We were close and he was always supportive. He was a friend and his door was always open and that was the type of relationship we always had. He helped me through it and I will always appreciate that.

Player welfare is very important and I know I have spoken about it already. Speaking to Cull was 'player welfare' back then and I was lucky because we were close. Several players since have had problems and not had the support that I had. It's well reported that Glees had issues but he is a free spirit. Some people say he is wild but he was a pro in a way. He looked after his body and always did extras to take his skill level to new heights. But he was a free spirit off the field, and perhaps if someone had spotted that and helped him then he wouldn't have had the problems at the back end of his career. I'm so glad he's got another shot. It's important in sport that we are proactive and that's why I applaud the State of Mind campaign.

As far as I know, the Rugby Football League doesn't employ anyone to look after player welfare as it is a club centric issue. At Warrington, we've had Brian Carney and Karl Fitzpatrick.

They have done a great job but they were employed by the club long before the well-publicised problems with Terry Newton and Gary Speed. I think there needs to be something where we can get money from the RFL to employ people as player welfare managers at all clubs. It's not hard but it needs doing.

I have been thinking about it a lot recently and I believe something needs to be done. I know when I split from Vicky I must have been suffering from depression. You try and battle it and I'm lucky that I'm a bubbly guy and positive. I don't know about other people and my team-mates though, you would hope if they are feeling that way they would talk.

The younger lads coming through know they need to talk if they are having problems and have grown up in a culture that has at least begun to address that. But I came from a generation where we were hardened rugby league players who were tough on the field and off it and not supposed to talk. I think Terry was locked in that culture too. I knew him really well and he was in his pub playing poker for charity the week before he killed himself. He was so full of life and I couldn't believe it when I heard the news. I called his phone as I didn't expect it to be true, but of course it was. You don't expect it to happen to someone you know; especially someone who was as competitive and tough as Tez. But who knows what anyone's state of mind really is like?

It should be a priority for everyone in the game and is one of the reasons a new players' association was formed in 2012. I know the RFL wanted to make it part of licensing but why wait three years to check it had happened? It needed to be dealt with to prevent another three of four players going the same way as Tez. Rugby league can be lonely if you're not being picked or are injured. The pressure is on then and it can be a very tough time. Also, what about the likes of myself who are now reaching that time when retirement is nearing? Is the RFL speaking to any of us? No. We will be spat out into the real world. Players who have known nothing but the sport will have to find money to pay the bills. I know that isn't the sport's issue but the least we can do is prepare players for what it is like.

It all means that these days coaches aren't just coaching rugby league. They need to do player welfare, manage the media – everything. I will hopefully be involved in that and will relish it. Having the responsibility of helping people would be amazing and I only hope I can pass on the knowledge of the good and bad times to make the players of tomorrow better.

*****

After the relatively successful 'Joey Johns' season our aim was not just to avoid relegation or finish mid table; it was to make the play-offs and make sure we got past the first round. In 2006 we did that for the second year in a row, beginning to relish life in the new stadium. Rome wasn't built in a day but we were building each year to a point when we could compete with the big teams in the league. Every year each team wants to win the Grand Final, but you need to be realistic. Back then the likes of Saints, Leeds and Bradford were looking to win it, and realistically the rest were aiming for the play-offs. We wanted to make the six and see what would happen from there. We'd never won a play-off game and to win one was our next goal. Travelling to Leeds for the first round wasn't the best place to try and do it though.

We boarded the coach in decent spirits but by the time we got on the M62 we were stuck in a massive traffic jam and already under pressure. We eventually got to the ground half an hour before kick-off and the RFL asked us if we wanted to put the kick off back. We said no and decided just to get on with it. England cricket were playing at Headingley the day after so we couldn't use the main changing rooms and were shoved in a shitty dressing room on the other side. We'd been stuck on the bus and basically had five minutes to get changed and ten minutes to warm up. But you know what, everything was so relaxed. When I saw us on the TV later that evening me and Cull were talking and taking in the atmosphere as we stepped out on to the pitch to prepare. There was no pressure on us as Leeds were favourites and that allowed us to play relaxed.

The game itself was really weird as we weren't in front many times but we were really calm. There are only so many times you're in the zone and it felt like that. Michael Sullivan had gone over in the corner and Benny Westwood had scored too. Then Leeds came back to level it up at 16-16. Kevin Sinfield dropped a goal and I replied almost immediately.

After Sinny put Leeds one point up, the Leeds fans really stuck it to me. Even though I wasn't with Vicky at the time, she was with my kids in the stadium and I was disgusted that they had to listen to what the fans were saying. They were questioning my sexuality but it went beyond the normal banter. So after Sinny had dropped his goal I kicked off and got it to touch to get the ball back. When I went to pick the ball up I flicked the fans the bird at the exact point Sky zoomed in on me and thousands of people saw it on TV. I don't regret giving some stick back to all those fans who had abused me for 50 minutes, but I did regret my kids seeing it as they shouldn't see their dad doing those kinds of things.

As I said, I kicked our equalising drop goal and then we both had attempts before I slotted the winner. Before the winning kick, they charged one attempt down and Ryan Bailey kicked through and looked odds on to score. But Rob Parker got back and smothered the ball. From there we drove down the field and I lofted over the winner. I know a lot of people talk about the goal that gave us the win, but if it wasn't for Rob Parker's massive effort, we wouldn't have got anywhere near winning that game. It was an immense effort from him and we won our first play-off game and it was fantastic. I was still in the mindset of getting blasted though so I didn't remember much of the celebrations afterwards.

We lost to Bradford in the next round but we almost pulled something off in that game too. We were a shed load of points behind and took the lead with about 65 minutes gone. It was awesome and we were confident we could do it. But Paul Deacon stepped Woody and went through to kill us off. It was still a very successful season for us. If you look at the year as a whole, the stats show we lost seven or eight games by less than a converted try, so our position in the table probably didn't do our overall season justice. You do get seasons like that and usually those games you lose by six points are the ones you need to be winning. But we did enough to get into the six and win that game at Leeds. Thankfully, we finished above Wigan too, which is always a bonus.

My season was a good one and you could say I had a break out year. But there's always somebody ahead of you and I didn't make the Dream Team. Longy was in front of me and he was awesome – as all the Saints team of 2006 were. I'm not in the game for personal accolades; if I was I probably would have played golf and been much richer too! But I still think I was the best six in the league that year and performed when it counted at the end of the season.

Incidentally, when I got back into pre-season training I was called in front of the RFL to explain that one-fingered salute. At first I told them I was wagging my finger, but they didn't buy that, so I owned up and got fined 300 notes. You don't play until you've paid up, so even though I thought it was nonsense, I had to cough up. I had been abused for most of the game and a two second salute earned me a fine while no one got punished at Leeds. At the end of the game I remember the true supporters in the South Stand at Leeds – a couple of hundred at most – clapped me off the field. That shows that not everyone is bad in rugby and with everything going on at the time it was a great gesture from them all.

I've had a lot of abuse at Leeds over the years, and at times it has been very personal. I don't mind some banter, but when it gets personal about family and things like that it is very disappointing. It does always seem to happen at Leeds. Sam Tomkins was booed for England when he was playing against the Exiles and nothing happened. I took it from all directions with some of the most disgusting abuse and I reacted and got fined 300 sheets! Are we too strongly based in Leeds' favour or what?

I've been taking stick since 1997 and sometimes it can be difficult to brush it off. But when it's personal and you have 3,000 people singing nasty stuff then it's different. That's not about the game, or not playing for GB, or not 'playing for a big club', it's something else. I think it is cowardly and if you confronted people they wouldn't admit it.

I know people think because we are professional we should be able to take it. But we are only human. We are professional and we have to be responsible, but how far can you go? I can handle the GB stuff, that's by the by; fatty and all that, that's a laugh, but when it is abuse then it crosses the line. How can the authorities condone that and then discipline the player if they respond? As for the Tomkins situation, someone higher up should have appealed to the fans as he was playing for his country. I stuck up for him as did Westwood and Peacock. But he was playing for his country and so someone from high up should have said something instead of relying on the players as they so often do.

The rugby league community is strong at times like this, but it is so often player-led. Thankfully though, sometimes we all join together to get it right. We had a benefit game for Mike Gregory that season and everyone pulled round to make it a success. I obviously knew Mike, he'd been involved at Saints when I was younger and had been coach of the GB Academy that I played for against France. He had an immense aura about him; his work ethic stood out and he was a lovely guy. He was a legend for Warrington and was a man's man who earned everyone's respect. You wanted to work for him, but you had fun with him too. So when he passed away it was heartbreaking. He still lives on in the club though. He is a Wire legend, and when you walk around the town, Greg is synonymous with it. He has a road named after him, a hall at the college and a lounge at the Halliwell Jones too. He was a superb guy and his legend will always live on.

A few years later Paul Darbyshire died too. Like Greg, Darbs went far too soon. I had the utmost respect for him. He was assistant coach at Warrington, and like Greg, his work ethic was amazing. The core group of Cull, Greg and Darbs would do anything for you. When he was weak with motor neurone disease, I just couldn't go and see him in hospital as I didn't want to be left with those memories of him. We were all pretty close and it was a real shock to the system when he left us. It was hard to see his wife going through that and seeing someone she adored and loved suffering. Thankfully, the whole rugby league community rallied round her and her family to give her some support in her hour of need. It doesn't replace Darbs though, as it doesn't Greg, but they are Wire legends that will never be forgotten.

At the end of the season, as Richard Horne was playing for Hull against Saints in the Grand Final, I took his place as reserve in the GB squad for the Tri-Nations comp in Australia and New Zealand. Although I'd been picked in the train-on squad only because he was at Old Trafford, I felt I'd been picked on form and had a really good chance of making the final cut to play in the series against Australia. Stat wise I'd been the top stand-off in the competition but I still had a lot to prove. So from day one I worked really hard to impress.

Unluckily, I shared a room with Glees and it was an absolute tip within about 30 minutes of being there. There were clothes on the floor and by the end of a week ordering room service there were plates all over the place. It was horrible. We landed on the Wednesday and although I was still in a drinking mode and looking forward to a night off on the Saturday, I made sure I worked hard in training. We trained in Manly one day and it was about 34 degrees, but beforehand we were supposed to be in a meeting and Glees forgot. In fact, he told me it had been cancelled. Sorry Glees, you're getting the blame. But he'd read the day wrong so we turned up late and were punished with extras on the field. It was red hot and we bashed the hell out of each other. At the end of training, me and Glees did our extras and I was spewing out of both ends. It drained and killed me but at least the carrot was there that you could have a good drink afterwards. But, as I've said earlier, the RFL wouldn't let us go out as there was a riot an hour away and so we ended up in the hotel on a ration of three beers. If you're up to this page by now you know the rest ...

Our warm up game against Newcastle was tough and we came out of it with a 40-6 win. Newcastle weren't the best team ever – almost a divisional side – but they sure did like to fight a lot. JP (Jamie Peacock) smashed a few that day and I got man of the match with five goals. Soon after though, I got told I hadn't made the final cut and was devastated. I'd worked really hard to impress when I got there and I had played well in the warm-up game but my face didn't fit. Some of the selections for the tournament were pretty strange though so I can't say I was that surprised looking back. They played Leon Pryce on the wing and he was a Grand Final winning stand-off. How you could put a guy of that calibre on the wing was strange to me.

That night I went out in Newcastle and then came back to Sydney to meet up with Nat Wood. I then planned to stay with Joey Johns and see the sights. He was surfing in Bali and was getting back two days after I was due to leave the GB camp. I got back to the hotel the next day and asked our tour manager if they could change my flight, but they didn't want me to stay in the hotel for an extra two nights, even though I would have paid. The team were going on to the Tri-Nations tournament but I wanted to wait for Joey. I didn't want to carry my bags around for two days. But they weren't playing ball, so I got on the flight and went home very pissed off indeed. If I'd stayed in Australia, I could have been picked if someone had been injured, but by then I wanted to come home. There was no point staying there for six weeks and not playing. Tours are about matches and if I wasn't going to play then I was off.

When I got home I went straight into the Welsh camp for

the first of a two-legged World Cup qualifier against Scotland. We led for a while and then conceded three second half tries to make the return leg the year after much harder. We ended up winning that by a couple of points but lost the game on aggregate. We then were defeated by Lebanon to end our hopes of qualifying.

9

A Decade of Service

I was officially an old bugger when I had my testimonial. When you think of celebrations, they're normally at the end of careers but here I was at 27 having a year to celebrate my life in the sport. Never in my wildest dreams did I think when I signed for Warrington I would be at the club for 10 years. I was really proud to have been at a club for that amount of time but I have to admit I didn't know much about running a testimonial, and when it began, it totally took over my life.

I know people have strong views about these sorts of things and some see it as outdated. I know rugby players can do well out of the sport but it's nowhere near what footballers can earn. A testimonial rewards loyalty for what you do for the sport and your club. You put a lot in to it and it takes its toll on your body.

A testimonial can bring in from around £60k to about £200k but it's as much about giving something back to the people and fans that have supported you throughout your career, and to be honest, the money has never really been an issue for me. Over the years I could have moved on to different clubs and I could have gone to union and maybe doubled my wage. So the testimonial probably offset the money I may well have earned elsewhere and rewarded my commitment and loyalty.

Some players are now getting three month testimonials and

I don't think that is right at all. A testimonial is 10 years if you stay loyal to one club and that is how it should be. Some Aussies are now getting testimonials because they have been over here a short period of time. They will have made a decent wage and then they are being rewarded by the sport. It's bullshit.

The most important thing about a testimonial is to get the right committee together. I know some players have done it themselves and it's ended up costing them a fortune and they've gone grey with the amount of work involved. It is hard; Mike Wainwright did his on his own without a committee and there is no way in the world I could have done that without one. How he did what he did without that support, well, he must have been fucking mental. Lee Penny had one and he did his own too and I think he ended up owing people.

I had Neil Smith, Roy Chicken, Alex Chicken, Pauline Nelson and Simon Bishop, whilst Vicky did a lot of work for me too. They took the pressure off with organising, getting invites out and events sorted. It is very stressful thinking about it and wondering if people will turn up to your forum or other event. They helped me concentrate on playing and I am very thankful for them for that. It was their first time on a testimonial committee too and they were amazing!

My testimonial game was against Wigan Warriors and they really helped me out. Wigan had just been taken over by Ian Lenagan and had this existing commitment for the game. Usually the gate money is split but Ian didn't want any of it. All he wanted was £300 for the bus journey and wouldn't even take food for the players afterwards. He wanted me to have it, and to do that was amazing and I have massive respect for the guy. We didn't know each other well and for him to do that was a superb gesture.

Although there is an argument that you have to earn as much as you can and as quick as you can, I wanted the testimonial to be directed at the fans so they could celebrate with me. I could have gone down the big corporate dinner route but that didn't fit well with me. The fans had paid my wage for 10 years and I wanted to give something back. I know a lot of players are going down the corporate route now and I'm not saying that is wrong, but the fans were the most important people for me. I wanted to make sure it was viable to everybody. So we held fans forums and things like ladies nights too. The single boys loved those as they could strut round with their vests on. They are also great earners too! Ladies get blind drunk and get served by the players! They are wild nights. We did a few dinners too – one with Andrew Johns – and a few golf days.

My team-mates were great; it was hard to ask them to support it all the time because there was a lot to do, but come the ladies nights and the hands went up pretty quickly that's for sure. You couldn't have a few beers though, well, ok, sometimes, but being pissed at your own do isn't great. The fans forums were very successful too. We did a few at Burtonwood Community Centre that were organised by Saints fan Geoff Cropper. He can sell a ticket that man can!

I do enjoy the forums and of course you get asked the same questions time after time after time. But they work if you're not too serious and have some fun. You have to try to have a laugh and to make fun of the guests. It all depends on what you are doing it for. I have done a lot for charities and amateur clubs and when you are making money for them it's good. I've done testimonial forums for Paul Wellens, Paul Wood, Benny Westwood – it's all great. There was no naked calendar for me though. I did one for charity a while back but not for my testimonial, although I guess you know by now I'm never afraid to get my gear off.

I did the *Super League Show* after one of the ladies nights and I was still pretty smashed from the night before. I paid our masseur to pick me up and take me to Leeds for 9am. I was rough as fuck and had to do the show live. Perhaps that's why only Robbie Hunter-Paul does it now! Damien Johnson was on the show and he was a great guy but I can't say I gave it my best appearance! It's always good to get asked to do things like that. I was asked to do *Question of Sport* but missed out because I went on holiday, and I have done the cup draw a few times. Once I was in a state after a bad night. You have to do a practice draw before the real one and I drew out Wigan at home to Saints. Come the real one I drew out Saints at home to Wigan! My Saints mates were happy with that.

It's good to get players on to things like that and on mainstream TV. Rugby union players are always on shows and it's got them very popular. I know their international set up is stronger than ours but we need to push our game more through TV. We can't beat them in terms of attendances for Test matches and even the Italians end up getting more than we do for Tests. Let's be strong for what we can be strong for. You've got me started now …

Some sections of our sport seem to like attacking union. I read a piece in *The Independent* in 2012 from Brian Ashton praising what I do on the field. That is how it should be. Let's respect each other's games. We should embrace each other and help each other out. We take pot shots and we don't need to. There are two really good codes and, yes, people argue each one is shit, but who cares, it's kids picking up a ball and running about. We can get better and we have to strive for that. There won't be one code in the memory of man, so why worry? Would football ever merge with Gaelic football? Would it balls.

Our club game is strong so let's build the international game and move on from there. It won't happen overnight but it can. In the early 90s we had 60,000 at Wembley for GB v Australia, 60,000 for a World Cup between Australia and New Zealand and 30,000 for a semi-final between Wales and England!

Back to my testimonial. One of the more ad hoc dos was through a good mate from Millom, a chap called Sconner who I met through Gary Chambers and Chris Rudd. He would come down to watch us play from all the way up there and that's a good two hours drive. When I started my testimonial he said he would organise a sportsman's dinner up there and I held him to it. Once we got the nod I persuaded a load of the boys to meet in the Lord Rodney outside the Halliwell Jones Stadium at midday and our kitman Bob to drive us up to Cumbria.

The plan was any time there was a do of any kind I would sort the lads out with a few beers for doing it. So we got a crate of beer from behind the bar and set off. Every time it got emptied we'd stop at a pub, have a few more and then grab another case. By the time we got up to Millom we were in a bit of a mess.

Like most places, people say Millom is the end of the earth and it is a really small village. We found Sconner's house, pulled up and he decided to take us to the pub first before we headed to the dinner later on. We looked up and down the street but couldn't see any bar. There was a row of terraced houses and by the time we walked down the road we thought we were being wound up. It turned out that the house at the end of the road had been changed into a boozer. It didn't have a sign, just a normal door and you walked in and you were in it. After that he took us to where we were staying. He'd sorted out five star lodges for us all out of his own pocket. They had saunas, Jacuzzis, the works.

The night itself was incredible. We were like superstars to the Millom people as they had to travel so far to see a game. There were 250 people in this small social club and everything went down really well. When the night was done, the boys were keen to kick on and take in the night life – and we found it. Basically, the tables in the social club were removed, the lights went on and that was the nightclub. It was one hell of a surreal night and party, but it was all down to Sconner. He's a rum lad and will sort you out with anything you need – venison, salmon – God knows where he got them from. He'd probably poached them! I ended up raising about £5,000 and gave £2,500 to a young boy I met who was severely disabled up there. I thought it was only right to pass it back to the young kid's school as a gesture for everything Sconner and the village of Millom had done on the night. They probably didn't know me but they came out to show their support and show the real spirit of the rugby league community so I gave something back.

I made a few donations from my testimonial to charities like Families United and other individual donations. There is always someone worse off than you and I have been brought up to help people wherever I can. If a cause is worthwhile and I feel attached to it I will give it my support. I have never wanted in my life really, and if I can pass something on then I will. I'd made a good living and I had that testimonial too so I was happy to help out.

I'm not here to do charity work and get the story in the paper. When I tie up with someone I don't expect 'Lee Briers is patron of this' to appear anywhere; that's not the point. I have been connected with five or six charities over the years but there are a lot of people who do a lot more than me. I'm fortunate that I am in a privileged position and that I can do something – and we all know people who won't do anything and I have no time for them. Rugby league players have been given so much, so to help a charity out with a few hours, then that's something we should do. My latest one is Rett Syndrome – a friend's daughter has it and it's a terrible disease for young girls. If I can play a small role to get them more funds or more publicity I will. It's not much to give a couple of hours a month and a few bits of kit, it's not much in life is it? There are people who feel they should get involved with things like this and do, but I want to do it. As I have said elsewhere, I'm not into God and things like that, although I have prayed a few times, but you can't keep taking in life all the time. If more people gave something then the world would be a better place wouldn't it?

I get pestered for kit all the time and I get a shit load of it and some of it I will never wear. I was privileged enough to be sponsored by Reebok a while back and they were fantastic with me. I was approached through Paul Cullen. His friend Dave Hutchinson was working for Reebok and they wanted to help me out. They were great and would sort out tickets for me, Vicky and the kids to Liverpool when I wanted them. I didn't abuse it but if someone needed something down at Thatto Heath and places like that then I would try and help them out. You can only wear so much so it clogs the house up otherwise. I like giving people my boots too – I could throw them in the bin if I wanted to, but what's the point? Adidas look after me now and if there is any spare, I will give it away. No point it staying in the house, is there?

After my testimonial I invested some of the money, around £50,000, into an apartment in Egypt. It was a good investment and sold to me brilliantly. I went over to see it when it was done and it was five-star, looking over the Red Sea in a new city. I changed the locks and made it a little bit more homely by putting in Sky TV and things like that. I even had someone renting it in the first couple of months and it was a nice earner, but the company who built it went bust and didn't pay the builders so we had to go to court.

At the time of writing this book, I am still waiting for that to be sorted out. It's like *Holiday Homes from Hell*. You might find me on that TV programme in the not too distant future! It was important for me to invest in something for the future and this looked like a good one. The investment is worth quite a bit of money, but we can't do much at the moment!

Whilst the testimonial was doing its thing, on the field at Warrington we recruited well once again but didn't quite hit it off. Adrian Morley's signing from Sydney was massive and we brought in Paul Johnson and Vinny Anderson. We had the makings of a solid team there so our performances that year were really disappointing. How the team didn't make the six I don't know. We started off well by beating Wigan, then lost to Bradford, beat Hull and London and then got hammered by Saints. It was like the last few years I suppose, too many inconsistent games and we couldn't get a run going. We had a number of young kids in the team too and I think their form in 2011 and 2012 was down to these tough times. The likes of Ben Harrison, Mike Cooper and Lee Mitchell. Chris Bridge was young too. They got the plaudits but we were pretty poor.

Kevin Penny exploded on to the scene in that season and did well. He made the Dream Team too. He was a great kid, who was confident and raw in his rugby. Because of his blistering pace, the media blew him up to be the next Martin Offiah. As soon as that happened, it was an uphill battle for him. Without having a go, he had a lot of flaws in his game and once teams found that out it killed him really. If he had been handled like Alex Ferguson looked after his young players – dipped them in and then out, that sort of thing – perhaps we could have nurtured his talent at that age.

But he was so good in 2007 that it was impossible to leave him out. Then, when his defence struggled, he paid the price for all that hype. The fans got on his back and he couldn't block it out. I wouldn't like to be a winger when you are marking Francis Meli. He was only about 10st. Meli ran all over him in the cup game that year and in 2008 he took a lot of stick. He wanted to learn and I think if he had been outside Matt King it would have brought him on a lot. He spent a lot of time out of Super League but now we have re-signed him. I'm sure he has learnt from those experiences.

We always scored well but needed strong defence to win matches and we didn't have that. Warrington were always pretty successful at moving the ball and playing entertaining rugby and we have borne the fruits of that in the last few years. Now we've added steel in defence but it was probably a bit too much to do both at the same time back then. Now we have that brand of football and Tony Smith has steadied our defence up. We are encouraged to play rugby too and this is down to Cull as he had us playing well in attack. Tony believes if your defence is good your attack will be right.

The pressure on Cull must have been massive back then, especially because of the new stadium and the increased investment in the squad from Simon Moran. It wouldn't have been a nice feeling to be him when we were losing. But knowing Cull as well as I do, he would have loved that pressure and would have strived for it and lived off it. I remember we played Cas in 2006 and we got a good thrashing by them at Wheldon Road. He was distraught at the front of the bus and I went to talk to him. It always transpired if we took a big beating on a Sunday there would be a board meeting on the Monday, purely by coincidence of course. It would be on the first Monday of every month and we'd take a beating beforehand. So Cull would have to go in on the back of a big loss. I remember on that day he was really down and I said to him, if it did come to him getting sacked, I'd follow him and I'd move on straightaway, with no hesitation. Thankfully it didn't come to that – but it did in 2008.

In those years we were happy to make the play-offs and then to see where we went from there. It's a different attitude now, but the pressure was still there. We took a step back in 2007, finishing seventh, but we were getting better and producing youngsters too.

I was a lot happier too both on and off the field, and the testimonial certainly helped. It was a happy year despite our season being crap. I felt a lot better about myself and although the depression was still there, it wasn't as bad as it was in 2006. They were dark days and I was wondering whether it was worth carrying on with rugby and life. Thankfully, I got past that and had a strong support group in my life with the committee and my family. Those guys became friends for life and I had something to focus on instead of just rugby.

That season I won the Parliamentary Player of the Year award after being voted top dog by the MPs who watched the game. It was a real honour and they invited me and Cull down to the Houses of Parliament to receive the award. We got the train down and the club paid for us to stay over. We had to be suited and booted and as I pulled on my trousers in the morning for the official visit, I realised I'd forgotten my socks.

It was pretty embarrassing walking to the Houses of Parliament with nothing on my feet apart from shoes. I knew that every time I sat down, people would be able to see acres of leg. When I got there I saw Big Ben and asked Cull where the Houses where. He pointed them out and I felt pretty stupid. Inside it was amazing and had a superb bar. It wasn't taxed and it was a pound a pint and 60p for a short. You could see the MPs in there – they would wait for the call to go to the Commons, vote and then be straight back in. Some of them would stay in for 24 hours we were told, but I'm not sure how true that is, but I will be standing for election as a result!

At the end of the season I played for Wales for the last time. We'd played Scotland the year before and had to beat them and overturn a deficit to make the World Cup. Before then we played PNG in a warm-up game in Wales, and when the lads were coming off they were changing shorts because we didn't have enough. I thought 'is this what I want to be doing?' It was a good game and I linked with Iestyn Harris which was always good but with losing out on the World Cup and then getting hammered by Lebanon, I thought what was the point. We'd beaten Scotland but couldn't overhaul the aggregate and then a few days later played Lebanon. We were on an emotional low and lost. Any other time we would have smashed them, so although it was horrible to think it, I decided it was the right time to move on and retire. It was upsetting to leave on that note.

It wasn't an issue of playing too many games; I was always in favour of that as the more you play the more successful you generally are. I just didn't want to go through the building process once again, and I think the changing of the shorts was the final straw. If we had got to the World Cup then of course I would have played. But with the injuries I was carrying at the time I might not have; I would have had to work hard to put operations off. For me, and I know I have mentioned it before, if we played 60 games and they all counted that wouldn't be an issue. It's the pointless ones we don't need so I would have moved heaven and earth to play in the World Cup had we got there.

When I came into Super League we were just coming out of a time when there was the Lancashire Cup, Regal Trophy and things like that and I think it would be brilliant to have more cups to win. Some teams don't feel the highs of winning a trophy, so how about the top eight that we have now go to the play-offs and the rest compete for a trophy instead of cutting their season. That means the teams that struggle financially and struggle to attract the big names can have something to play for. Maybe it might be a bit of a second rate cup, but those teams that are in that comp will draw a crowd and take advantage of the financial boost. If you'd asked me six years ago about a tourney like this I would have taken it. It means more money and the chance of a trophy. Seems pretty easy to me!

The hangover of that close season cast a shadow over the following year. I didn't feel in a good place and as a result I gave up the captaincy. With the disappointment of not making the Super League play-offs and then the World Cup I thought seriously about quitting the game. I went back into the depression I really didn't want to be in. I was that disappointed to miss out on two major things that I did think about giving it up.

I phoned Cull and told him where I was at and that I'd thought about quitting the game altogether. We spoke for a long time and he convinced me to sleep on it and not make any rash decisions. He told me to think about what I was going to give up. So after a while I went back to him and agreed but said I wanted to relieve myself of the captaincy and then I could just concentrate on the game. We had a month or so to think about it and we decided the best person to do it would be Moz.

To give up the captaincy was massive, but I couldn't think of anyone else better to give it up to than him. It was great for the club and me. Moz is a leader and is inspirational. When he was told, the first thing he did was to come over to me and asked if it was ok or if I had any objections. I told him straight I couldn't have been happier and history has shown it was the right choice.

I was 28 and the sport that I'd loved since I was a little boy kicking cans and balls around on Peet Ave was getting me down. Would I have actually done it and quit? Hindsight says not, but to have those thoughts in the first place and the thoughts of leaving the sport I have grown up with, showed there were a few issues. I had a long off-season to get my head sorted and perhaps I had too long to think. I suppose it was the start of a new era for me, Warrington and Moz.

I can't praise Moz's attitude enough when he was offered the captaincy; in fact, I haven't a bad word to say about him at all. He is a bandit at poker and if he doesn't win, will sulk. He's a gentleman and a big soft git off the field. He's not a massive talker but when he does, you listen, and he leads by example. Our families are close as his dad is from Clock Face and went to the same school as my mum. Our backgrounds are similar so we just seem to hit it off. When he plays, he is a roughhouse prop who always goes to the whistle. And at the end of the game or training session, he just goes home to his family. There are not many people who have gone over to the NRL and ripped it up like he did. When we were in Sydney, he couldn't go 20 yards without someone grabbing him for a picture – that just shows the impact he's had over there.

You notice that NRL experience in the body language of pretty much every player who has played in that league. Moz didn't want any of us having our hands on our knees, heads and hips, even when we couldn't breathe after a session and it's clear he learnt that tough attitude over there.

Our trip in 2012 showed we are just as fit as the Aussies and we did a lot of their training, especially a lot of running, and we blew them apart. But we can't match them in intensity internationally. I think the mentality of playing tough NRL games week in week out makes all the difference as you can't have a minute off. Sometimes some of the top teams over here can have lapses and get away with it. In Australia you can't and you see that in Moz.

It's not arrogance, it's just they have a swagger, a different lifestyle and it leads to that way of holding yourself. And if you put an NRL player and a Super League player in the same room, you just know which is which – and not by the accent. NRL players are media trained from a young age and are more outspoken. We can be a little shy and sometimes look a bit scared of doing things wrong – and you notice that on the pitch too. Our lads seem to go into their shells against them and that leaves you asking why don't we play against them like the way we do in Super League. Our players are better than theirs for me but they play tougher games and know what they are doing.

On our trip to South Sydney in 2012, we did some coaching over there and I would say our under-nines are so much better than what they had. There were a couple of lads on the Roosters under-14s and 15s sides but I could pick players from Thatto Heath and Crosfields who were better. That shows we are just as skilful as them on a one on one basis. Basically, they have confidence in their abilities which is something we lack!

Once again we recruited well that year and it was really the start of the successful period we know now. Adrian Morley, Chris Hicks, Michael Monaghan – you're talking class individuals who were great assets to the club. Matt King also came in and that was a huge signing for us and Super League. He was at his peak and was still playing for Australia. I think the signing of Andrew Johns a few years earlier had shown how big a club we were and how we could attract players like King from Melbourne. He was allegedly on a massive contract and we'd wind him up about that all the time. At the end of the day he was an Aussie centre, had played Origin and therefore you'd expect him to earn big dollar wouldn't you? He was in his prime and was an outstanding bloke. But he struggled a bit that season. Perhaps the price tag on his head was too high and the expectation too great. But when the team isn't playing very well or is inconsistent it is hard for anyone to shine.

Monners was brought in at scrum half but played most of his time at hooker, and I think him, James Roby and Cameron Smith were the best in the world. Hicks signed on the wing and was quick as anything. When he came over he put out a statement that suggested he wanted to finish with his mates and win a Grand Final. I wasn't too happy with this as it questioned his commitment to Warrington. I went and saw Cull and had it out. We'd let Henry Fa'afili go for him and I didn't like that attitude. It's fair to say Chris shoved it up my arse really! He finished tries for fun and was something else. Louie Anderson also came in and he is one of the toughest players I have been with. When we trained, the coaches would play left versus right which meant I would be up against him. He always trained at 100 per cent too, no half pace, and I would be buggered after a session as he never backed down. He was religious, didn't drink and was an unsung hero for us so many times.

It was hard to lose Henry. He was a mate but the club thought they had to move on and we needed to strengthen in that area. I'm sure Henry could have played back row for us but Chris Hicks came in and did an awesome job.

Once again we got off to a shocking start and had a horrific injury list to go with it. We had a number of top players out and then with only one win in seven matches, Cull decided to call it a day. We had the team to compete but we weren't firing. Sometimes it isn't the coach's fault but rather it is the players, and I thought on this occasion it was ours. When he left we went on a bit of a roll, and a year later we won the Challenge Cup. Perhaps we needed someone fresh behind the scenes but it was soul destroying for myself and for him of course. That's life though in sport.

I felt guilty for a while afterwards. I think he lost the dressing room, which was a real shame, and it hurt me to think that. It hurt me to think that some of the players just didn't trust in him anymore. He wasn't only my coach, he was my confidante and my friend. I was real close to him so it hurt me to see people question him and lose faith in him and I think that is why he lost his job.

We'd started the season with stability, Cull had been with us for five years and we had four top players come in and join us.

Then, we suffered the injuries of Stuart Reardon, Chris Bridge, Paul Wood and Paul Johnson. When you have a lot of injuries, unless you are a top side you tend to struggle. At that point we weren't one of the top sides and weren't mentally strong enough to cope with injuries. And that's why we struggled … and then the coach went.

Players thrive on pressure and expectation. It makes you work harder and you become more mentally prepared for it. Warrington are now expected to be a top two, top three team and we know we will be. But it still means you have to work for it. Our biggest downfall could be expecting that to happen every year. We could beat ourselves but we practise daily for it not to happen. If you don't train well enough then it can happen. Now we can sit in a meeting and tell each other where we are going wrong. I can say to the coach I don't think the gameplan is right because we are strong enough as a group to do it.

So what if Cull had stayed? Who knows what would have happened but it has been proven, where facts are concerned, that we did have to move on. We progressed and won trophies. Whether that would have happened regardless, well, if I knew that I'd go out now and stick a lottery ticket on. The facts are we won trophies beyond him coaching us. Cull was a strong character, a good coach and a friend and I respected that.

*****

Jimmy Lowes had the arduous task of taking over from Cull. He was a legend as a player but I had contrasting thoughts about him. As a player I thought he was an absolute arsehole – but only for one reason. At Bradford he had a massive pack and Jimmy was an awesome player. He could marshal his troops around like something I aspired to, and for the full 80 minutes whenever we were playing Bradford he would be screaming: 'Run at Briers, run through him and run over him'. That would put me off my game and after a while I would be shouting: 'Fuck off, leave me alone'. They were big enough to tackle anyway and with Jimmy pointing them my way it was pretty bad! I dare say we didn't get on as competitors because he just destroyed me really. He was an old head, good at what he did and I had a lot of respect for him as a player. But I really hated his guts. Ha!

When he came on board I wondered how it would work. It actually worked pretty well. It was like we'd just met and we became good mates. We had the same banter too. It was like the old days. We were starting a new era, but we'd come from the old era – me the late 90s and him from way back (only kidding) – and it went well. Whilst we were in the same mould of how to get teams around the park, we certainly had different thoughts on fitness. Jimmy is a fitness freak, still is, and loves his long runs. He'd be first in the gym doing weights and his pre-season for the following year was all long running!

No one could blame him for taking the job given the resources the club had but I just thought it was a bit too early for him. You can't blame him for wanting to have a go and stepping in the deep end; that is what Jimmy is all about, he loves a challenge. But in the end it didn't work out for him as I will talk about later. I think he needed a better backroom team behind him. Better perhaps isn't the right word; more experienced backroom team maybe.

It was hard for him to come in halfway into a season and he tweaked a few things but essentially left alone what was Cull's team. He has a strong character and his own thoughts, and the season after he changed a few things around to his way of thinking. He was always going to do that as you don't want to be a clone of what has gone before – you want to stamp your authority and footprint on the team. He has a view and whether it is right or wrong he stuck by his convictions. That made him a good coach for me but it was the experience as a head coach he probably lacked.

He was around 38 when he took on the head coach role and that is young to coach a side, especially with the pressure in Super League. Added to that the expectation at Warrington was high. Jimmy is a proven winner and was loyal and gave everything that season. When he stepped down for Tony Smith in 2009 he went back to being assistant, and I know how I would feel if I had been in his shoes, but he put aside any feelings he had about what had happened, was professional and got on with his job. Fair play to him for that.

Jimmy inherited a team full of injuries but we made the play-offs and had to go to Catalans in the first round. We were down to the bare bones on that trip. Antony Jerram got a game as did Taylor Welch who was an American who'd only played a handful of second grade games. We were down on numbers and France is hardly the place you want to go when you're depleted. In the end it was a case of trying to go through the motions but we got thumped 46-8.

It was another frustrating end to a disappointing season. Somehow we made the play-offs but ran out of steam, energy and motivation. On the plus side we had our Mad Monday in France which was a result – if a little dear on the wallet.

I also went on a stag do for a mate to the Isle of Man of all places. We were in a mess before we got there. We were pretty blasted and got ourselves kicked out of most of the pubs in Douglas. Once one doesn't let you in, they put in a call to all the others and that's that really. We were in bed for 10pm and the lad who was getting married thought he'd got away with the usual stag fun. Our ferry was leaving at two the next day so in the morning we found a pub to wait in and the daft sod left his wallet on the table as he went off for a piss. Easy. We lifted his card and when he went to pick up some more cash he noticed his card had gone. I took charge and told him because he was pissed I would cancel his cards for him. He was delighted and not suspicious when I asked him for his pin number too! We got on the ferry and because of his 'loss' I said I'd get his beer and look after him. So me and Danny Whittle went off to buy a few pints for everyone on the boat who wanted one. Pizza? No problem. The stag thought this was ace when we brought back pizzas and beer for him. Two months later he got his card bill and wasn't as happy; we stung him for more than £600.

It was a good end to a shit season, but at least I could put the full year behind me and have a carefree pre-season under my belt. Looking back on it though, it was horrible, we did nothing but long running – and fucking hell did Jimmy make us run. We would be running for hours without seeing a ball and it was really tough. I think he enjoyed watching us suffer. We would warm up with a two minute drill. You had to hit the line – every line – on a full pitch. 10, 20, 30, 40 50 up to 100 and then back – and keep going for two minutes, hit the line with your chest. And that was just for a warm-up! It was horrible, especially when the ground was cold and you had to hit it with your chest and hands.

Warm weather training had been canned that year too – Jimmy was old school! We went to Lilleshall and it was freezing, Baltic cold. We didn't enjoy it and the Aussies less so. One night halfway through the 'trip' we had a social night and each group had to do an act. One was Take That, one was Blind Date and one was some other boy band. We were all put in groups and everyone had to take part. I ended up being Cilla Black from Blind Date with high heels, tight mini skirt, make up, the works. I think I enjoyed it a little too much and some of the lads fancied me for sure. When they got changed I kept the gear on and gave them all a thrill.

When I am head coaching, we will spend about three and a half months in Spain! Touch wood, I can get a job like that but I have picked up enough over the years to know what works and what doesn't. The more enjoyment you get out of it the better of course, but you have to do the hard work. It's three or four months of pain and for anyone who has not done sport as a pro, there's nothing like pre-season; they are disgusting. It is groundhog day, waking up, breakfast, gym, out on the field, lunch, out again, getting home, eat, sleeping, eat, waking up, gym and it goes on ... I think this is why people go abroad and it does refresh the mental side of it and works wonders. The massive thing is if you have a good conditioner and they know what they are doing, it doesn't really matter what you are doing as a head coach in pre-season. It's still hard work and you know it's your job when you are pounding the hills. I wouldn't do it if I didn't like it though. I have done more than 18 pre-seasons now!

I had a couple of offers in early 2012 from other clubs but at the time I couldn't talk about them because there is a rule that states a club can't speak to a player if they are under contract. That's a bollocks rule. Let's face it, all clubs do it and if one club says they're not, I'll show you a liar. By the end of 2012 I would have been out of contract but I have always thought the best possible way to get a new one and not worry is to perform on the field. If you get your performances right then someone will look for you.

Rugby league needs to get rid of this rule though. If someone is out of contract in their final year then they should be allowed to speak to other clubs. It couldn't happen in any other job! If you're out of work in October and now it's April you're going to talk to people and check the job ads aren't you? But now we have the problem of the rule and the negative headlines if someone got caught doing it. I guarantee it would make a full page in the press. If a player moves you can make a big story out of it ... but if they get caught it is negative. It seems daft that you have to wait until September if you're out of work in October! Where is the logic in that? Isn't that a restriction of trade? It is harder for rugby league players to find work because they haven't got anything else to do. We play rugby and there's not that many places on a team – twenty-five places on fourteen teams at present. When you add the ridiculous issue of the quota when Crusaders lost their licence then it makes it worse. The young Elliot Kear was very close to not getting a job and he is a home grown Welsh player. But he almost lost out because clubs were allowed to take Crusaders' quota players off quota. How stupid. We now know this rule has changed – God I'm good.

This is one of the many reasons League 13, the players'

association, was formed. League 13 isn't here to fight against rugby league; we are here to assist the RFL and to help the players. We aren't here to say we want another two million on the salary cap. We live in a realistic world but we want the sport to be fair and want the players to be recognised as having a voice.

We believe there should be a player welfare manager at every club. I've spoken about putting a quid on Wembley and Grand Final tickets and that would do it. I know some clubs have them already and at Warrington we were one of the leaders on this. It's important to have that support for players, young and old, in a club. There needs to be a system for getting players into colleges and to thinking about what happens when they retire or suffer a career-ending injury.

Reaction has been great and as of April 2012 we had 86 per cent of all Super League players on board. That's around 300 of 350 players. It took a while for the RFL to listen to us as they said the players already had a union in the GMB. I know that union has looked after players in the past and they do a great job. But we want our voice and if the RFL think the players are happy with the current situation, we wouldn't have the majority of Super League players with us would we? In the end they knew they had to listen to us as the figures don't lie.

Anyone who has tried to form an association of any kind knows it is hard work. We were helped as the players clearly wanted it. It isn't a talking shop and we jumped through a number of hoops to make sure it was set up correctly. We identified fourteen players, one from each Super League club, to talk to and held a meeting in Brighouse. We then pitched to them and had Mike Denning from Hattons Solicitors, Ernie Benbow who works for the NHS and the Wigan Past Players Association and Terry O'Connor. It was decided at that meeting to send a ballot out to each club to see if they wanted change and to be part of a new association. The delegates from each club took that back and it came back 94 per cent in favour. We then had another meeting of the fourteen delegates and voted on the people for the committee.

Jon Wilkin was elected as chairman, Ernie as CEO and Jamie Peacock, Clint Newton and myself. Clint is now back in Australia and was a massive part of setting it up and knew what it was like in Oz to do something similar. Mike Denning came on board as a non-executive legal advisor and Terry as an ambassador for past players.

From there we went round to each club to talk to the players and give a more detailed plan of what we intended to do. What we did was give people a choice – either stay with the GMB or come over and join League 13, and the numbers haven't lied. Now we are putting a package together for our members with deals and things like that and by April 2012 we went live. The next step is speaking to the Championship clubs and then taking our combined voice to the Rugby Football League.

Rugby league is a great game but can it be better? Course it can. We are here to make the game better, not to make it worse. We are the only major sport who doesn't have our own professional union and we've received backing from the PFA, cricketers and the rugby union associations. We have 12 months free membership with the Professional Players Association. We are well backed and we just need to keep knocking. We are not so daft to think it will be smooth and that it will always be easy. I have no doubt I will still be playing when it is all up and running, but this is about making sure the players of the future are looked after and have a good career. The players promote the game every week as they are the ones who play the game; they are the front line.

There will be a number of issues that come up but the main ones seem to be the rules and a minimum wage. We know the NRL has a minimum wage but we aren't stupid enough to say it should be £40,000, that isn't viable. But we want something set in stone that can be realistically achieved. The RFL could come back and say a minimum is not viable so we could go back to our members, tell them that and can look into another way of doing it.

One thing for sure is that we have paid average Aussies good money over the years. We need to get to a point where there has to be certain criteria to come over here. We have had some shocking overseas players at Warrington who have no doubt been on top dollar. The ones we have now are superb quality, but in the past you wondered how the hell some of them were getting a start. When you add up what money they have been on too, it was a joke.

We have to start by making sure those players have have appeared in so many games in the NRL. If not they should only be in a certain wage bracket, say 50 NRL games you get £22-40k, something like that. That is what the Aussies are doing with the British players heading over there and I think it is something that we should be looking at. That would keep more money in our own competition for our own players. We can then look to the Championship and bring more Chris Hill's and Alex Walmsley's in.

The players will be represented by players and people who have been in the same position. We will look after any issue and that is when the likes of Mike Denning and the experience of the committee members will be crucial. We only want the best for our game as it is the best product in the world and we need to promote it. We need to get players out there and use their image to promote our game. We need plans in place for players whose clubs drop out because of administration for example.

Player drain is a big issue going forward as we can't afford to keep losing players to the NRL or rugby union.

10

Cup Dreams

Ok, straight into a cliché – good things come to those who wait. I'd waited 13 seasons to finally get my hands on a trophy and when it finally happened it was very sweet indeed. Lifting the Challenge Cup at Wembley is the stuff of dreams. kids who grow up with rugby league as their sport, or any sport come to think of it, want to turn around after walking up all those steps at the national stadium and hold up the cup in front of a packed house. I'd tasted a little bit of the build-up in '97 before I was cruelly denied the chance to really get involved. So to do it after 13 years of playing the game that kept me off the streets and out of prison, well, it was more than I could have hoped for.

But if you look back at 2009 and everything that happened, and how special it was for the club and the town, you'd never have seen it coming at the start of the season. Our record was pretty bad, we lost our coach, and when the new chap came in, we were hammered 60-8 in his first game. Hardly the stuff of legends.

Jimmy had put us through easily my toughest pre-season to date. We ran, ran and whenever we did alternative training or at a different venue ran some more. It gave us real confidence to head into the season as fit as we could be and challenge for some silverware which was becoming expected. But after losing our first three games to Saints, Catalans and Wakefield he was relieved of his duties. We then lost to Leeds and the club brought in Tony Smith – with Jimmy as his assistant. Normally you get a bit of a jump when a new coach comes in and the week of his appointment we were set to play Harlequins away. But we were pretty dismal in that match and lost 60-8. The fans gave us a load of stick in that match and a lot of it was focussed on Matt King. He reacted by flipping the bird at them and had to apologise later in the week. As I know from experience, we are human and can only take so much. He reacted in the wrong way but quickly made amends.

I had probably one of my worst games for Warrington in that match. I made a number of uncharacteristic errors and I wasn't really arsed with how I was playing. I was pissed off with all the upheaval and it affected my performance. Quite rightly I was dropped to the bench for the next match against Hull KR. That was a big wake-up call for me and made me think I had taken rugby league for granted as something that would always be there. So, I decided to give my mate Danny Whittle a bell and carry cement up ladders for him on a building site after training. It stung me back into what reality really was like and it helped. There would be no repeat of that performance for the rest of the season.

Tony perceived me to be a wild man and someone who liked partying and I perceived him to be an arrogant Aussie and a real disciplinarian. I'd never crossed paths with him but it was a perception I had. The only time we'd talked was in 2007 when he asked me to play for GB against the All Golds but I'd been playing with injections and I was going on holiday so I couldn't commit. When he came into the club though my opinion changed, even after he dropped me for the Hull KR game. He sat me down, we exchanged frank views and then wiped the slate clean. He told me what he expected and I told him what I expected and we moved forward from there. From then on, we've had a really solid and great relationship. We are very similar in the way rugby league should be played and we bounce off each other.

He came in with the openness to listen to my views; he is a coach who always wants to learn and if that's learning off his players he will. He is all for his players and if he can do anything for them he will, and that's what makes him successful. That confidence flows into the players as a result. Did I think he was the right man for Warrington at the time? His track record was awesome. Other than getting relegated at Huddersfield he got them back up without losing a game. Well, they did lose a game in the cup which we took great delight in telling him on a quiz night. He asked us which was the only team that had gone unbeaten throughout a season and never lost. No one got it and he said Huddersfield, so we had to remind him of that. He'd turned Leeds around to what they are now and brought that winning culture to the Rhinos. It was a good appointment.

It is always a worry when a new coach comes in. You ask yourself whether they like you and are their perceptions going to keep you out. You have to knuckle down and impress. But if you have faith in your own ability it looks after itself. No disrespect to any other coach I've worked with but I wish Tony would have come in earlier. If he'd have come in five years beforehand, I believe he would have made me a better player. But that is no disrespect to any other coach because I have learnt a lot from them. Tony's taught me lessons on how to play the game differently and not be as one dimensional.

It was a lot of upheaval at the time, particularly for Jimmy. He moved aside to let Tony come in and became his assistant. That shows the character of him really. To do that professionally can't have been easy, and he was a true pro. But it was an appointment that needed to be made. I think in the end Jimmy perhaps lacked the experience to be a head coach, and his backroom staff certainly did. Perhaps if he'd have had more old heads behind the scenes it could have worked.

A couple of months later Martin Gleeson moved on too. He never seemed unhappy, but when your home town club comes knocking – in his case Wigan – and you'd always wanted to play for them, then it's difficult to say no. I was gutted when he left as we had a great understanding on the pitch and were thick as thieves off it. Can't blame him for taking the opportunity though.

Stu Reardon also left, and that was a bit harder to take. It was the fault of the medical team really as he didn't have the right rehab on his Achilles and he got pushed out. He was going through a bad patch with his wife too and was on a charge as well. It was a tough time for him and to be let go in the way he was was disappointing. His situation affected the whole squad so we had a whip-round for him and raised £3,000. He had to have another operation on his leg and this money helped him on the way.

Ritchie Mathers came in from Wigan and he was outstanding. He took and still takes a lot of stick from fans but he is one of the most professional players you will ever come across. He was great for us, really enthusiastic and that was what we needed. He was perfect for the club and a great bloke too.

It had been nine months of turmoil at Warrington and I suppose being dropped to the bench after the Harlequins debacle could have tipped me back into the dark days once more. I felt totally different this time though. Although it was the first time in my career I'd been dropped, I thought I'd take it on the chin and train a lot harder. I took it as a challenge to prove people wrong and show Tony Smith what I was all about. I didn't sulk as that would have shown I wasn't there for the team. I trained hard, helped the boys out who were also in my position and did as much as I could for the team. I think from then onwards the respect grew between us. And you know what? With that mindset I played well against Hull KR when I came on the field and set up a couple of tries. I actually liked coming off the bench because I could watch what the other team was doing and pinpoint the gaps – and it worked in that game as we came from behind to win 24-12.

After all the changes though, 2009 will go down as a historic season for the Wolves. We missed out on the play-offs as our league form was shite but we won the cup! That made it the best season by a country mile in my career. Yes, we were disappointed with our tenth placed finish and that wasn't good enough, but would we trade a play-off spot for the cup? Would we bollocks.

It's difficult to balance a good run in the Challenge Cup and your league form. When you win the cup you want to go on and finish the season strong, but it takes so much out of you. You play the final in August, you then play two or three games and you're in the play-offs. The emotion from a day at Wembley is immense and it takes a lot out of you. It shouldn't affect you as you should be able to carry on winning, but it just does. It can be done because Saints did it in 2006 and Wigan have also done the double in the 2013 season, but it's unbelievably difficult. Anyway, that's enough about the double because I really want to explain how good it is to get to Wembley and do the business.

But first, just a little on the comp itself. I have spoken about the Challenge Cup a few times in this book and how I think it should change. I always preferred the cup to be in May because you work all year round to win Super League. With it being in August now it is difficult to come out of that and back it up in the play-offs. Therefore, all that work to win Super League and getting yourself into a position goes out of the window. If you play the cup final in May, then you have four or five months of the season left and everyone can focus on that competition – including the fans and media.

At present you play until the quarterfinals in May and then the semi-finals are not for six weeks. Then you have about two or three weeks to sell tickets for the Final. What other sport in the world would do that? What other sport would have an eight-week break between the rounds? It doesn't make sense. Get it over and done with, have a separate cup comp and don't try and run it parallel with Super League. Having a two or three week break between the semi and Final means you can't really make the best out of it commercially. It's like people don't want clubs to make money on the Final. How can you market it in that short a time span? We take fans for granted and after they've paid for a semi they have to fork out a load of money to head down to Wembley almost straightaway.

I'm getting on my soapbox once again so back to 2009.

Any player will tell you that they are nervous when the first round of the cup is drawn. Whether you're at the draw itself or listening on the radio you will feel the butterflies in your stomach go as soon as you hear: 'Gentleman, the draw.' One thing I can tell you about the draw though is it isn't fixed. I've done it, there are no hot or cold balls, and you aren't told who to choose! Sometimes you do a practice one beforehand and I have pulled out Wigan v Saints in that, and then drawn Saints v Wigan in the real one. It is the luck of the draw.

In the first round you want a home draw for sure and then a lesser team. If you get both then you are happy, although there aren't any 'gimmies' in rugby league. So to draw York at home was perfect for us. We wanted to stay away from the big teams as in the past we always seemed to get Saints at Knowsley Road! York put up a good fight too but when you have a Super League team over a Championship one then there is ever only going to be one winner. From there we drew Featherstone away and I thought that was a good omen as the last time we won the cup, we played them along the way and won it. I didn't play in that game but we won pretty comfortably and I remember Ritchie Mathers getting two tries. After his second he threw the ball into the crowd and punched the air, he was that pumped up. We gave him a lot of stick for that!

It was good to get York and Featherstone as we were struggling in the league. We didn't have any consistency in our performances and it was a good distraction for us. Our next match was at Hull KR, and that's when things got a bit serious. I decided to go 'hard' and shave my head but when we got to Craven Park it was a red hot day and I looked like a tit. The game was up and down and they were ahead about 24-12 at half-time. When we got into the sheds Tony Smith began his team talk. Normally – and I don't know why – Moz farts a lot during the break but this time round he just let rip the loudest fart I have ever heard ... everyone burst into laughter, despite the fact we were getting beat. I was sat a few seats along and I can still feel the ripple heading along the bench. Hardly the best preparation for the second half having your eyes stinging, but perhaps it took the heat out of the mess we were in.

In the second half I kicked for Kingy in the corner and Bridge converted from the touchline. Then Moz went through, I got the ball and I hit Bridgey. That drew us level and we went into extra time and the golden point for the first time. It had never been done before. As we were in the huddle before the period kicked off I remember saying to the boys, 'Get me to the halfway line and I'll hit a one pointer over.' I think they got me there about three times and I couldn't get anywhere near. On the fourth one the field position was too good not to shoe it over and the rest is history. As soon as I struck it I knew it was over and it was pure elation. I think it was the best one I've ever hit, including that one at Leeds which was pretty much perfect too. The celebrations were immense in the changing rooms because we'd got through and showed we could handle the pressure.

I'm known for kicking drop goals and I always believe if I'm in the position to do it, I will get them over. You just want the forwards to get you in a position to do it. Then, if you get a quick play the ball it is a lot easier. As long as they can do that it makes my job easier, and that's what I get paid for. If someone is flying out at me I find it easier to just kick, but when I get more space and more time to think, I can spoon them a little. A lot of people talk about when I kicked five against Halifax and still got beat. We were struggling for points and Dave Plange told me that every time we were down in their zone we should keep the scoreboard ticking over. But we got done in the last minute. I get embarrassed when people talk about it; I don't want to be known for kicking five drop goals in a game and bloody losing.

As for the drop goals, you have to know when to do it and not. For instance, if there's five minutes to go and you're winning by four, then there's no point going for one. If it goes over they'll get the ball and go for a short kick off. That's pressure on your line and you don't need it. You need to play for field position. But if the chance is there, and it benefits you, then why not?

So it was down to us, Saints, Wigan and Huddersfield in the semi-finals and I wanted Saints in the Final. It didn't matter to us whoever came out and it happened to be Wigan. Like us, the Warriors were mid-table at the time so we were pretty happy with that. Our game plan was to run at Feka Paleaaesina and keep on running to tire him out. We scored three tries going through him and he couldn't handle the traffic coming his way. He got dragged off and never came back on. We were 24-0 up at one point and they came right back. It took a Chris Hicks try to seal it at the end and I kicked a drop goal at the right time … to make sure.

Earlier in the match I scored next to the posts. It was my brother's birthday too and it felt really weird to do that on his day. To go to Wembley, score and win, well I'm not a big believer in God but something happened that day. He was on my shoulder and looking over us I think. Jon Clarke had an amazing day too – he'd been playing for eight weeks with a broken ankle and produced a magnificent performance. So when the hooter went and we'd made it at last to a final, every emotion came out. On the lap of honour afterwards, I gave my dad a massive hug and we both started crying. It was amazing to see so many faces who were elated for us. It kind of made up for all those hard years and those 'nearly there' moments. We'd lost three times in a Challenge Cup semi-final and to get to the final was not just about me and the team but the fans too. The Stobart in Widnes was packed and we'd paid back the support of our passionate fans,

It was important not to get ahead of ourselves and our focus was on winning the final. After the game in the changing rooms, we had a talk about what we wanted to do and there was no champagne. We didn't want to make up the numbers at Wembley. In the other semi-final, Saints unexpectedly lost to Huddersfield, and although I wanted to face them, I wasn't too fussed. It was nothing to do with the people there but I wanted a bit of payback really. I still know a lot of people behind the scenes and I have a lot of friends at Saints. But I just wanted to put things to bed in a final.

After the semi we had two league games to play as well as all the build-up for the big day. We faced Wigan and then Wakefield, then had the biggest thing to happen to the town for 35 years! As a professional rugby league player you have to focus on the game in front of you. If you get too far ahead of yourself then you can get injured or completely lose the plot on the field. But we were due to play in such a massive game and that meant we couldn't whole-heartedly focus on what was in front of us. We knew there was a huge expectancy around the town and everyone was buzzing about getting to Wembley. We also knew we weren't going to win Super League as we were pretty adrift of the play-off spots. Our focus therefore was squarely on the Final. In the weeks before I was hoping Tony Smith would wrap me up in cotton wool as I didn't want to miss the big day and I suppose it did affect how the team approached those last two league games. Unsurprisingly we lost both.

You don't go into games wanting to lose but when you have a final around the corner, your focus changes. The last thing you think about before you go to bed is running out at Wembley. When you wake up you think the same. Anyone who tells you anything different is lying. You always play 100 per cent because anything less means you are more than likely to pick up an injury. But mentally it is different. Normally my sole focus would be on the next game and then focussing on the one after when the first is over. But when you have a cup final around the corner, you lose some of that focus. You try your best but it is hard not to think ahead.

After we lost 40-28 at home to Wakefield, the build-up to the final was already in full swing, but we tried not to get completely caught up in it. I knew a little of what to expect as I'd been through it with Saints back in 1997, but this was a totally different experience and was very full on. It was mayhem from start to finish. There were Warrington flags everywhere – banners, posters, you name it. It was off the Richter scale. A few days before I went for a haircut and I got a call from Vicky who said I needed to come home straightaway. Fearing the worst I drove back like a loony and when I turned into my drive all my neighbours had decked it out in primrose and blue and there was a 25 metre banner across the close wishing me all the best. Sky TV were there too and I was embarrassed really. But I made a promise to myself in those weeks up to the final that I would take it all in as I might not get there again. And that was the attitude of all the squad – we didn't want the occasion to spoil what could be a historic moment for the club. We treated it like any other game, even though the whole town was totally mental and we'd all been given nice shiny suits for the occasion!

We travelled down to our hotel on the Thursday and as we pulled out of the Halliwell Jones, there were thousands of people cheering us off. Shoppers couldn't get anywhere near Tesco as it was jammed with well-wishers. It was an unbelievable feeling as the fans were proud to be part of something big. But, and I know a few of the lads would agree, the well-wishers and the magnitude of the occasion never put us under undue pressure. We were struggling in the league and I don't think people expected us to win. We were there to enjoy it, and we did, but we had no intention of just making up the numbers.

We stayed at The Grove in Watford, where the England football team have been in the past, and prepared in the best way we could. We played a lot of poker to relax and I lost a fair bit too. One time I went back to my room to find a few more quid and as I looked round I knew someone had been in. All my stuff was hanging up and my used toiletries had been neatly put away. I thought someone was winding me up. I went into my bedroom and there were slippers by the side of the bed, the covers had been pulled back and someone had drawn the curtains. Apparently this is what happens in posh gaffs. I'm not used to that at all and I'm surprised no-one came in and made sure I was all tucked in and read me a bedtime story to be honest!

On the Friday we had some breakfast, did a little training and went to look round Wembley. It was eerily quiet inside and it did look as big as it does on the telly. Some of the kickers did some kicking to practise, others were taking snaps and then we went back into the changing rooms. Tony spoke to us, then he gave us a few minutes to think, and after that told us to go outside and stand as if we were getting ready to receive a kick off. It was all designed to get us ready for the game and the occasion, and so our minds were focussed on the match and not the event itself. We then headed back to the hotel, had a meal, I lost more money on poker and then bed.

At no point in the build-up had I experienced any nerves about the final, and the morning of the game itself was no different. We had breakfast and then walked around the hotel. It had a golf course attached to it and all I really wanted to do was have a round. Apparently, Tiger Woods had broken the course record with something like twenty-two under in 2007 and I fancied having a go at beating it. I then went and got ready, had a shower, shave, brushed my teeth and went downstairs for a quick meeting. Once again Tony said a few words then he played a motivational video which had the Black Eyed Peas belting out. It gives me shivers down my spine thinking about that now.

It took about 25 minutes to get to Wembley on the coach and you could see the seriousness of what was going to happen. We had our game heads on and some of the lads were doing what they would if they were off to Saints, Wakefield, London wherever. There were jokes, others were playing music at two million decibels in their headphones. In my head I just kept repeating: 'don't play the occasion, play the game'. Too many people have played the occasion, had a shocker and never been again. So what if there are 80,000 there watching a game ... realistically what difference does it make?

We'd done what we had to do and prepared well so we had to put that into practice. Our lead up was perfect and we had done everything we could to make us play at our best. No stone had been unturned and all the other things, like pissing about with tickets, had all been sorted by the club. Simon Moran had done a cracking job with the hotels for us and our families and all we had to do was train and play. We were fully confident everything we had done would lead us into the game and if we could stick to the gameplan we had a very good chance.

The trip to Wembley was everything I dreamt of. As you wind your way through that shitty industrial estate you're hit with a sea of people banging on the coach and singing. It was like that 25 years ago too. And it was all Warrington fans. From the fist pumping to the banners this is what it was all about. I'd played at the Wolves for 13 years and seen a lot of heartache. This was our chance to pay them back.

Once you get through the crowds, you swing a sharp left and the bus has to negotiate the tiniest entrance known to man. That lightened the mood as we all watched the driver back up and inch through a tiny gap. Then it gets pretty surreal. From the hustle and bustle of outside you're now underneath the stadium and it's deadly quiet. It really is the last few minutes you have to yourself before you jump off the bus and the cameras are on you straightaway.

Dressing rooms are usually pretty quiet places until you are just getting ready to head out. The ones at Wembley are vast, and every player's need is looked after. Whilst we were getting our gear on and getting strapped up Tony was getting some of the finer points across, little bits of the gameplan and trying to keep us focused. On my right was Michael Monaghan and Chris Hicks was to my left. I always spoke to Monners before a match, just idle chit-chat really. Hicks was a bit of a weirdo anyway and was doing his own thing. Only kidding Spider!

The call then went for us to go out and warm up. Although the stadium was only a quarter full we soon got an idea of the atmosphere and what it was all about. It was a beautiful sunny day and looking around you could see what it meant to people and how big the occasion was going to be. But we had to keep our feet on the ground and focus on the warm up. You hear stories that the Wembley pitch saps it out of you as it is so big. It is the same size as everywhere else. It's the emotions that get you and that means you cramp up. We tried to take the emotion out of it and make sure we hydrated properly.

Once back in the dressing rooms there wasn't much time to do anything other than listen to Tony and then get the knock from the referee. It's a bit weird really, but normally I am sick before a game with nerves. It happens whether it is the first round against York or in the semi-final. In fact, after 400-plus games I don't think I have ever been as nervous in my life as I had been before that game against Wigan. I was shitting myself. But once I got to the final and got out into the tunnel I was really relaxed. It was like it didn't bother me in the slightest.

In the tunnel I was second in line, and next to me was Huddersfield's Keith Mason who was shouting: 'Just run at Briers, get him and we'll win the game.' I turned round and said: 'You wanna be careful Keith as we are coming straight for you ...' And in the end he didn't have the best of games. I often wonder whether he remembers that moment or if he was just so psyched up. It kind of backfired for him in a way.

I was so calm and it also helped that I had Reece, my son, with me as mascot. When we walked out on to the field he was taking it all in and was like: 'This is great dad.' He was buzzing! He was only young and perhaps he didn't really take in the magnitude of the occasion. He's a privileged little lad having done that and I thank the club for making it happen. He'll realise in years to come how lucky he is.

Once we had lined up and the firework smoke was beginning to clear I was reflecting on how far I had come. I wasn't nervous at all, we'd prepared well and trained well and I'd waited 13 years to be at Wembley. There's no way I was going to let nerves spoil the occasion. In the meeting on the Friday, Tony had had us in a circle and we each had to say what we were going to do on game day. Before the meeting, I told Tony I wanted to get the Lance Todd out of the day; not for selfish reasons, but because if I won it, it would mean 99.9 per cent that Warrington would win. He said keep it to yourself and I did. I knew what I wanted to do and wanted to prove to people I could do it.

The game itself started perfectly for us. We knew that if we kicked off, they would play towards our right hand side and kick through Brett Hodgson. And they did just that. The ball went through the motions and then Louie Anderson charged down the kick and a couple of plays later Richie Mathers went under the posts. That was a great start, there's not many times in your career you are in the zone, but I believe that day we were and the start put us in it. After Mathers' score, and his usual fist pumping because he was so fired up, Huddersfield almost hit back. They got into our end and Shaun Lunt plunged over, but was called back for a double movement. It was of course, but someone was looking down on us for sure and we got away with it. Within minutes though David Faiumu put on a step, hit Hodgson and Lunt scored to tie it up. There was a bit more pressure from them after that but we got the breakthrough again when Monners jumped out at dummy half, took on the line and went over.

We'd done a lot of work on Huddersfield and we knew their centre Paul Whatuira liked to come up and then move towards the middle when he was defending. We had a set move to beat this which basically had Benny Westwood running through, Mathers out of the back, and I would miss both and hit Bridge. The idea was to draw the centre on to Mathers and I would go across them both. It worked like a dream and Bridge had the simple act of getting it to Hicks who scored. We were in control then, but after we had a try disallowed Hodgson popped up and made it 18-10 at half time.

In the dressing room we reiterated what we needed to do. We were always two scores ahead and were pretty relaxed. Everything had gone to plan. We were calm but buzzing.

The second half began really tightly and was a bit of an arm-wrestle for 20 minutes. Then Monners made a break and hit Vinnie Anderson who made no mistake. He'd been playing at six on a number of occasions and was awesome that day. At 24-10 we were out of sight and although Bridgey missed a conversion and they scored a consolation, we never looked like losing from that point. But it wasn't safe until I kicked a drop goal at the death. I suppose we knew we had it in the bag but that one-pointer sealed it. It was more about me wanting a point at Wembley I reckon!

Monners won the Lance Todd, and after the match I had to explain to him what it was all about. He was made up with it, but when the hooter went I was only interested in going mental with my team-mates and celebrating. The elation was unbelievable and it rose from my boots and just came out. Everything I'd ever dreamt of as a kid had come true, and everyone was going mental at the same time – it was really surreal. I guess that's what happens when you're so elated and you're not used to it and you don't really know what to do. So I just basked in it with my team-mates and hugged anything that moved.

After a few bumbling interviews we all just wanted to get up the steps and pick up the cup. And just as I was celebrating Moz came over to me and said he wanted me to lift the trophy with him. I thought my time had passed and as I wasn't captain, it didn't really bother me. But when he said that I started crying and there's no way I will ever be able to repay him for that. It speaks volumes for the character of the bloke.

So what's it like? You know not many people have done it before you and it's difficult to put into words. You walk up 100 odd steps in your boots and you're proper knackered by the time you get to the top – I was looking for the lift to be honest.

You walk along the balcony and it's bloody high up for sure. Then Moz grabbed one side, I grabbed the other and it was total euphoria. We were stood there with this massive stadium in front of us and half of it going bananas. My first thought was I want more of this. 13 years of hurt, always the underachiever, and now we had done something. We made sure we took it all in and took our time too. It had taken us long enough to get there and we knew it might never come round again.

The lap of honour was very special. Try as you might you can't pick people out in the crowd but you can see faces. So much joy and happiness; kids, adults, people crying. It showed how much it meant to the supporters and I was so proud to be part of bringing that moment to them. It was for them. We were also lucky that our families found a way down to the tunnel and we had our pictures taken with them. I look at those pictures from time to time and they send a shiver down my spine. Success can become routine for some people but you should make the most of moments like this, whether your a player, or if you're a fan, or work behind the scenes, or are part of the coaching staff.

It took an age to get off the field and into the dressing room, but it was well worth it. Those times when it's just you and your mates are moments you cherish. We cracked up the team song, the clothes come off and we went proper mental and threw beer all over the place. I know the BBC come in and film those celebrations but I'm sure they'd need their extra zoom cameras to see everything! Once that was done we just wanted to get our gear together and get out on the piss. We ate upstairs but the bars were shut so we got on the coach, stopped off at the nearest offy and made the owner's day by clearing him out.

Simon Moran had sorted out the hotels before the trip and the families stayed at the Intercontinental on Park Lane. We were due to join them after the match but couldn't get through the crowds of fans who were banging on the coach and just loving what they had seen. When we got to the hotel it was an amazing place and Simon had really come through for us.

People might read this and say I am kissing his arse, but he is genuinely one of my mates and is an amazing bloke. There was a tab behind the bar and once we'd used it up, I called him and said it had finished. He said if I put a grand behind the bar, he'd see me right and true to his word he did.

Simon's waited so long for us to win something that he just wanted us all to have a good time and we did. After that grand went, we headed off to Tiger Tiger and they let us in there. The bouncers had seen us win on the telly and treated us like VIPs. We were taken off to our own special area, filled with champagne and we partied until the small hours. We fell out of the bar late and me, Woody and Vicky got on one of those rickshaws and I paid the driver a few quid so I could drive it. He was in the back and I was pedalling around on it. The hotel was about four miles away and I'd knocked off a couple of them for sure when I saw a massive hill coming up. Woody had been mithering me to have a go so I jumped off and said it was his turn. He leapt on and, pissed out of his head, sped up the road and hit the hill. We were laughing in the back as it took him about 10 minutes with his legs pumping away to get up it. As for the rickshaw driver, he was chuffed to bits as he earned about £60!

The next day was filled with more of the same. I stuffed as much breakfast down my neck as I could, jumped on the coach, filled the bus up with beers and then had the best trip home ever. By the time we hit Birmingham we pulled up at the services and had run out of beer. The lads jumped off the coach in search of a Burger King and I scoured the supporters' coaches for a few tins. I ended up getting six cases off a bunch of Saints fans and loaded up the coach and all the ice boxes. The lads got back on and I was sat on the back seat with my feet up and a tin in my hand. They were going mental looking for where I'd got it from and I simply pointed at some bin bags. Cue the boys jumping up and down and continuing the trip up the M6!

When we pulled into the Halliwell Jones Stadium to get on

an open top bus we were all pretty pissed and didn't really know what to expect. It was crazy. From there all the way through to the Golden Gates it was packed. They reckoned afterwards that 50,000 people turned out to see us, and at the Town Hall itself another 15,000. It was superb. That's when it all sank in really. We had a few interviews on the bus, a meal with the Mayor and a few beers and I thought 'this is what the town has been waiting for'. The boys went off to Stockton Heath to continue the party and I went home.

My party was done. In my younger days I partied longer and harder after a loss. Now, I'd won the cup and had a few scoops on the Saturday and Sunday and then went back home to the family. I guess it showed how I've changed. I would have enjoyed the trip with the lads, but I wanted to have some time with Vicky and the kids and enjoy it for what it was.

*****

Tony gave us a day off on the Monday and then called us back into training a day later to prepare for our trip to Hull KR. I can't say it was the best session ever but we wanted to end the league campaign on a high. We got dusted at Craven Park though and I think that was expected considering the highs of the Saturday before. We'd got the monkey off our backs and achieved something and I could have retired there and then a very happy man for sure. But I remember Kevin Sinfield saying when you get the winning bug and you've done it once, you want to do it again and again. And that's true.

Without that cup though in 2009, it would have been a shocking season for Warrington. We finished tenth in the league and that wasn't good enough. We weren't happy with where we finished and we were upset we hadn't been consistent enough to do better. Although there are only three trophies you can win, and we'd won one, the most important for me in the sport, expectations were high and we wanted and needed to do better.

But that was for 2010 and before that I organised a trip to

Tenerife for 20 of us. It was a bloody nightmare sorting out 20 flights and hotel rooms and I was pretty nervous about anything going wrong. It was for three days and it was mental. Nearly all the squad went and that made it special. In the hotel, we ended up buying all inclusive bands for 35 Euros for three days and after just three hours the manager cut them off and gave us half our money back. We'd drunk too much!

When I got home I went in for surgery on my shoulder as we suspected I had a tear of my labrum. I'd had my wrist and fingers done in the past but never had anything major. Before they put me to sleep I expected to come out with a normal sling on and be out of action for about three months. Groggily, I woke up and tried to move my shoulder and my arm was stuck out straight in front of me and I had a fucking big box under my arm. They asked me what I wanted to drink too so I asked for a pint of cider! Turns out I had three tears in my shoulder and a ligament had pulled a piece of bone off. Any shoulder operation is serious, but this one certainly was. It was horrible and bloody hurt for days afterwards.

I had to sleep on my back for two months in this sling, looking up and constantly on painkillers. It was a shocker and if I had to have another I would retire there and then!

I'd had problems with it for a few months and had needles to kill the pain so I could play, but I didn't realise it was so bad. Having needles is part and parcel of the job, even though I hate the bloody things. In 2012 I played with five injections for a bruise on my hip just to get me through. You do it for the team because you want to help your mates. A lot of players do it and fans don't see that. I would say the majority of players are carrying niggles here and there and sometimes the fans think you're playing shite when it's not the case – half your body is hanging off!

It took me a while to get through the rehab but I was ready for the 2010 season – the first full year with Tony Smith in charge. Pre-season was a lot more fun too as he was into more game type conditioning, rather than running and running. We'd do little games to get us ready and it was something different to the other ones I had been through. The hill sessions were still there of course and I still hated them. Tony also brought in a new conditioner in Chris Baron and he is excellent. Bubble knows his stuff. Tony lets him get on with his job and they work really well together as a result. Jimmy was still around too and he flogged us to death as was his style, but it was still an enjoyable pre-season. We went to Tenerife for pre-season and Joey Johns came over to coach us.

Expectation at the club was high that season as we were classed as big-spenders and we'd won a cup. The pressure was on. Fans always expect no matter what team you are in, but the realisation from the players that we could deliver was a totally different mindset … we now knew how to do it.

There was a lot of continuity on the field too. Just three players came in and three left. Paul Johnson had had some unlucky seasons with us through injury, Paul Rauhihi who retired and Steve Pickersgill who is a Warrington lad through and through so it was hard as anyone for him to leave. We brought in Ritchie Myler and Ryan Atkins – two young English players who were awesome signings, wanting to make their mark in the game. We also took a punt on David Solomona (Sol), who had been injured a lot. By the end of the season he'd paid us back in spades. On his game, there's things he can do that are like magic. We probably didn't get on before he came to Warrington as he was down my side and I always had to face up to him. I remember him and Stephen Kearney chasing me around the Millennium Stadium because I was winding them up and I always tell him he was a bully for that.

Ritchie was an interesting signing because he was a half-back. Although I hadn't signed a new contract by the time he came in I knew he was signing in 2009 and I took it as a challenge. I thought I had to up my game and I'd like to think he's learnt a lot from me since. I've always been someone who the lads could come to if they've needed some help and as I was now one of the senior team members, I was a mentor to the younger kids on the field.

As well as bringing in those three good players, we moved the club training facilities from Wilderspool to Padgate and the Chester University Campus there. We had our own purpose-built gym and it's probably the best facility in Super League. Everything is there for us to succeed and it has certainly helped move the team forward. We've come a long way since the crap facilities of the 90s. A gym is a gym though and whatever fancy equipment there is, I still don't fucking like them. A £10 million gym or £10, I hate them all, and that will never change.

Ironically, I have now done a PTE course through Fit UK, to help train people in the future. When I finish I'm not sure if I will ever go to the gym again. I've thought about this a little bit though and probably in a weird way I will look after myself more when I don't have to. It's when I am told to do something that I don't like doing it. It's the rogue in me perhaps. When I'm told I have to do this and that, it makes me not want to do it. When I don't have to do it, I'll do it probably! I think that's why my form has been better over the past few years. I've had conditioners who keep on hammering me in the weights room. Van der Velde was probably the first one who wanted to put weight on me and he tried making me do different stuff and it didn't work. Others wanted me to lift massive weights and it just isn't me. Bubble knows what I need to be doing to get on the field. I have to give credit to Tony for that, he's allowed Bubble to look after me in the gym and tailor my programme to what I need. It's all about maintenance more than than muscle. If he wants me to put 10kg on the bench, he knows it isn't going to happen. As a result it makes me work that little bit harder in the gym. Of course, if I needed to do those things to get on the field, I would, and when I'm out on the field I put in as much as I can.

So five years after I've retired I can't see myself ripped. You don't see many coaches ripped to fuck now do you? Let's put it one way. There is one thing I guarantee I won't do when I retire and that's another fucking hill session and that is a promise. I will be barking orders from the bottom. In fact, no, I won't even be at the hill. They are done and make me ill.

That season we got the consistency we craved. We had it in the league and in the cup and we finished third. The main thing was our defence was getting stronger and we squeezed the life out of teams. In the past, we could always score points, but conceded a lot. Only two teams had a better defence than us in 2010 and they were Wigan and the Giants. Unlike in the past, we had a good start beating London 58-0 and that got us on a roll. We ended up winning 20 games and missed out on second spot on goal difference.

At one point it looked like 2010 might have been my last season with Warrington. I was pretty close to Kevin Walters and he offered me an awesome deal to go over and play for Catalans. I love France ever since I played for Carcassonne when I was 18 and I was very close to agreeing a deal. There were a few issues though, one being they wanted me to go over there and then. That would have been tough although I don't know if they'd spoken to Warrington. There were also no English speaking schools in Perpignan and that was an even bigger stumbling block. My daughter was 12 and my lad six and it would have been a huge deal for them. But I still was interested and the money was excellent, as was the tax regime over there too. It would have set me up for life. As I was thinking about the deal we had a game in Hull and afterwards in the tunnel Simon Moran came over and offered me a deal there and then. As I have said before, when Warrington become interested in signing me back on, it doesn't take long for me to agree to it. We did the deal there and then, five minutes max. I didn't say I wanted this and that, Simon is a good judge of the value of his players and I trust him and trusted his judgement and that was it.

We played Catalans a couple of weeks later and I told Kevin I had signed and he wished me well. Back in 2009, Barrow came in for me at a similar time of the year and that was an amazing offer. It was top Super League wages! But, in the end,

I got out of jail as if I had joined them I would not have won the Challenge Cup. It was the same in 2010 with Catalans and in 2011 when Crusaders made me a great offer too. I dodged three bullets I suppose!

Sometimes I don't help myself though. During the year I was locked up for being drunk and disorderly and I had only myself to blame. I was on a golf trip with some friends, we teed off at 10am and we were drinking all day. I was in a real state and afterwards one of the lads said I took my shoe off and threw it at one of my mates, landing perfectly in his bowl of soup ... so they say anyway.

We went to Nantwich on the night and they wouldn't let me in the pub. I asked them what I had done and they said they would call the police if I didn't move. I said fine, go ahead then and they did. The police arrived out of nowhere, asked me to move and I walked up to a pizza shop with a cab rank next door. I must have been there two minutes when the police flew in and arrested me. My friend ended up persuading the police officer to let me go but I said go on arrest me, being a dickhead, and they did.

I remember waking up in the early morning in a cell in Whitchurch. I rang the bell in the cell and they asked me what I wanted. I asked them if I could leave but they refused so I asked for a blanket. They said they had given one to me as I'd already asked half an hour earlier. I must have been in a state. They were good to me in the end though and arranged a taxi for me later on. That cost me £80 to get home.

One thing that didn't change that year despite how successful we were becoming was our record to Saints. We led at Knowsley Road in the league and lost, and then at the Halliwell Benny Westwood missed a kick at the death that he would have kicked any other time. We have a laugh about his kicking as he only took it up two or three years earlier. As with anything with Benny, you have to know him to get his humour. If you have something like FIFA on the Xbox, he won't have played it. But he'll say 'It's easy, I'd probably beat all of you.' That was the same with his kicking. He missed that kick against Saints and one in the Challenge Cup Final in 2010 too. He also missed a kick against Hull in 2011 that would have beaten them. I tell him it's ok kicking when there's no pressure, but he's missed a few big ones now and he laughs it off. He knows we all love him.

I'd given up converting with the boot as I felt if someone was better than me I was more than happy for them to have a go. I just could never get used to kicking the Steeden ball. I know that sounds weird but when I heard Jonny Wilkinson say the ball's pressure is off, I can understand him. The way I kicked it I couldn't get it over. But now I have changed my style and I can bang them over from all over the place. I didn't miss it at first then did and now I'm easy either way. Brett Hodgson is a great kicker anyway – even with his skinny little legs.

Obviously a massive part of 2010 was the Challenge Cup and going all out to retain it – and our campaign started in the best way possible. I am a big believer in superstition if you haven't guessed already, and the last time we won the cup before 2009 was 35 years back and we played Featherstone. We did the same in 2009 and then we pulled them out of the hat again. I thought here we go, it's our time again. They gave us a real good fight but once our speed as full-time professionals got on top of them there was only ever going to be one winner.

Next out of the draw were Huddersfield – a match-up of the final and at their place too. A couple of weeks before the tie we'd beaten them and you could tell they were hell bent on revenge for what happened at Wembley. One thing is for sure, I am glad I am on the edges in games like this. Their forwards are always big and powerful, physical too and if we didn't show up they would walk all over us and leave us sore for days after. We have a right good rivalry with Huddersfield. We've played at the Millennium Stadium and that was a great tussle and we played in the cup final too. There was a pretty decent crowd on at the Galpharm, but to be honest it wouldn't have mattered who we played as we put 60 past them. It was one of those games. It didn't matter if it was Brisbane Broncos, we weren't losing that day and giving up our cup. Bridge scored three and we were once again in the zone. We worked hard for each other and to win like that was a sign of how we wanted to retain the trophy.

Next up in the semis were the Catalans who'd done us a couple of weeks back in Super League. In a way it could have put a seed of doubt in our minds, but it gave us the kick up the arse we needed. Our gameplan was to run at their right and take on Casey McGuire and Brent Sherwin. They'd ripped us apart down that side in the league fixture and the plan was to make those two do as much tackling as possible, then we'd see how good they were in attack. And like Feka Paleaaesina the year before, I wouldn't have liked to have been in their position. We never moved out of the left hand channel and when they pulled in we'd shift it and pull on the other side. Louis Anderson scored three tries down their side in the first half and we didn't see McGuire or Sherwin again in the second.

The gameplan was spot on in front of 12,000 Warrington fans at the Stobart Stadium and what made it even more special was that I scored in the same spot as I had done the year before – on my brother's birthday – and they say lightning doesn't strike twice. It was the same spot, same ground, same date. I have goose bumps thinking about it now and you can't tell me there's not something going on there! We put in an unbelievable effort that day and it all just came together. We won 54-12 and the Dragons couldn't live with us. It is harder to retain the cup the second time out, but we stepped up a gear when we needed to and it showed. We had a tougher qualification than in 2009 and proved in each round how much we wanted to get through and retain it.

We all knew what to expect in the build-up to the cup final but the excitement and hype around the town was twenty-fold. Simon Moran looked after us all again and we stayed in the same hotels as the year before. We didn't want to change our preparation in any way. This time round though, I made sure I took a video camera with me to capture the fans as we left and we had someone recording the day itself too. We were more prepared and as a result, I didn't feel the nerves again because I knew what was happening. I know what it is like to lose in a semi-final. To get to the final, half the work is done and you can enjoy the experience. We were relaxed and confident in what we had done and trained very well in the lead up. We prepared at Wasps rugby union with Shaun Edwards and the facilities were fantastic.

Everything was pretty much the same and I think that is why we thrashed Leeds. I think the emotion got to them. They had banked everything on the cup and it affected them on the field. We were led out by Tyler, Benny Westwood's little girl, and from minute one they couldn't handle us. It was like it was meant to be and we cruised to a 30-6 victory by following the gameplan. Although Leeds were full of experience, especially in winning Grand Finals, we were confident in what we wanted to do and comfortable in our surroundings and I think we shocked them in how slick we were.

Towards the back end of the match they had to drop out and I was getting ready if it came to me. Then over the tannoy it said I had won the Lance Todd Trophy. I was really shocked as Chris Hicks scored a hat-trick and I reckon it should have been him. I pointed at him as if to say that should be you and he smiled. But I'm glad it was me. It was something I had always dreamt of and dreams do come true.

Other than the Man of Steel, the Lance Todd is the most coveted personal trophy you can win. My goal the year before was to win it and this was no different. I thought I'd had a good game but I've never been interested in Man of the Match and things like that. As long as I can look myself in the mirror and say yeah, I've had a dig and the lads and coach are happy, then that will do me. I'm also not bothered what the press think after a match either, but on that occasion I was as they picked it with a record number of votes, so I loved them all very much!

At the end I took a backseat and let other people get on the photos and lift the cup. It was still an unbelievable feeling and we made sure Simon Moran lifted the trophy in front of the fans too. It was just a very special moment. Warrington are judged on trophies now, not league positions, and people have to take us seriously. Without being arrogant, we are something of a benchmark. People are chasing us. Saints, Wigan and Leeds have set the standards in the past and then recently, we've been doing it too. Hopefully another team can do what we've done by slowly working their way up the table and winning things. It would be excellent if six to eight clubs were in with a genuine shot of the title.

At the semi-final I was drug tested after a red hot day. I was so dehydrated I couldn't piss and it took five hours after the final whistle to do the business. They collared me again at Wembley, so once I'd done the celebrations and stepped one foot back in the tunnel, they pulled me straight into the testing room and I missed some of the good times in the dressing room. The boys did some singing and then went out on the field, had a beer and took it all in. I missed that as I had to have a piss and I was pretty upset.

I've been tested 20 times or so in my career and it is something you get used to, but there is a time and place to do it. If I was going to hide something, I could have done it on the lap of honour. If I was going to mask something, I could have done it then. I thought to test me at that point after we'd won the cup was unreasonable. It is a special time for a player and you may never get in that position again. The testing spoilt it.

Tony Smith mentioned it in the press conference after the game and said it was disgraceful. He wasn't having a go at the testers, but he was the system, as I had missed out on something special. They could have sat with me and enjoyed the celebrations too but we had to do it and I missed it all. It got a lot worse though because, as Tony said, I had been tested because some fucking idiot made a rumour up that I had been done for drugs. It was some stupid, jealous fan and they clearly didn't realise the problems they caused.

My kids go to school, people know who they are and they took a lot of stick they didn't deserve. I knew I was clean, but it bothered me that my family were getting hurt by it. I was 100 per cent clean but people were coming and asking me and my family.

The system is that you don't get your test back for six weeks, but if you are positive then you will be told in about ten days. The first I heard of it was when we played Saints in the play-offs. One of my mates phoned me up and asked me if I was ok. I was at Ryan Atkins' engagement party and someone phoned me up and said I'd been done. I hadn't a clue what they were talking about. I phoned the RFL to find out what was going on but they couldn't tell me as it was against their policy. They said if I had failed a test, I would be told in ten days. This phone call came after nearly two weeks. I was going to put that out but I thought balls to it, I am clean, why should I defend myself against some jealous keyboard warrior. It really didn't bother me, but the constant talk around my family was very annoying. Thankfully, it died away.

After the final we went to the hotel but changed venues and we were in a smaller room. All the beer was put on though and there was plenty of food. We were on a rooftop and when you went out you could see all over London. It was a superb setting. I took Adam Fogerty, aka Gorgeous George, as my guest and all the boys were buzzing because he was there. He can't drink so we got him pissed! Kasabian's manager was about too, as was Gary Barlow. The girls were all over him and he was a top bloke. David Solomona's dad came over from New Zealand and all the families from overseas were there too. It was a great do. After the party finished, we went back to Tiger Tiger and they recognised us. Cue more champagne, a VIP area and Steve Broomhead, our chairman, dancing on the table.

The Sunday was more of the same and the trip home was fun. Unless you have been on a team bus coming back from a final you can't really explain it. The music is banging out, there's beer everywhere and you're just letting yourselves go.

At Woolston once again there were even more fans out to greet us, and the Golden Gates were a sea of primrose and blue. More speeches, a feed with the Mayor and off the lads went to Stockton Heath … and I went home again!

We were back in training on the Tuesday and worked hard all week to make sure we got past London (away on Friday night – great fixture planning) and hit the play-offs in the best form. We faced Saints at Knowsley Road and in any other season we'd have beaten them that day. It was the final year of Knowsley Road and with all of the emotion tied to it they'd sneaked into home advantage with a great try from Kez (Keiron Cunningham) in the last minute the week before to give them a points difference of just two over us.

We were 8-0 up against Saints within minutes and it started raining. We were flying, buzzing, and thought it was our time, as we had done before. Keiron Cunningham was on fire and he wasn't going to let them get knocked out or go down on a whimper. He was an unbelievable player and did what he needed to and lifted them to the max. He killed us. It was a great game to be involved in, a massive atmosphere, but it was the Knowsley Road curse for us and we couldn't come back.

We had another chance though and that was a week later against Huddersfield and everyone expected us to win. But we'd run our race and perhaps the cup had done us. The highs had been so high that it was so hard to get back up for it. I'd love to try the challenge again though! We'd whimpered out of the play-offs once again but it was a cracking season for sure. We finished third which showed the consistency and won the cup. It was a progression from 2009 and we were determined to continue to improve.

*****

At the end of the year we decided as a squad to head to Magaluf. I was given the job of organising it and they all gave me their money to get a good holiday booked. Me and Matt King ended up in a tourists' shop for about six hours trying to find somewhere to go. Once again it was a great trip and we had a lot of fun.

To my way of thinking, if you have a testimonial you should sort the lads out with free beer. I treated the boys to a day at Ripon races with beer thrown in. On this trip Paul Wood was coming off his benefit and we said to him he should tip up some cash. We were in a nice bar on the front and he put his card behind the bar for a full session, it was unreal. We stung him massively for it and I'm sure he'll never trust me again ... only kidding Woody it was a great, if expensive, gesture.

One day we were in the bar on the beach and I walked into a shop nearby and got a pair of those bright orange Speedos, whacked them on and walked back. The boys were in fits!

After the tour I played for Wales once again. I'd met with Iestyn earlier in the year and he asked me to come out of retirement and play with the sole aim of winning the European Cup and getting into the Four Nations as a result. I was a little unsure as I had retired but they said I could coach with them when I finally finished with the game. I was sceptical about going back, especially as he also asked me to be captain too. In the end I went back because I felt I had a little unfinished business from the last time I was there and I wanted to see what I could do for the team.

It was a great competition. First up we played Scotland in Scotland and smashed them 60-22. That set us up then to face Ireland at home and they gave us a really tough game. I did my medial ligaments about 30 minutes into the first half and I knew I had done them pretty bad. But I strapped them up and managed to get out there in the second half and rely on adrenaline to get me through. I kicked a drop goal and in the end we needed it as we scraped through 31-30. It was a great camp to be involved in, we were more like a club team and there were no superstars – apart from Gareth Thomas of course! The first time I met him I just got sense of what an inspirational bloke he really is. He is a leader of men and when he speaks people listen. For the month he was with us someone followed him around, I think they were doing a book or film.

That got us to the final against France and no one gave us a chance. The French played all their games at home. I think someone wanted them to get to the Four Nations! I couldn't play of course as my knee was fucked. I tried running after keeping off it for the week leading up to the game but it gave way on me. I was devastated about that, it was really tough. I shed a few tears as I wanted to play and get us into the Four Nations.

The night before the final all the coaches went out and superstition dictated that we had to have a quiz. We all had to bring five questions to it and pop a tenner in. The pot was about 100 Euros and I ended up winning it and I have no idea how. Well I do, I was sneaking a look at my colleague's answers! I put the cash behind the bar and got blind drunk again. The next day I got up for dinner and the coaches were having theirs outside. Gareth Thomas was being interviewed for Welsh TV and I was watching him, turned round and full on butted the glass doors that were separating us. Everyone was in stitches.

At the match, Iestyn gave me the privilege of giving the boys their shirts and it meant the world to me for to do that. I wished them the best and they went on and won it! To win the European Cup was nearly as good as winning the Challenge Cup, especially as no one had given us a chance. And then I lifted the trophy too as Alfie wanted me to be involved in the celebrations. That night was a great party, some of the players were semi-pro and it was special for them. Mark Rowley, chairman of Wales Rugby League, put a free bar on and we ripped into it. We had a great time.

I should say that where we were staying in France was run by a young couple called Audrey and George and we got to know them very well. They looked after us like their own. They would get the best food for us and wash our kit. George was crazy and when he met me he thought I was a superstar. He played third division in France and I was his hero. I gave him my training gear and boots and when we left he was crying. When we won the cup he came into the dressing room in a shirt with press studs. After shouting at us all to watch, he ripped it open and it said: WALES ARE THE BEST. He then started singing with us in his French accent. They came out with us afterwards too.

The piss up continued late into the next day and as our flights were late, Iestyn said we could go into Albi town centre. We headed for an Irish bar and put on a tab. I ended up negotiating with Rowley and said we'd earned him a lot for Wales Rugby League and he needed to put his card behind the bar. He flatly refused but started to look curiously at this big fountain in the centre of the town. He said if I got naked and ran around the fountain he'd sort the tab out. Well, I didn't need asking twice – or once really. Clothes off, out in the middle of the centre, round the fountain and back in. As I came back to Mark, half the lads had stripped off and were doing the same!

Like I said we were all pretty close and that moment summed it up. It was one in, all in. All through the trip we didn't fine people for being late or fucking up, we drew balls out of a hat for a forfeit – the Cymru Court as we called it. As I'm about to reveal this I'm sure I will be selecting a number very soon. Number one would be eat dog food, two would be glasses drawn on your face in marker pen, three was wear women's clothes, four, get a Mohawk haircut – and about six lads had Mohawks for being late – and number five was walking down the centre of the coach with your kecks round your ankles having your arse slapped, and that hurt.

There were several others that I can't reveal or I will be pulling balls out for the next six years.

By the way, my knee was pretty bad – I had a grade two medial tear which kept me out for about six to eight weeks, and I ran round a fountain! I looked like a one-legged duck going round in circles.

11

Wire On the Map!

When you talk about perceptions then people's view of Warrington pretty much matched their view of me before those great 2009 and 2010 seasons. My wild days were behind me and as I began to realise that every game could be my last then my form got better too. In the past I was expected to carry the Warrington team, and if I didn't play well then nine times out of ten the Wolves didn't play well either, or that's what people said. I always grew with that pressure, but when Tony Smith came in and transformed the mentality of the team, my performances on the pitch were better too. In 2009 and 2010 I was playing some of the best rugby league of my life – certainly since that 'dark season' of 2006 – and we were winning things which made it more worthwhile too. I was settled off the field and enjoying every day of being a professional rugby league player.

People began to sit up and take notice of Warrington too as we weren't the side who promised much but failed to deliver anymore. Our fans expected us to be challenging on all fronts and the press and pundits were predicting big things too. To be honest, as a squad we'd gone from thinking we were also-rans into knowing we could compete. The mindset was totally different and heading into 2011 our focus was turning from being a side that could win cups, into a team that wanted to win every game and get to the Grand Final. We believed we could do it and that wasn't arrogance, it was just confidence.

Our goal at the beginning of the season was to go unbeaten as we had the personnel to do that. So after a really good pre-season we suffered a massive reality check as we lost to Huddersfield at the Magic Weekend. That goal was out of the window but at least we didn't need to worry about having that pressure! Then in the next game I got hauled off the field against Hull KR at home as I wasn't playing very well. I think that may have been the first time it happened to me in my career and was another reality check. I suppose I wasn't playing well enough to stay on but the team wasn't playing as well as it should and I was the fall guy. We didn't have the leaders on the field, and as a half-back I was expected to lead. I wasn't, so had no arguments with coming off.

On the sidelines it was a different way of watching the game. It was a learning process to see where we were going wrong, and after 20 or so minutes Tony threw me back on and I guided the team to a win. I could see what we needed to do and I made use of that when I got the chance. In the past I might have been a bit pissed off at what happened, but I took it as a challenge and knew I had to continue to learn. My maturity showed once again!

Our next match was against Saints at Widnes, their temporary home whilst their new stadium was being built. We'd had a real curse in Super League at Knowsley Road and I think a lot of our fans thought this could finally be our time. The lads thought so too, but we'd done that about 30 times before so I didn't get too excited. But the confidence was justified as we blitzed them off the park. I scored twice and we finally exorcised the hoodoo to beat them at last. Before the match I thought if we did it we would all be celebrating like we'd won a final, but once we did, it wasn't a relief or anything like that, it was just two points. That probably showed how far we'd come as a team even though inside I was leaping up and down like mad! The fans, outsiders and the media obviously made a massive thing about it, but to us it was a game we'd won, nothing special. We didn't go out and rip it up afterwards, it was two points, job done and let's move on. We were outstanding in that game and the scoreline flattered Saints but we then went on a real run. We beat Leeds, rested players at Wakefield and still dug out a win, then turned over London 82-6 and then faced Wigan.

I've been on the wrong end of a few thrashings like that, and whilst it's not good for the league for Harlequins to lose so heavily, someone had to do it and it was us. The Wigan match was tough though and the forwards knocked lumps out of each other. But the first time we got into their zone we scored and then did it the next time as well. We were lethal in attack and teams couldn't give us a chance or they would be punished.

Catalans were next up and they give us a bit of a pasting at our place. We had three or four disappointing games through the season and that was one of them. The next one was a week later as the Giants beat us for the second time. Once again, it was a shock to the system and perhaps one we needed so we could refocus and continue to push for the title. We beat Crusaders and Salford in our next two games and totally hammered them. There were games that season we knew we would win as soon as we got off the bus. Winning bred confidence and we would be buzzing heading into matches. I know from experience you can turn up at games and be beaten before you play. But our body language was so much better than the opposition's on some nights that you could sense we were going to win. It was scary really.

As the season went on the fans fed off that and came in their numbers whilst the media kept up the hype around us. We knew we needed to work hard on the training field and every player knew their role within the side. And when we suffered a defeat or a setback, we would regroup and bounce back.

It was one of my best seasons and the consistency in performance I had been seeking was starting to appear too. That's what got me through the year and I bagged 21 tries too which wasn't bad for someone who doesn't run with the ball and has no speed! Like I said, the days of staying out for days on end getting hammered were long gone; it was more about having confidence and having a great team around me. Monners was unbelievable and took the pressure off me. His own form meant I could be a little more off the cuff when I wanted and concentrate on defence too. There was also pressure in knowing my place wasn't safe. Players were coming into the club and in the back of my mind was the memory of being dropped after the game against Quins in '09 and earlier in the season at home to Hull KR. I needed to earn my place as I wouldn't get in on reputation. Players wanted to play in my position so I needed that consistency to earn my place and I did that. As a result, in April of that year I signed a further year's contract and there were a few other clubs sniffing about too.

After some more wins we beat Saints for only the second time at home in Super League. It was important to show the rest of the comp the victory earlier in the season wasn't a fluke, and show our fans we could do it. It was a real ding-dong of a match and we sneaked through at the end. I remember Royce Simmons saying Saints had been penalised a few times when they were on a roll down at our end. It's true that you never want the ref to give pens at that point as it stops the game when you have momentum. Saints ended up getting three in a row and I went and stood in front of the ref to ask why he was giving them. But I also knew it was giving my players a breather and on Saints' next set, with their energy deflated because of the stoppage, they knocked on.

I did something similar in 2012 when we beat Wigan at the DW Stadium. There wasn't much time to go and I noticed they were packing down on their 10 to stop the clock. I thought if I get in there they can't get to the 20-metre line where they should have packed down, and it would waste a few seconds. It worked and we won. Sometimes you need to do things like that to win a match. Call it experience, call it my natural charisma – I have no doubt that some people think it's cheating.

I would disagree with that. You've got to keep your eyes on the ball. I don't really talk to the refs as much as I used to do and when I do it looks worse than it is. I am quite expressive and it gets exaggerated by people because it is me. I have no right to talk to refs as I'm not captain, so when I do it becomes more obvious. I have a laugh with them more than anything! There's no point being a hot-headed player. I need to be calm, to get my team around and if I am angry then it is impossible for me to concentrate on the game.

I always remember Shane Cooper playing for Saints and a fight broke out on his 10-yard line. As fists were flying everywhere he picked up the ball and went the full length whilst his team-mates were brawling. That stuck in my mind; I would rather have a laugh and a joke than getting stuck into a fight! Fuck that, I couldn't fight my way out of a paper bag! But I do fancy fighting a keyboard warrior if they want to come out and meet me somewhere. Come and show your faces! Everyone knows where I live, come and meet me and see me. I might get battered a few times, but I would love to meet these people who hide behind anonymous names and abuse players. They are cowards. I can take constructive criticism, but once it gets personal, it is cowardliness.

I don't get drawn back too much on the negative shit anymore and I won't allow myself to be held back. The past is the past and everyone makes mistakes. No one is perfect, it is how you learn from your errors and I believe I have done that over the last few years. So in a game I will try and enjoy myself as it could be my last one. If you enjoy your rugby, you play well, and a team that is enjoying itself usually plays well. I am a competitor, I'm not there to make the numbers up and I want to win. You need to enjoy your time on the field as it could be your last game.

Some players and fans take the sport too seriously sometimes. We have to have an air of seriousness as we are role models, but we are also in the entertainment business. In a way it's like if you're a rock star – if you go out on stage and are flat, people won't enjoy it and you won't either. I like to go out, enjoy it and express my talent and strengths. That's what people want to see and enjoy. The problem is that rugby league has become a bit robotic and dour and it is difficult to be the entertainer in the current system. The fun is taken out of our game sometimes. But it works both ways – would we like to be amateur or semi-pro and still working? No. The sport is better professional and we have to be serious as it is our living. But people pay their money to be entertained and we need to remember that. As a club we want to entertain and enjoy it. And to beat Saints was good!

The morning after the first win, all the Thatto Heath junior teams were training down at Sherdley Park. I said to Bobby our kitman not to clean my kit as I wanted to wear it stinking at training. I jumped out of my car at Sherdley and ran round in my gear to show all the Thatto Heath kids, all eight teams. They'd given me enough stick over the years so I gave it back on a great lap of honour. I had about 100 kids chasing me around the fields and when they caught me, they jumped on me and gave me a pasting. It was good fun. When we beat Saints the second time, I did it again. But they turned it round in 2012 with pretty much every kid running around me at training. Swings and roundabouts!

Everyone knows I am a Saints fan and they will always be my second club. I am from St Helens and through and through a Saints lad, and I take my lad to the matches if Warrington are not playing. I do a lot of coaching in the town and presentations. I don't think it ever leaves you where you are from. It's just that I work for a different team and that team has been so good to me. Warrington are my first club. I left Saints in sad circumstances but I have a lot of good friends there, from the kitmen to the office staff and the players too. I'm not saying when I finish I will be a home and away fan once again, I'll be at Warrington cheering on the lads and my team-mates. But if they're not playing, I'll be at Saints … hoping Warrington turn them over.

Anyway, as we proceeded through the season we continued to play well and at midway we were flying and it was a great place to be around. There was a realisation that we could win matches and be up there with the best. We are good enough to match it with the top teams and took the step from being inconsistent to being consistent. We were scoring points for fun, in a great style, much like a top team but our defence was tight.

After we thrashed Keighley and Swinton in the fourth and fifth rounds of the Challenge Cup we pulled out Wigan at home in the next round. It was our first real test of how far we had come in a winner-takes-all game, but I didn't know if I would make it or not. I had torn my calf in the lead up to playing Castleford a few weeks before. In the Captain's Run the day before that match I jumped up to catch a Brett Hodgson cross kick and as I landed I felt it pop. I missed three weeks but came back for our trip to London. I played 80 minutes in that match and it felt great. Then, on the Monday before we took on Wigan, I was doing some light running and I felt it go again. I thought it might be cramp or the effects from the game, but knew deep down I'd torn it. My worst fears were in front of me and I would miss the cup quarter. I kept it quiet until just before kick-off, and then watched us lose. To be on the sidelines and not be able to help your team is frustrating, and it was magnified about 200 times because we couldn't retain the cup too. Wigan were the better team on the day, and as we know, they went on to win the comp.

A lot was said about Michael Maguire at Wigan and how he set them up. They were very regimental, had a system, and I dare say they didn't stray away from it. One thing you can say is that it worked! Not many people liked him or the way they played, but in the end, you're assessed on trophies and they won the Super League and the cup so he did pretty well. They were ruthless in the tackle and squeezed the life out of teams. I thought the way they would put three men in the tackle and have someone coming in to smash knees and ankles, was a terrible way to defend. They took it to the limit but they weren't breaking any rules so weren't cheating. The rule was wrong in the first place! They played by the rules and you can't blame them for that. They played to win and I suppose if that meant injuring someone on the way, well, that was that. I don't think it was right for the sportsmanship of the game though.

I am ok with Michael Maguire, he was a great coach over here but even though he's in South Sydney they don't adopt this style. It's because they aren't allowed to do it and the quicker we do the same, the better for our game. There's nothing worse than when you have both feet planted and someone comes in at your ankles. It is pretty much a coward's way to attack someone. It was effective, no one can argue with that, and the people at Wigan are probably not losing much sleep over it as they look at their medals. Wrestling is part of the game now though, and all teams do it. If you slow the ruck down and win the ruck, then you are more than likely to win matches. It does piss me off though. I like to be attacking and with the ball. On the flipside, it has to be done as the game would be too quick without it. But if you don't police it correctly the game suffers.

We probably need to look at the two referee system that the Aussies have. Tony Smith mentioned this to the RFL about 12 years ago and it is a sensible option. Some would argue that we don't have the refs but we do. The main experienced referee could be looking at the ruck and anything around it. Then you could have a junior referee who polices the ten yard area. I'm sure we have referees who can do that and they could then step up and we would have better referees. But again, have we got the balls to do it? I'm not sure. At the moment they have too much on their plates as the game is just too quick. I really do pity them. I wouldn't like to be in their shoes. If they get one thing wrong then it is blown out of all proportion.

We got back on track after the cup and unlike the previous two seasons we could solely concentrate on Super League which was a real goal at the beginning of the year. We secured the League Leaders Shield by beating Wigan after they won the cup.

We know how hard it is to back up after the Wembley experience, especially with the emotions around winning the cup. We got the Warriors on a good day and performed really well. We went to Hull after that and sealed the Shield. It is a massive effort to finish top of the pile after 27 rounds and it isn't celebrated enough. We knew how big an achievement it was. We had scored more than 1,000 points and had the best defence in the competition too to show how consistent we were. It was massive for us, and at the final whistle we celebrated on the pitch in fine style.

Our first tie in the play-offs was against Huddersfield. Tony Smith and Nathan Brown are good mates and it added a little more spice to it. We'd beaten them in the Challenge Cup Final and they'd turned us over in the play-offs at the end of the previous season. We'd then had some epic battles that season too and it made it a very tasty contest. From the first minute though, we were red hot and they couldn't live with us. We thrashed them 47-0 and had the chance to pick who we wanted in Club Call.

If you're not a rugby league fan and don't know what Club Call is, I'd suggest you hit the web. Basically, the highest ranked team coming out of the first round of the play-offs can pick one of the winners of the second round to face in the third. Yes, it's daft isn't it? It's a gimmick and gives nothing but motivation to the team that is picked. We were always going to pick the lowest ranked team, as every club has done since it was invented, and that was Leeds.

Once again we went into the match confident and following the win over Huddersfield we had every reason to be. But Leeds were too good on the night and edged us by two points. Kevin Sinfield was fantastic in that game and they showed us how to play play-off rugby. They were experienced in it, had done it for years, and they did what they needed to on the night. Every one of their players stood up, and we were off. In a way it was disappointing to lose like we did, but the season overall was massively successful when you look at our record.

We were upset to lose – gutted, devastated – but when you look back and reflect, especially after four nights on the beer afterwards. Yes, it's frustrating not being champions after finishing top. If you finish top of Super League, as a player you don't actually get anything for it. Bonuses are paid on where you finish after the play-offs, so finishing top of the table meant jack shit to us. Instead of us earning perhaps £15,000 each, we ended up with about £3,000. It's daft I suppose and you don't really realise what it's like until you are in that position.

*****

At the end of the season I had a few beers. I wanted to get away from the sport and have a couple of weeks off after the Grand Final. I couldn't go too wild and forget about rugby though as I was going to play in the Four Nations and it was something I was looking forward to. But I did end up in Magaluf on a mate's 40th and it was a great trip!

Playing in the Four Nations for Wales was a fantastic experience and I am pleased I came out of retirement to do it. We lost in every game but didn't let ourselves down. For our capabilities we played above our weight; from our kitmen to manager, players, fans, we all dug in. You have to when you are a small country, have scant resources and have limited players to choose from.

In our first game, we had England at 14-0 and they struggled to break us down when most people expected a walk over. In that game we faded after 50 minutes and that was bound to happen when we were playing against some of the best players in the world. Against New Zealand at Wembley we were down at half-time but showed great spirit in the second half.

After the match we went to Harrods and I was eyeing up a purse for Vicky. I saw one I thought she would like and asked the girl behind the counter how much it was. She said £850. I replied that I only wanted one not all of them, so I ended up getting her a bag instead. That was much cheaper. I'm not on that much money!

My final match in a Welsh shirt was against Australia in Wrexham and it couldn't have worked out any better. We were leading 8-0 at one point but went in losing at half-time. I looked around the changing rooms and being in there with your mates and knowing everyone has had a good dig doesn't get better than that. We ended up losing but the experience those lads will take into the World Cup is invaluable.

When I had previously retired from international rugby I was injured. I went back in 2010 to help Wales get into the Four Nations and we did that. It was a great team achievement. This time to finish on my terms against Australia in Wales was super and I couldn't have asked for much more. I got Jonathan Thurston's shirt after the match to go alongside Benji Marshall (New Zealand) and Bennie Westwood's from the tournament. I've had them framed and they're on my wall at home. When I finally do retire, I will look back on them all with great memories.

12

So Close ...

Learning the lessons of previous campaigns was really important if we were to be successful in all competitions. We had the pressure of being a big club, but also being a side that expected to win week in week out and play in finals. Whilst writing this chapter I wondered how best to describe it ... it was quite simple in the end. We felt we were ready to win a double, but had to prove it.

I played the majority of the 2012 season with two knackered Achilles tendons and did pretty well I thought, even though I was week to week with rehab to make sure I was fit enough to play. I didn't miss a game because of injury in the entire season and towards the back end of the year I felt I was on top of my game. In fact, the whole squad was. We again lifted the Challenge Cup and then finally got to Old Trafford, giving Saints a good hammering in their own back yard on the way. That felt good too.

Tony Smith used his entire squad and many people wondered if he was doing the right thing. We didn't mind being rested and swapped about as the lads that came in were expected to be as good as the pros they'd replaced. He used me well too. He made sure I was fresh for every game and I was. His man-management and the work of the physios made sure it happened.

A lot of people asked whether we adopted this approach because the league wasn't as important or if it was because our squad was good enough to be rotated. Finishing top wasn't our priority, that's true, and unlike the year before when we wanted to get the Shield, that didn't really matter. It was about form and playing well to finish in the hunt when we got the chance. And the squad did really well. The fringe players weren't expected to be a few feet behind the 'older' blokes, they had to do the same job. That gave them confidence and in the years to come Warrington will reap the benefit.

I know this makes it sound like we didn't mind not finishing top, or losing matches, but that's wrong. It wasn't our attitude to lose matches and if you look at the two games we lost heavily – London and Salford away – we wanted to win and put in a performance. Ok, one was before Wembley and the other before a semi-final, but we were pissed off at losing those games despite what came next. Fortunately, I didn't play in both games so I got over the defeats quickly ...

We believed our squad was good enough to beat anyone and the attitude was to win every game. There was no 'we can afford a loss here'. It annoys me in football when people say a draw is a good result – no it fucking isn't! You can't go into games wanting a draw; you have to go in to win every game. What comes after, you deal with, and it's a load of bollocks to have any other attitude.

Our success was based on a really settled squad. Trent Waterhouse came in and was a big presence in the team – and a big dopey bastard too. Some of the guys were wondering how we would replace Catalans-bound Louis Anderson but Trent came in and did more than that, even though he got some stick early on for his performances. He did a lot of the stuff no one really sees in matches and towards the back end of the year you could see how special he was. NRL players tend to struggle early on in their England careers – whether that is the weather, the fact that families have to settle in, the change in beer, I don't know. Probably a bit of everything.

We started off the year with a cracking pre-season trip to Australia where we played the Bunnies and had a good laugh. It was pretty hard with training every day and getting ready for Super League and the temperatures were in the 30s. You don't believe me when I say it was hard do you? Well it was, but even I wanted to train as I woke up next to the beach at Coogee Bay every day ... it was great.

On the way over I was sat on the plane with Paul Wood who is hardly the brightest player at the club. His head kept bobbing back and forward as he tried to stay awake and after they brought his food out he was inches away from a face full of grub. As it arrived I watched him place his false front tooth on the tray and then crash out, missing his meal. About an hour later he woke up and I said: 'Where's your tooth gone?' and as he found out they'd taken the plate, tray and tooth and thrown them away. He spent nearly the whole trip with a big gappy grin.

All the fun was dealt a really bitter blow though when David Solomona broke his leg in training. We were working hard in a fitness session and Sol took the ball in, stepped past Karl Fitzpatrick who nudged him with a tackle pad, and he went over. I was 30 metres away and I heard his leg crack and a lot of the boys heard the same. Sol was in agony, his leg was in a mess and the boys and physios did a great job to stabilise him and keep his spirits up until we could get him to the hospital.

To see someone go down like that, a team-mate and a friend, frightened the fuck out of me. It was very scary. David eventually got taken to hospital and as he went off, we all agreed to finish the session off. I think the mental toughness we showed that day to continue training was important. We were all close to Sol and it was tough to see that happen to him. We ripped in that day and I believe it changed our attitude while we were over there. We certainly used that to motivate us when things got tough. I remember early in the season at Huddersfield when Benny Harrison did his knee and I thought I'd broken my jaw, we used that Sol incident to say, look lads, look what we did that day. We were down to 14 players at half time, Sol's injury was mentioned and it spurred us on to a great win.

Sol was in hospital for two or three days and when he came out it was hard for him. We were training a lot so he stayed in the hotel and couldn't really be a part of what we were over there for. We ended up getting him a disabled scooter so he could tootle around with us. He loved being on it and even gave it some bling. He had a basket on the front with an iPod and speakers, and tunes were blasting in and out of the hotel. You'd hear some faint song in the distance then next thing you knew Sol would be flying in and giving us a laugh. It made the trip for us as he showed great character to remain so positive.

Sol couldn't get up the hills at Cronulla though and I very nearly didn't too. Most players have done sand dunes but these were different. It was steaming hot and there were miles of the fuckers. Ben Sammut, the ex Hull and Gateshead fullback took the session and said it would be a 500 metre run to the hills. It was actually about a mile there on soft sand in trainers, then up the hills! Until you've done it, it's difficult to explain how bad it really is. You weren't allowed to stop. Chris Bridge had just come back from a serious knee injury and this was one of his first sessions. I can still picture him being dragged up the dunes, spewing up whilst running. Looking back, perhaps it helped to get us through the year but I'm not jumping into my car to go to Ainsdale Beach.

We had a couple of belting nights out to freshen the legs. We went powerboating on the harbour and had a good drink. We also had a superb booze cruise around the harbour in Sydney which was excellent, leading us perfectly into the week when we faced South Sydney. We trained with them during the build-up, and to be honest we were a little wary of playing them as we didn't know where we would be as a team. We also heard they did a lot of long runs in pre-season training while we mainly do short ones and a lot of sprint work, but we surprised ourselves and blew them apart with our fitness. That fired us up for the match and I swear to you my old team-mate Matt King pulled a hamstring in that session because he knew how good we were going to be! Ha, only joking big man.

On gameday we raced to something like 26-0 up and they couldn't match us. We then made a few changes and edged a win 34-28. We showed what we could do and it also sent out a message that Super League wasn't that bad compared to the NRL.

After the game I met a few of the guys from back home who I hadn't seen for a few years – Ste G and his dad and brother who'd moved to Adelaide. I asked Tony if I could break the booze ban and have a few beers with them as I hadn't seen them in so long. He said it was fine and trusted me not to go overboard and not have too many. But me being a dickhead and not seeing my mates for years, I had too many and I should have known better. I didn't do anything which was overly wrong, but I was rooming with Rhys Evans who I needed to set an example to and I woke him up when I came in. I told him he needed to wake me up for 10am for rehab and then went to sleep not realising what I had done.

Next morning I did my session, but towards the end it got back to me that Rhys wasn't impressed. He'd gone downstairs and made his feelings known and it got back to Tony. The gaffer had words with me and said I had to come up with my own punishment by the time we got back home. I thought it through and decided it was only right to drop myself for the first game of the season. I had a standard to set and I'd crossed the boundaries. I'm not sure Tony thought I was going to do that. Perhaps he expected me to ask for a fine, but money isn't the most important thing in my life – playing rugby is – so it felt like a proper sacrifice to make. As for Rhys ... I looked after him for three weeks, let him use my phone and washed his clothes and he dobbed me in; only kidding mate. It was my fault though and another rare blemish on an impeccable record. Only a minor one I suppose considering my past.

Our first game of the season was away at Hull where we

notched up a draw despite having several chances to win the game, which would have been special after coming back from Australia. But I was down to play in the 20s the day before and was getting ready to be the oldest under 20s player in the history of the competition. I was actually looking forward to it. I was training with the 20s up on the 3G pitch and it was great. It brought me back down to earth. But the game was called off because of a frozen pitch and perhaps I dodged a bullet. I would have happily played though.

It was a fair old year in the end and despite those losses at Salford and London, it was business as usual. As a club we were consistent – we weren't as up and down as in previous years. We didn't suffer back-to-back losses because we learnt from our mistakes and put things right the week later. There wasn't any finger pointing after losses, we were honest as a group, but it was more about the team moving on. Wigan finished the year on top, but we entertained and expressed ourselves. We had different game plans for whatever situation came up and our defence was much keener which gave us a solid base to play rugby. I probably made more tackles than in any other season and it was something I had put my hand up to do. I ain't ever going to be the best tackler, but I've learnt to make the right decisions and hopefully it pays off. The Axe wasn't finished in 2012!

As I said before, we used Sol's injury throughout the year to get us through tough times. But in the match at Huddersfield I thought I was going to be out for a long time. I was taking a ball forward, stepped and Tommy Lee smashed me flush on the jaw. It didn't hurt at first but once the shock subsided the pain flew right into my ear. The tackle had hit me on the chin, pushed my teeth back and when I closed my mouth the pain was immense. I thought I was done for but bloody hell I got away with it.

I felt sorry for Tommy. I've coached him since he was very young and we are good mates, I'm friends with his parents too. He got a lot of stick for that tackle but I knew it wasn't on purpose. He's stayed at my house a few times and unless my breakfasts are crap, I know he wouldn't have done that on purpose. It was a mistimed tackle and rugby league is a pretty honest sport in any case. I said that at his RFL hearing and did the same when Saints' Paul Wellens caught me in their win over us at the HJ. I went to the RFL and said it wasn't intentional as he isn't that type of person, but they didn't listen and banned a player with no previous for a match. I thought that was a very odd decision.

Our run to the Challenge Cup Final was special and seemed to flow from one match to another. It was tough though as we had to go through Catalans at their place when it was red hot too. We had been there a month previous and got a good thumping, and prior to our cup meeting they were unbeaten at home. No one gave us a chance as we had Michael Monaghan and Moz both out. But, we have this knack of turning it on in the Challenge Cup and playing for each other and we did just that.

It was in the high twenties and humid but we drew on the experience from the Aussie trip and were awesome. We were on top of our game and kept them at arm's length throughout. You know when your name is on the cup and that was one of those games. We were massive underdogs and with the crowd screaming at us we pulled off a win. The changing room afterwards was something else. We were buzzing and knew we had done something special. It wasn't like the year before when we were winning by 60 and 70. They were good wins and it was a case of job done, but there were games in 2012 when we had to put a lot in and work extra hard for each other. That then made for a better changing room after the match and the traditional post match nude sing-along.

When we got back, Benny Westwood's car battery was flat so he banged on some jump leads and drove home. When he got there he decided to leave the engine running to boost the battery but at 11am the next day he remembered he'd left it running and went outside to find it had no petrol ... Brains!

That reminds me, in 2005 we had a weekend off and organised a party at Bennie Westwood's house in Warrington. It was a pretty manic night and by the time 3am came round there was only me and him left. We'd run out of beer so we decided we would head round to a few of the guy's houses, wake them up and get some beer.

Danny Lima was first up and we managed to grab a bottle of wine. That was a success so we continued on to Graham Appo's gaff. There was a lamp post next to a window so I shimmied up there, got through the bedroom window and landed on Graham and his missus. I was making some stumbled apologies and then Bennie came through too. Appo thought he was being robbed and went crazy. He had no beer though so we left him alone and ended up at Jon Clarke's house. Again, we were up the drainpipe but he heard us and thought we were burglars. He flew down the stairs and offered us out. As I jumped off the pipe I landed on him. He was screaming and not happy but in the end we sat up with him all night and had a good drink. It was good fun but really stupid.

We faced Huddersfield in the semi-finals and unlike matches between us in the past, they were on the decline and the game came at the wrong time. We won 33-6 although it was tougher than the scoreline suggested. That set us up for another Challenge Cup Final with Leeds Rhinos and another cracking game. In the two years we won the cup we had stayed in the same hotel and tried to keep the same routine but that changed as Leeds won the toss and got the pleasure of being the 'home side'. We stayed at a totally different place which was a little further out and it took a while to get to Wembley. But things like that only matter if you let them, and in the end we had been there before, knew how to play at the stadium, and ultimately that was the difference.

The turning point I suppose was when Kylie Leuluai hit Brett Hodgson and the ball came out and Brett Delaney scored only for the ref to give a knock-on. That just kicked us on even more but I thought we were always on top and deserved the win. We took it out and it was an amazing experience. To not win one for about 400 years and then lift the cup three times in four, well, that's special. People ask which one is the most special for me ... basically they all are. To win a cup, not many do, and to win three, that will do me!

Cup finals are usually played in balmy conditions but that was one of the wettest games ever. It was scarily wet. You could hear a bang, then one drop, and then you couldn't see 20 metres in front of you. The only thing I had in my head was Don Fox missing that kick in the 1968 Challenge Cup Final and Eddie Waring going 'He's missed it, the poor lad has missed it' ... I remember that from *101 Great Rugby League Tries*! I couldn't shift it out of my head and Sinny (Kevin Sinfield) was kicking us to death. We took a foothold though and won the day.

The after match celebrations were special as usual and I ended up with the cup in my hotel room. It was passed from pillar to post and our chairman Steve Broomhead was worried about it so I put it up there to keep it safe. Tony Smith wanted his picture taken with it so I ran up to the room to get it and Reece had put his massive Wolfie (our mascot) head on top of the cup, and on a chair facing the door. When I opened the door I shit myself. Little git!

It was a great day for the club and a great session too, so I decided to break with my tradition and go out with the lads around Stockton Heath. I went out with my Wembley t-shirt, shorts and flip-flops, didn't buy a beer all night, and then got home without my flip-flops and black feet. Great times!

We got into the play-offs and everyone was talking about how we could be the first club since Saints to win the double. We'd had our eyes on it all season and felt we had a great chance heading into the last few weekends. Our first playoff match was against Saints and although we trained really well during the week, they played their best game all year and gave us a thumping. But we had learned how to come back from defeat during the season and we did. Next up were Hull and they were on fire coming into the final eight and were dark horses for the trophy. Their line speed was rapid and we had to adapt, doing enough to set us up for the semi-final. And as soon as Wigan could choose between Leeds and us we always knew we would be off to Saints.

This time we made no mistake. We had learnt from our last meeting and dominated. For 30 minutes they looked like they could break through but we got a foothold just before half time and the momentum changed. From there they couldn't live with us and it was a good result. We played the percentage football a little more, not a lot of offloads, and were more controlled. We completed our sets, we played better and demonstrated we'd finally worked out how to win playoff games to set up a Grand Final with Leeds, who had shocked everyone by turning over Wigan.

I'm not a fan of the top eight system and I think it has outlasted itself. You are rewarding average teams with a shot at the title when realistically they don't deserve it. If you don't win half your games then can you really win the title? It's not good for the sport and it should be a top five or six for sure. I reckon my view is shared by many across the league.

Early in the season we found out that Bradford Bulls were in real financial trouble. They needed £500,000 to survive past the first week in April and then another £500,000 to secure their future. They managed to reach the first target by the first deadline of course as the rugby league community always pulls together in times like this. Some of the pledges to the club and offers of support were incredible, and it was amazing so much was raised so quickly.

But let's not beat about the bush on this one, it was a fucking disgrace the game allowed the Bulls to get as close as they did. Only six months before they announced they were in trouble they'd been given a licence for three years to be in Super League. Surely the Rugby Football League, their auditors or someone knew the situation? In any business you have to know your outgoings and incomings and someone clearly must have known. For it to happen again to another club, following on from Crusaders and Wakefield, means we are a laughing stock. How can it happen in the best league in our sport? It makes a joke of the franchise system.

What was scary about the situation is that they signed up Elliot Whitehead for five years about a week before the club announced they were in trouble. How can that be allowed when they must have known this was looming? Was it to get an asset on the books? The RFL clearly knew what was happening as they bought Odsal to effectively claim the club's main asset to pay a debt owed to them. So if that was the case then how could the Bulls have been given a Grade B licence? The situation stinks, especially when you consider the RFL didn't step in to help the Crusaders, Halifax or Leigh.

Bradford are a great club and headed our league for a long time. Everyone wants the best for them, but you have to ask how this can happen under licensing when you need to meet minimum standards. It made a laughing stock of our sport as not only had they got a licence, but this was a team that used to be one of the greatest in the league. It would have been a massive shame for them to go out with 12,000 plus crowds. I'm not a businessman but something must have been wrong there and it proved the franchise system had massive flaws.

I thought the players showed amazing resolve to do as well as they did, as did Mick Potter and his coaching staff who worked for nothing for most of the season. As a player there are opportunities to move away, but not knowing if your mortgage is going to be paid is very hard indeed. People think we can afford not to be paid for six months but that is bollocks. It's tough for some players, they're not like footballers and it must have been a very worrying time. But they turned in, cracked on and nearly made the play-offs but for a six point deduction.

It's a real shame as we have a great product. If we get the marketing right then it will be the best game in the world. But we have a natural tendency to do our game down. Every time we talk about our game being good, after a cracking match for example, then we always get a negative story. We announce the venues for the World Cup in 2013 but we don't announce where the final is going to be. Saints beat Leeds 46-6 a week after Royce Simmons was sacked and people go mental because the Rhinos' players dyed their hair for charity. After a match we will talk about disciplinary incidents instead of a great game. The players have forgotten about it so why can't some of the press? We shake hands and move on. Let's celebrate the game, its intensity, spirit and get it out there. Stuart Pearce was in our changing room for a match in 2012 and was in awe over what we went through. He loves his rugby and is gripped. We should be selling the game like that, not which player has hit someone else with a forearm.

It's a British trait isn't it? We want to focus on the negative and bag people when we should enjoy what we have seen – the effort and the skill. Players don't go out to hurt each other, they mistime stuff. If we have an incident in a game the commentators will bang on about it for 10 minutes. They could see blind passes, a great tackle and a chip over the top but still harp on about something that happened five minutes ago. We know rugby league hasn't got much money but we need to sort it and be proud of our game. We need a title sponsorship with money involved ... but no, we get a load of trucks with my face on! How's my ugly face going to sell anything?

Anyway, we approached our first Grand Final like any other game by training well and working hard for each other. When we lost in the first round we decided to go into 'camp' and stay in the Marriott Hotel in Manchester before our game with Hull. We then went to Liverpool and did the same before we took on Saints. It worked and so we did the same before the Grand Final too. It isn't like Wembley in terms of build up because it comes a week after you play the semi, but we trained well and were buzzing heading to Old Trafford. We didn't play well on the day though and deservedly lost. I can't say it anymore truthfully than that. Sinfield kicked well and I was utter shite.

Leeds did a job on us and it was a horrible feeling. From where we have come from to make the final was a real improvement. To win the double would have been dream world for the club and our fans. I was disappointed not to be able to do that for them. I didn't match my standards and I felt very lonely on the pitch.

I've been to three finals and won them so this was a different experience and I probably drank a lot more that night than after all the previous cup wins! I wasn't as blind drunk as I would have been in the past as I needed to feel the pain of losing to make sure I remembered it in crucial times the season after. In years gone by I would have hammered it for a few weeks too.

We were back into training on the Tuesday to watch the video of the loss – that was pretty tough – and then it was the traditional trip to Magaluf. It was another great few days and we met up with a few players from other clubs too. Chev Walker turned up, with his and Nick Scruton's stag do and ripped in. It will be my last one I think though; I was so rough on the plane that I thought if we crash now, I don't care.

On my return I went straight into camp with Wales as assistant coach for the Autumn International Series. It was good fun but really hard work. It was 7.30am starts and still up at 9pm doing videos with Damien Gibson. It was strange being a coach and not a player ... and tough not to be a player!

We put a decent performance in against France and were then hammered by England, but for me we shouldn't be playing England on that stage anyway. We'd like to compete but we aren't there yet and it's hard to ask some of the lads who are part-time to do that. To take on a full-time England squad isn't fair, yet it was a good experience for us. We got together for a full week and completed loads of fitness testing, and now the players know they have a scale of where they need to be in readiness for the World Cup. We set standards for Welsh Rugby League and four of that first team squad played in the under 18s too.

We should have played Fiji or Samoa, teams like that, and I

don't know what England got out of it. It didn't benefit anyone. It was on live TV and didn't really do our game any good. England's football team beat San Marino 5-0 but you wouldn't see them organising a comp against those guys would you? England Rugby Union wouldn't play Romania ... we need to think about what we are doing.

13

MY Great Britain

I firmly believe if I had been picked for Great Britain, I would have done a great job. I would have provided the team with something different and hopefully shown the rugby league world how proud I was to represent my country and prove my abilities. It wasn't to be for various reasons so I've done a lot of thinking and decided to come up with the 16 guys I would have loved to have played alongside me when I pulled on the jersey.

Full Back – Paul Wellens

His consistency is unbelievable and he rarely puts a foot wrong. He's a St Helens lad, like me, and is a good friend. You can always rely on him to do the right thing on the field.

Wingers – Jason Robinson and Anthony Sullivan

Was there a better finisher than Jason? I'm not sure. He was powerful and had pace to burn. I played against him about five or six times and he was almost impossible to mark. Sully was the Welsh flyer and if you got the ball to him he would finish it off. He had frightening pace.

Centres – Martin Gleeson and Paul Newlove

Glees had everything and made my job a lot easier! We had

a good understanding and I don't think anyone could match us when we were on form. He was untouchable. Newy was a complete player, a big strong centre and was a good as they came.

Half-backs – Lee Briers and Sean Long

I would have loved to have partnered with Sean Long; we would have buzzed off each other. We are similar in so many ways but totally different in others and I reckon that combination would have worked very well. I know people say you can't have two off the cuff players in the same team, but why not? We are both capable of guiding our teams around the park. It's a real shame I never got the chance to give it a go.

Props – Adrian Morley and Jamie Peacock

Moz would be in there for obvious reasons. He is a leader, an immense player and someone who never takes a backward step. Jamie Peacock in his prime was the same too. I know who I would have liked to have been with in the trenches.

Hooker – Keiron Cunningham

Simply the best player I have ever played against. He had unbelievable talent and every time we played against Saints, he was the reason why we got killed. He was way above anyone in that position.

Back Row – Ben Westwood and Chris Joynt

Ben would be on the right hand side. He is a machine of a player who was underrated in the past, but is now getting the recognition he deserves. Joynty was a leader and an exceptional player. He had a non-stop work ethic and was someone I looked up to when I was at Saints. I'll never forget that he stood up for me before Wembley in 1997 as that showed the true qualities of the man.

Loose Forward – Paul Sculthorpe

I'm torn between Andy Farrell and Scully, but I would choose the latter because I had played alongside him until he left for Saints. When he left Warrington I was gutted – but I was also happy as it kick-started his career and he went on to do everything in the game.

Subs – Andy Farrell, James Roby, Terry O'Connor and Gareth Hock

Had to put Andy in here for what I said above. He was a cracking player. James Roby is one of the best around and Tez was tough as old boots. He'd never take a stride back, did nothing fancy and was hard working. I also loved the way he got his head punched in by Gordon Tallis too. Gaz Hock could prop and go in the back row. He is ridiculously talented. When he has the ball he can attract two or three people and offload.

Coaches – Tony Smith, Iestyn Harris and Paul Cullen

14

Grand Finale ... Almost

At our play-off game at Langtree Park in 2012, I walked into our medical set up to get a rub and saw that our doctor had 13 needles lined up. This is what a number of our players were doing to simply get through such an important game and do their jobs. After the match, one of our players was also pissing blood. Our sport is tough and physical. A lot of fans slag players off during the game but they don't realise what they go through to play the game they love. These are injuries that will probably affect players for the rest of their lives.

I don't think players ever take to the field 100 per cent fit. There's always a little niggle, whether it is the pain in your shoulder from tackling or some other bump or bruise. The game is too brutal for you to be totally fresh each match. Players are hard as nails. Look how many injuries Paul Sculthorpe had and yet he came back time after time. On occasions he must have been in bits. I think the fans need to appreciate that before passing an opinion on how someone is playing.

In 2012, I had problems with my achilles and I went to see the best medical specialist there was for that type of injury. He told me I would never be 100 per cent fit and asked about my contract and how long I had left. I'd just signed for 2013 and he said I should just get through it and take the money. I had been thinking of retiring but it was quite striking to receive advice like that. He told me I would only ever be at 80 per cent and should play when I needed too. I couldn't just take the money and not give it my all though.

I have never been worried about my health after rugby until I had a neck problem in 2013. There are niggles I will take into my future life like I can't bend my fingers properly, but that's part and parcel of my trade. But the neck was serious and I thought I might be fucked for the rest of my life. I never wanted to retire injured, I wanted to go out my own way, but it almost pushed me to the brink.

In 2012, four games before the Grand Final, I took a whack and felt a slight pinch in my shoulder blade. I thought it was just a trapped nerve so had it massaged each day. It seemed to work and I would have a jab in the spot to get through a game. I didn't have a scan or anything like that as the massage and injections seemed to be doing the trick. Over pre-season it was fine, and then leading up to Bennie Westwood's testimonial match I did some contact training, went into a tackle and jarred my neck. The pain returned behind my shoulder blade and I thought the nerve might have been playing up again. But after we played Wigan two games into the season I got pins and needles down my left arm into my hands and fingers. At that point the physio said it wasn't a trapped nerve and it must be my neck.

I went for a scan this time, and as soon as I saw my specialist's face I could tell something was wrong. His facial expression said everything to me and I started to panic, fidget in my chair and feel hot. He was pretty stark with me. He said I had to stop playing straight away and it was lucky we had caught it in time as another big collision could have left me in trouble or in a wheelchair. I couldn't believe what was happening.

We agreed to leave it six weeks and if it hadn't settled down they would do a procedure. That would involve going into the back of my neck and fusing some of the vertebrae. That would get me through to the end of the season and then they would go through the front of my neck and take three discs out. It turned out I had two bulging discs leaning on my spinal cord and another one had prolapsed. It was in a pretty shit state. I was gutted and had no insurance for finishing injured because I never thought I would need it.

I was being told I couldn't play for six weeks, and then maybe if it didn't get better I would have an op to get through to the end of the season. I got a second opinion and they said I couldn't play for three months, and if it wasn't better then I would need the operation through the front of my neck and that would be it, career done. I'd gone from playing week in week out, to a six week injury, then to three months and possibly career over.

I was numb. Even though I had been planning to retire, once someone takes it away from you, on their terms, it is different. I broke down, was in tears and was shaking. The specialist was being tough with me; he had to be, as he was telling me the truth. He said it could be worse as I could have been in front of him in a wheelchair. That hit home because life isn't just about rugby is it?

To say I was in a dark place was an understatement. For the next two weeks ... well, I feel ashamed really because it was like I was going back to my past. I didn't care about rugby and neglected my family. I was being selfish: drinking, taking diazepam, sleepers and painkillers because my head wasn't right. I couldn't sleep and I didn't know what to do. Those prescription drugs stayed in my system, and when I had a couple of drinks on a weekend, I wouldn't have any control over myself. I'd wake up next day, look over to Vicky and she would say I was an idiot. I'd look at her and not realise what I had done because the pills had worked against the booze. I knew I had to get a grip because to have any chance of playing on I needed to sort my head out.

I went and saw Ben Stirling who is our Head Physiotherapist and talked about what I needed to do. Ben is a close friend and we set a few goals. I'd put a bit of weight on and my first target was to lose 20 per cent of my body fat. And you know what, for someone who doesn't like training I did it. I stopped drinking for twelve-and-a-half weeks and worked hard. Ben gave me freedom with when I had to do my rehab and we travelled up and down the country looking for techniques to get my neck stronger.

I had six needles in my neck to see if that could help. Only thing was, it was done in an operating theatre and I was awake through it! I was paralysed but it really was one of the best feelings I have ever had. I remember when I was in the theatre, you could see what was happening on the TV screens and I asked if they could put Sky on. I then asked them to let me have some extra as it was great stuff! We also went down to London to see a neck specialist who worked with Red Bull F1 and Mark Webber.

It was a long rehab process and because there were no symptoms of pain – just the pins and needles – it was hard to know if it was getting better. After a while that sensation started to get less, and ten weeks in we felt it was worth getting another scan. I was sat with Ben watching the specialist go over the results. He seemed to be taking ages but his body language was more positive this time. I had also pulled my calf running the kicking tee on for Brett Hodgson and the specialist was looking at that scan too. But I didn't care about that one at all as I just wanted to know about my neck. In the end, I couldn't wait any longer and I asked him outright, could I play. He looked up from the scan and really casually said 'Oh yeah, you can play'. It was a great feeling and Ben and I were in tears. It had been a long three months. I had given myself a good shot because I was disciplined.

From being given the all clear I couldn't play anyway as I had done my calf. It was only a pinhead tear but it kept me out for about four weeks. And when I came back from that I damaged my ankle ligaments and needed jabs in that too. All in all I spent about 16 weeks having injections, and when you get to my stage of your career, that is the last thing you need to be doing.

Thankfully, I came through it but it was really tough. There were times when I found it hard to get up in the morning and go through the training I needed to do. I love my sport and job but I was very close to jacking it in. I felt my body giving in but I had to meet the challenge head on. It was the first time I had really doubted myself and questioned if I was good enough to play. I felt a yard behind everybody, but that could have been because they'd had around 12 weeks playing which I'd missed. I thought I wasn't doing the team justice and they would pick up on it but maybe I was being paranoid. But it was a struggle and a battle to get myself ready to play.

I know that I will need the neck operation when I am finished, but for the time being it is 100 per cent ok to play. I will have a six inch scar at front of my neck and when it's over, I'll probably look like the cricketer, Gladstone Small.

*****

2013 was an odd season for me but one which will make me stronger as a player and a coach. We began the year with no new signings, and whilst that might not have pleased some of the fans, it was a big confidence boost for the players that remained. In the past we built from the top down with the likes of Nikau and Langar, but over recent years we have developed the team from within, which is something the successful clubs have done. Ben Currie came through in late 2012 and he was fantastic throughout the year, and if it wasn't for a bad illness he would have been pushing for a Grand Final spot. Rhys Evans was great too. He was unlucky with injuries but when he came in and played he showed us his quality. My understudy, Gareth O'Brien, also got vital experience out on loan which will stand him and the club in good stead going forward.

It also meant we naturally gelled and could approach the year looking to learn the lessons of the past. As a team we are a lot more composed than we used to be. We know how to close out games, but above all, each person in the squad has developed. Over the last couple of seasons it is really noticeable how grown up and mature we are. We do a lot off the field in the community and for charity and that never gets publicised, not that we want it to. Where we have come from is massive.

We were in good form all season but when it came to the semi-final of the Challenge Cup we just didn't turn up and play. It was gut-wrenching to lose to Hull FC as we usually turn in a good performance in the big games. It was devastating but we had to come back from that and focus our energies on getting to the Grand Final.

In our first play-off game against Leeds at the Halliwell Jones, I almost cost my side the chances of winning after I punched Carl Ablett. It had been building up for a couple of games. Carl is a real competitor and I'm sure part of his job is to get under my skin and that is what happened. He has given me a few sly digs in games gone by and before I snapped I'd got caught on the last when he'd put me to the ground and gave me a dig. I decided if that happened again I wouldn't take it any more. Later in the game he caught me on the jaw – intentional or not – and the referee didn't give anything. The red mist came down and I have to admit I don't remember much after that. It was totally out of character for me and I don't think it will happen again. Thankfully, I wasn't sent off and I didn't get banned.

Our semi-final saw us picking Huddersfield in Club Call, and as soon as that is done away with the better. It is a dogshit system, and I totally backed Tony Smith's stance in not wanting to be a part of it. Of course, we had to say who we were going to play and we went for the Giants because we had confidence in playing them; that and the fact games between Leeds and Wigan would normally see them knock ten bells of shit out of each other. In the end we were right to do that as we progressed to the final. Whoever you are going to pick will result in a tough match and it wasn't done to disrespect Huddersfield; we just had to choose someone.

We got through and the build up to the Grand Final with Wigan was excellent. We prepared well but things didn't go quite to plan for us in the match. We had a commanding lead but we lost Joel Monaghan, then they scored and it turned the game. If the Warriors' Blake Green had gone off the pitch when he was injured we probably would have won but he didn't and was excellent. In the second half we lost Stefan Ratchford too and I ended up at full back. I can't do much from there so we lost a pivot as a result too. The boys never gave in but when I was talking to them from full back, I could see they were just looking through me. They had run their blood to water and had nothing left. Ben Harrison was out too with what was close to a dislocated pelvis, and with no rotation in the forwards we were knackered. Wigan were too structured and we couldn't handle that. It was disappointing but it didn't feel as bad as the year before as the circumstances were different. Against Leeds we just didn't turn up.

The lads went out after the game, and when I said I felt a yard behind them earlier, I certainly did after the final. It took me two days to recover from being out, but to be honest, I didn't really want to go. I didn't feel I should be celebrating a Grand Final loss, especially considering the season I'd had. But we had a good drink and some of the lads wore some great fancy dress!

In the end I'd rather be in a final and lose than not be there at all. It is an experience and you have to suffer that pain and disappointment to get better. We'll learn from that and be back stronger. Losing is difficult but it's easier to take when you know you've had a good dig. It is tough and hard to overcome but it is what makes you hungrier for success.

We will learn and move on.

15

New Chances

That's my story for now but I know I have many more years to come when new chapters will be written. I thought it would be over in 2013, but I signed another year with Warrington and I'm going to go round again in 2014. The way the back end of my career is going you can certainly say it has been unpredictable, much like my life.

I'll take whatever is around the corner and face it head on. I have never planned too far ahead but now I'm in the latter stages of my playing career I'm certainly giving my future some thought. I've not planned a date for finishing playing but I certainly don't want to have to retire through injury. But in rugby league you are a long time retired and I want to bow out when I feel ready. I have spoken to a lot of people who have retired and they are right when they say you are a long time out of the game. They've told me you have to go on as long as you can. But I won't put my health at risk, it's not worth it. I want to be able to knock about with my kids and my grandkids and I don't want to be hampered for another 40 or 50 years and not be able to walk or carry them. Too many players have gone out like that and it must be soul destroying. My health must come first and my family too.

It will be tough; I will struggle when I do call it a day as it is all I have ever known. The wage drop will be another thing.

I haven't saved a lot of money and I live day by day. Whether that means I struggle when I finish, then I will have to take that. It will mean I will have to work hard to provide for my family and I know that will be another challenge.

Above all, I know I will miss the buzz. My team-mates, scoring tries, setting them up and getting smashed in the tackle … well, I won't miss that one. But I get a real buzz from setting up tries for my team and seeing a move that has taken weeks and weeks of training and preparation come off. That camaraderie is special.

Having been part of such a close team for many years I can't see how it won't be difficult not to be involved. There are so many different personalities in a team and we have a great laugh. They are my extended family. There's no way on earth I could have worked in an office and had the same craic I've enjoyed over my career. How am I going to fill that? I have promised myself I will turn out for Thatto Heath Crusaders and play with my mates when I have finished. If my body is willing I will definitely do that. I owe it to rugby and to the club and to have a few guest appearances would be awesome!

I know I won't have the same buzz coaching but I have started on that pathway with Wales and Warrington. I have done a few sessions and enjoyed them but I can't get involved as much as I would like. I'm still a player and I want to take part in drills. I've done a few attacking sessions and I want to run in, take the ball and spin a pass. When I finally pack in I don't know if I will be able to stop myself still getting in the mix.

I have been involved in the game all my life and been a professional for nearly 20 years. If I am honest I couldn't have ever expected this. I haven't looked after my body, like the so-called true professionals. I've never been the strongest of people and I have never planned year by year or month by month, rather it has been day to day – I am more into short term goals. But for somebody who has partied all his life and not trained hard and hasn't looked after his body, by the time I have finished I will have played more than 450 games in my career – and that's not too bad for someone who has supposedly pissed his life away. I know there are players who have been model professionals and not got that far. Maybe it's fate, maybe it's how my body is set up. I have no regrets though.

Over the years I have grown up and would love to jump in a time machine and talk to the young Lee Briers. I'd tell him to enjoy every minute of it because it goes fucking quick. I can still remember the day I started and it does seem like yesterday. I have no doubt the young kids don't realise how quick it will be over and they need to plan. It took Mark Forster to tell me it would be over quickly, and I'm here now and it isn't far away. You need to make the best of every opportunity.

Of course, with hindsight I would have done a few things differently. I would have worked harder at school for a start. I would have done the odd thing differently in my rugby career too. But I don't have any real regrets. There's no point living life with regrets is there? I have loved every minute and it has been a hell of a time.

I hope people read this book and the stories go some way towards people understanding me. I didn't write it to change people's minds as I know you guys will have your own opinions. I'm not looking for sympathy either. I'm here to get my story across, and above all I want my kids to know what I've done and I hope they are proud of me and what I have achieved. I'd be a liar if I said I hadn't partied and pissed a lot of money up the wall, I have. There is a lot of pressure in sport and maybe those pressures got to me at times. But there are no made up tales in this book – the stories are all true.

A lot of you will only see Lee Briers the rugby player, whereas my friends and family see the other side. I hope this book gives an insight into that part of my life. People will see I'm not an angel, it's not in my personality to be one, but I haven't done too badly along the way.

My family are important to me and have turned out to be

everything I expected. My son, Reece, is definitely mini-me. He's sport mad and when I watch him play on the field, or in the front garden, it is like I have been cloned. It's scary as he is exactly like I was as a kid. He isn't out and away from the house like I was at four-years-old, but taking that away he is like me. If there's a ball about, he's got it and is banging it about the place. It's great. Sophie is a wonderful girl and has grown up ridiculously quick. She gives me attitude and has plenty of tempers, but then I was the same! I either ignore them or snap back. But, like every good daughter she knows how far she can push me and she is good at it too – just like I was with my family. She'll take me to the edge and let go, whereas with Reece I can tell him he's not playing sport anymore and he's daddy's little boy again! I love them both to bits

I still pinch myself knowing I have a 16-year-old daugther and a 10-year-old lad. Sometimes I think I am still young and without a care in the world. That was my problem a while back; I didn't understand what being grown up was all about. When you're living your dream you're in the bubble – training, drinking when you can – and you're untouchable. You're still that kid on the local park with a nicked Mitre Multiplex. My life was training, coaching a local amateur team and having eight pints on the Tuesday, I'd then train Thursday and have another four or five. I couldn't live like that forever so I cut myself off from it. It took 10 or 11 years for me to realise it but that's what I did – I didn't train with my mates and the local open age side. Now I am coaching the kids and there aren't too many of those asking me to head out for a pint afterwards.

Thatto Heath Crusaders are a massive part of my life and I will continue to put something back for as long as I can. It's great seeing Reece at a good club and watching him improve each week. Like me, he isn't the bravest player but his skill is immense. He can spin out of tackles – like Robbie Paul in his prime – and he can pass off the left and right. He was kicking the ball over the goals at Warrington at the age of four too. He won't be a forward though and he's so laid back it's like his head is on the floor. He's very much like his Uncle Craig (Hall) in that respect. He can play football too and at some point he'll probably have to make a decision between football, rugby or golf! Sophie is sporty too. She is a really good gymnast and can run a fair bit. She doesn't do anything with it, but I would support her with whatever she chooses.

I took Reece down to Thatto Heath when he was five and I had no intention of getting involved. He was coached under Mike and Steve Kilgannon and they were great for him. After a couple of years Steve left and they asked me to help out. It has been great ever since and I love watching the kids develop. The style of rugby league they play is unbelievable. Some teams will just have big lads who they get the ball to and they walk over for a try. But we have a rule that the kids have to pass. That means they develop teamwork and a good skill set. They give me and Mike a lot of cheek too – it's like looking at 20-odd little Lee Briers' from years back! You tell them something and next thing you know a huge pile of mud is flying past your head.

The under-nines section has burgeoned since we were there. We were doing well and everyone wanted to come down and train with us. That meant we had 27 players and had to play with nine in the first half, another nine in the second and nine on rotation. That wasn't fair really, so we split the age group into two teams meaning they have eight coaches for 27 players! That's like a private school! I have also used my sponsorship with Optimum to help them out. Pete Moran from the firm kits them out if I wear some branded stuff on the field. I could take money for that, but don't and we get kits and tracksuits for the kids. To see their faces when they get new gear is superb.

In three years we've lost just two games, even though we coach them to go out and have fun. The whole environment is based on them enjoying our great sport. If I play for Warrington on a Friday or Saturday, after Thatto Heath's games on a Sunday me and Mike, John McGiven, Paul Bolen, Ste Connolly, Dave Reed, Shaun McMahon and all their families will stay and socialise afterwards. It is a good club and that atmosphere makes it work. Mike Denning does a great job as chairman as does Tracy who runs everything from the teams to charity events. She is brilliant; everyone should have a Tracy! I didn't have a set up like that as a kid coming through Saints Crusaders and it's a great base for the players of the future to develop – including girls as the team coached by Geoff Alford is excellent. Please come down and see us, you'll be most welcome.

Like I said, once training is done I head home or to Thatto Heath and I can switch off from the pressures of being a pro. Luckily enough, my two great kids and wonderful missus help me do that. We have a lot of fun together. I have no doubt they think I am a lazy bastard, which I am, but I live for them and they are all I live for. Family is very important and I have the best!

My mum and dad mean the world to me and Stephen, Julie, David and Brian are the best siblings I could have hoped for.

Stephen is my eldest brother and when he was younger had a missus called Karen. They had a daughter, Danielle, and it must be 16 years since I last saw her. We've shared the odd glance when we've been out and about but we aren't as close as a niece and uncle should be. Sadly, the same happened with his second partner too. They had Megan and we don't see much of her either. It's a shame for him as he's done it hard, not seeing his kids, and it would be great if we could all catch up.

My sister Julie is married to Gary and he's been like a brother to me. We are very close and he shares my passion for Liverpool FC. Every Christmas I get a mate round and we take on Gary and his son Jordan in a snooker match. There's a trophy up for grabs too and it's very competitive. Holly is their eldest and she is an unbelievable niece. She's so kind and has looked after Sophie and Reece since they were born. Jordan is a little younger and he's sport mad like his dad. He's getting to that size now when he's after all my gear. Every time he is round at our house he's asking for boots and trainers. It's good to help him out as he's a really nice young lad who will grow up to be a top man.

David is married to Debbie and we get on really well. I always remember that she would do my artwork when I was young to get me out of the way. When she and David would babysit they would offer to do my homework as long as I went upstairs. That was a great way of getting it done! David would also say: 'Lee, it's cowboy time' and I never understood what he meant. I later found out it was ten to ten and that would be the sign to go to bed.

Their daughter Toni is my second oldest niece and is a wonderful girl who has grown up so quickly. She has also just had a little son. She's a stewardess and is great to be around. Her brother Craig was a great footballer when he was younger and I mentioned him earlier in the book. He would score 60 goals a season for Bold and signed on with Blackpool. But they let him go when he was 16 and that was tough as he'd lost contact with most of his mates from Bold. Now he's at college and is working hard on a different path.

Vicky's family – her mum Christine, David, Donna and Craig, have been great as have her grandparents George and Hilda. I would have loved to have met mine and it's sad that I don't have that. But Vicky's family have more than helped. Hopefully, with our extended family, we have the tools for our kids to be successful and if I can help them on the way, then life really is complete.

I have done some pretty amazing things in my career. I have won three Challenge Cups, a Lance Todd Trophy and played in amazing places like South Africa and Australia. It really has been everything I dreamt of. The three Challenge Cup Finals at Wembley will of course be my stand-out moments. People always ask what a final is like and it's true when they say it goes in a blur. I made sure, especially the second time round, that I took it all in and I can still remember every single minute. That will live with me forever. It took a long time to get there but it was well worth it. I wasn't dwelling on it never happening; I wanted it to happen, but when you've been to three semi-finals and lost, then it would have been easy to think it would never go my way. But it did and the rest is history. Success is based on medals and cups which is unfair as there are only so many you can win. If you're not in a top side then you haven't got much chance of winning anything – as I found out for the first 13 or so years of my career. There are legends who will never experience what I have, and that's a shame.

Over the years my sport has changed so much and since I started in 1997 I reckon it has evolved three or four times. I'm not here to blow my own trumpet but I have had to reinvent myself at least twice. For someone who has supposedly pissed everything up the wall, ate shit and didn't train, I must have done something right! But the game has changed massively and you only have to see the athletes on the field today, and like you I'm stood in awe of some of the people I play with and against.

I really do think the game can go from strength to strength, but we need someone with imagination to take it forward. I would think that more than 75 per cent of players haven't got faith in the current system, and that needs to change. We are moving in the right direction; we have a fantastic game, but we must exploit it.

Rugby league is in a better state than when I broke on to the scene in 1997 and it won't take massive changes, just tweaks, but someone needs to stand up and make those decisions. We know there isn't any more money, we know we can't double the salary cap, but there are things we can do. As much as we talk about a European game, we are a northern sport. Catalans are strong, but we are a northern based league and the quicker we come to terms with that, the more we can build from within instead of looking to outposts, even though I love the Crusaders' teams and what they stand for.

I know promotion and relegation is a topic on everyone's lips and it could be coming true at the time of writing. I'm not sure how it could and would work in the modern system we have now. In the past teams have come up and then immediately have gone back down. There isn't the money or the player base to go out and recruit if a Championship team came up. In soccer if you get promoted you have thousands of players to choose from – it's not like that in rugby league. It's hard on Leigh, Halifax, Featherstone, Whitehaven and Workington as they are all good clubs who have been around for donkey's years. Unless you have a new stadium and are in the right financial state, you aren't getting in I suppose, but there are teams in Super League who don't have that.

I do think we miss the drama of relegation and promotion though. People like to enjoy those moments of extreme elation – and the media can latch on to stuff like that. But if your club has no chance of competing in the top flight then what's the point? We do need something for the lower teams to latch on to though. At present, you have clubs who won't finish in the top eight with more than half a season to go. What is the point? We probably need a comp to keep those teams interested too. It's all up in the air and that's why rugby league is pretty complex at the moment. Thinking about it, I would have the top half and bottom half of Super League play-off in separate competitions.

So what else haven't I told you? I'm not a big lover of music but like going to gigs. I've unashamedly watched Take That a number of times. Oasis at the Etihad were amazing, as were the Kings of Leon. I also tried to play the guitar once, but with plates and screws in my fingers I couldn't get my brain to direct them correctly. That's the same with computer games – I can't get both thumbs to work in unison. I'm also a shit cook.

Alongside my cup medals I also proudly won the St Helens Pairs Dominoes in 2005 with Saints' kitman Alan Clarke. Our deadly duo beat 90 other pairs to lift the cup and we bagged £120 each. Alan put the trophy behind the bar at the Boars Head but one of the regulars pinched it and brought it back a year later! He was upset but it served him right for saying I could lift the cup as it would be the only one I would see!

When I'm 60, if I live that long, I want to be reading this on a beach somewhere, in a nice hut the kids have built for me and Vicky out of their millions. Sophie will be a lawyer earning big bucks and Reece a pro-golfer or footballer. I will be his caddy or agent.

After that, well, I just want to be known as someone who was entertaining, a little unpredictable and who always played with a smile on his face. If people remember that, with a pint in their hands, then that'll do me.

Tributes

When you're putting a book together, many of the characters of the subject's past proffer their words of wisdom. Ours was no different! Although we wanted the book to be in Lee's words, we spoke to a number of people about Lee's career and what makes him tick as a person.

Below are just a few of the many stories and we apologise if we've omitted some belters!

Clive Griffiths, Wales Rugby League Coach in 2000

He's a nutcase when he's had a few as you well know! Who isn't? But Lee is wicked and funny as well. Back in the 2000 World Cup, we'd run Australia very close in the semi-final at Huddersfield. The bookies gave us 60 points start! Well, Lee played a blinder and was one of our men of the match. After a long, tiring World Cup campaign, we all returned to the Holiday Inn team hotel at Runcorn after the post-match reception. The lads understandably let their hair down! As the night progressed well beyond midnight, Lee decided to turn the reception area into a one man nudist colony. He sat there drinking wearing just his Welsh tie. He then decided to jump on anybody in our party who looked away for a split second – I remember ending up in a heap with him on the reception floor when my chair tipped over as he launched himself at me. The hotel staff just ignored him in the end as it was priceless. I should have asked for the security footage to blackmail him. People returning to the hotel in the early hours were treated to a real show!

One of the best lads I've had the pleasure to coach. He always gave me and Wales RL 100 per cent – why do you think Iestyn Harris was so keen to get him out of retirement? Why he failed to play for GB on a regular basis still mystifies me. Top guy, great memories. He still does the business and the Wolves are a 'different' outfit when he doesn't play for them.

Alan Hunte, St Helens and Warrington

I first met Lee when doing my very first presentation evening at the then UGB Crusaders back in 1989. I was with Gary Connolly and we decided to take turns presenting to the different age groups. It was all very new to both me and Gary but we were both pleased as punch thinking we were kind of big deals handing out all the trophies. How wrong could I have been as the biggest star of the night was a certain young Lee Briers.

Lee would have been 10 or 11 then and he walked back and forth from the stage with a swagger neither Gary nor I could match. He cleaned up at the awards winning everything available, and even commented on how they wouldn't let him play up an age group otherwise he would have won all their trophies too. You couldn't help but laugh as for all his confidence you could just tell that this little lad would have no problem backing it up.

Five years later I got the opportunity to see how he did back it up. It was the pre-season of 1994/95 and back then Saints trained at Ruskin Drive. As always the training was tough but Eric Hughes, coach at the time, always finished every training session with small sided games and I got to see Lee play. Wow ... here was this 16-year-old kid ordering round seasoned pros and internationals, and quite frankly taking the mickey out of the opposition in general and a certain club captain and GB scrum half. All the lads knew then he was going to be something special and he certainly didn't let us down on that prediction.

From a personal point of view I was pretty close to Lee travelling a lot to training together in my time at Warrington. I couldn't have had a better laugh because however hard training was or the opposition in games, Lee just looked forward and got excited about playing and you could see the look then as a pro that he had that the very first time I met him. Cheeky, confident and with a pure love of the game written all over his face; it was contagious and was just so much fun playing with the guy and sometimes he even made you look better than you were.

Simon Moran, Owner, Warrington Wolves

Lee has been a tremendous player for the club and has been with the Wolves through thick and thin. I have no doubt he has had a lot of opportunities to move on but I am glad he decided to stay with us, which is testament to his loyalty. Thankfully, over the last two or three seasons he has experienced the highs to repay that commitment to the club. Everyone knows Lee is a joker in the pack, but he is great to deal with. He has always given his best on the field and when he finishes, he will be an all-time legend of the Wolves. But there's a couple more years in him yet.

Chris Baron, Head of Strength and Conditioning, Warrington Wolves

I have been working with Lee for the last couple of years and in terms of his career I have probably seen the best bits. To prepare for a game he does just enough to get through. He ticks the boxes to get himself on the pitch and it seems to do the trick. To be honest though, I would have liked to have had him when he was a bit younger as I could have done something with that lovely frame of his – especially that foraging rat running style.

It's always fun seeing him get ready to do a big hills session in pre-season. He'll be putting his trainers on ready to go and he'll be talking to everyone about it – almost talking himself up to take it on. He'll ask how many reps and then by the time the session starts, it has gone through the squad like Chinese whispers and were doing double. He is a bundle of frenetic energy and has anxiety attacks at the thought of doing it and he's almost sick before he gets up the first hill. Afterwards, he will call me up from a lay-by throwing up and saying he's seeing stars ... that's the greatness of the man really!

I have to chase him up to get him to do things but he always does what is asked of him. At this moment in his life he isn't looking to become the next Usain Bolt, it's about him doing enough to keep that rugby brain ticking over and keeping him on the pitch. Saying that, over the last couple of years we've given him the nickname of the 'Axe' because of all the tackling he is doing. He's up to about six or seven good shots now in a season. Smithy [Tony Smith] shows it in video sessions and I think Lee secretly likes it on the sly. People say he's been lucky with injuries. Is that because he's someone who avoids being injured or someone who doesn't get hit?

I'm being harsh of course. Lee is far ahead of anyone on the pitch and leaps and bounds ahead in his head. He's never been caught when he's intercepted and we know he isn't the fastest on the field – that shows he processes the game quicker than most. He does enough to make sure he can continue that. Although I haven't known him long, the years of being excessive have clearly gone and he's more of a family, darts and dominoes man down the local now. I know some people haven't got a good word to say about him, but if you take him to amateur clubs outside Warrington, he gets nothing but praise afterwards. He does everything he can for them and will put himself out. I help out with England and in the dressing room before our Four Nations game against Wales, the coaching staff said expect the unexpected and that is Lee all over.

He is good person and will do anything for you and I wish him all the luck in the future.

Graeme Swann, England Cricketer.

I've always been a fan of Lee Briers. Firstly, he plays for the greatest team in the kingdom of rugby league, the mighty Warrington Wolves, and secondly he is the best player to hail from these shores in a generation. I once referred to him on Twitter as 'the Lionel Messi of Super League', and I didn't get many people disagreeing with me (apart from a few irate St Helens fans who questioned my parentage and sexual orientation). My thinking was that both are small, quick and very tough to tackle.

Many people ask why I support the Wolves. My mum's side of the family hail from Bewsey, and so it was from an early age that Granddad would sit me down and explain the rules of this strange northern game that Jonathan Davies had switched to. I loved it from the word go and still watch whenever I get the chance nowadays, and there's nothing I like more than watching Lee kick, pass and tackle his way to another famous Warrington victory.

For the record, my tweets were: 'Another good win for Warrington tonight. They are the Barcelona of Super League.' Then 'Lee Briers=Lionel Messi. Small, quick, great on the ball and hard to tackle' and finally 'Yes I know Briers didn't play tonight, just love winding up St Helens fans. There's only one Saints in rugby, and that's Northampton'.

Shaun McRae, St Helens Head Coach 1996-98

When I first saw Lee it was clear he had exceptional talent and would make it as a professional rugby league player. He had all the skills and a great ability to read the game – all at a young age. He played a number of games for us but the difficulty we had was an offer came in from Warrington, with a lot of money, and his personal terms were going to be increased too. He was also playing behind Bobby Goulding and it made good business sense to accept it. It also was a good personal decision for him to make. Lee was ready to play Super League week in week out and I couldn't offer that to him as Bobby was at his peak. Lee excelled when Bobby was out of the side but it was always going to be hard to maintain that with Bobby at the club. I think looking back now his decision was the right one and he has gone on to have a stellar career.

He has been able to control games almost single-handedly at times and he has adapted to the changes in Super League over the years. I fully believe longevity is the hallmark of a player and Lee has succeeded in the game because of what he did as a young player and how he has learnt to acclimatise and adapt to any changes.

I reckon as you get older and you know your time may be coming to an end you get a fear of failure. You're not as agile and quick and you come up against stronger, bigger and more mobile players. I think players who excel in the back end of their careers say I want to go out on my terms and almost play every game like it is their last. Lee has that. His approach to the game and training has changed and is culminating in that longevity.

He has always been a successful player. I know people measure success by trophies but that is only one form of success. I think if you look at a rugby league player, they are very much like those who make an Olympic final or swim a personal best. They couldn't have performed any better. He's had wonderful accolades when he hasn't won anything but lately has reaped the rewards of surviving in the game and improving and striving to be better. That means he has all the hallmarks of a champion player.

Off the field he's shy and not one of those who outwardly expresses himself. He likes his privacy. Any game he has played in when I have coached the opposition he has come over to shake my hand and have a chat for a few minutes. That's the type of guy you get with Lee. He has matured from the 17-year-old that hit the scene.

Even though I was only with him for a short space of time in terms of coaching, I am very proud of him and delighted to be a part of his career. He is a credit to the game of rugby league, himself and his family and I can't speak highly enough of him.

Paul Cullen, Head Coach, Warrington Wolves 2002-08

Creativity and vision are skills that are very difficult for any coach to instil into a player who hasn't already worked out for himself, that looking, feeling and listening are as vital as running, lifting weights and hitting opponents as hard as they possibly can in defence. Lee Briers has the ability not only to see a play four phases before it is attempted, but to create the opportunity to facilitate it.

I'm sure his schoolboy midfield soccer skills opened his eyes and his mind to the importance of space and time and never being caught on the ball or giving it away cheaply because he hadn't positioned himself correctly. And at 10 stone wet through he couldn't afford to be clattered on a regular basis.

I always used to use small sided one/two touch soccer games as part of our warm ups advancing to left foot passes only. It was hysterical to watch rugby players literally falling over their own feet when taken out of their traditional training methods comfort zones, (especially the Aussies and Kiwis). Lee would run around like a big kid, thinking he was Stevie Gerrard organising everyone and stroking passes from midfield. That's where he was in his element, having fun, thinking fast, playing in a time zone that was minutes in front of his team-mates. Training without a ball was tedious for Lee, with a ball he ran harder and played faster than anyone.

Andrew Johns was the master of the play before the play. Lee Briers understood this method as well as anyone I've seen or worked with.

Playing professional rugby league is like playing chess in a car crash. Thinking while exhausted and being physically assaulted is not as easy as those who sit on the other side of the safety barrier think it is. It takes a certain type of individual to be able to not only manage these difficulties but to thrive on it.

Lee developed these skills over the years as his career progressed, he accepted that if he couldn't outfight his bigger opponents or outrace the faster ones, he could certainly outthink them.

My experience tells me that players who are classed as visionaries or instinctive geniuses have simply worked out how to process all the relevant information far more quickly than all others which allows them to make better decisions.

Rugby league essentially is moving your 13 players into a position to out move 13 of theirs. It was a pleasure to watch Lee don his dinner suit and orchestrate his players without a finger being laid on him. Never afraid to make contact when it was required and never afraid to square up to anyone who was taking liberties either.

His partnership with Martin Gleeson formed an attacking edge that was unrivalled for skill and guile, even though in a team that was not quite ready to take the next step up to glory. I'm sure Lee will remember with great pleasure the combinations he had with the legendary Alan Langar and briefly Andrew Johns, but I'll wager his time playing alongside Nathan Wood, a diamond of a bloke, a maverick and equally as daring in his views on life and sport, will be up there with his best memories of his career.

To be able to enjoy your work is a privilege in life that most people don't get to experience. To jump out of bed with a smile on your face, anticipating the fun and challenges that the day is about to bring, is extraordinary. Lee Briers provided that environment in bucketfuls; the good days outweighed the bad. His talent was recognised by all the coaches that went before me in Lee's time at Warrington and all those after. His drop goal to beat Leeds in Warrington's first ever play-off win in 2006 and his drop goal to beat Hull Kingston Rovers in the Challenge Cup quarter final that paved the way to Warrington's 2009 Challenge Cup were special moments that ended years of frustration. Simply examples of Lee's ability to think and plan when others couldn't.

I hope and trust that Lee matures into a coach and he has the ability to pass on his knowledge to help our creative players of the future. Mistakes made have to be lessons learnt because if not, they will be rendered worthless and the talent we have had the pleasure to watch will be lost to the next generation.

Andy Wilson, The Guardian

'Yeah, belting.' Lee Briers had just completed his international career with a memorable cameo for Wales against Australia at the Racecourse Ground, and been congratulated by Darren Lockyer and Tim Sheens, among many others. He nearly fell off his chair when he joined Iestyn Harris, a former half-back partner turned coach, for his farewell press conference. Not because he was overwhelmed, or surprised in any way. Just a bit clumsy.

After confirming how much he'd enjoyed those last 80 minutes against the men in Green and Gold, in which he rolled back the years to that unforgettable World Cup semi-final at Huddersfield 11 autumns earlier, he praised the efforts of the young Welsh forwards for 'knocking the Aussies around a bit', stressed the importance of maintaining momentum ahead of the 2013 World Cup – and then admitted he wasn't too bothered what happened in the following weekend's Four Nations Final, which he would be watching, he told us, with a beer in his hand.

Briers, always so watchable on the field, has become increasingly good value off it, growing into a role as elder statesman at Warrington since the arrival of Tony Smith, who had been widely expected to usher him quickly towards the exit – but instead proved the catalyst for a glorious Indian summer.

Dry statistics could never capture his impact on British rugby league, and Warrington in particular, over the last 15 years, but they are pretty startling nonetheless. His position so high up Warrington's all-time try-scoring chart is arguably the most remarkable for a scheming half-back who has set up so many for others – although at least a couple of dozen of his own scores have surely been poached through the interceptions in which he has always specialised.

All this for a St Helens lad who ended up in Cheshire by accident, snapped up for £65,000 by Darryl van der Velde in April 1997 after helping his hometown club to their second consecutive Challenge Cup Final at Wembley during the suspension of Bobbie Goulding – only to lose his place as soon as Goulding had served his ban. Warrington needed a half-back, and had a bit of cash to play with, after selling Harris to Leeds.

'I signed on the Friday and made my debut at St Helens on the Sunday,' he reflected from Tenerife during an interview for the *Forty20 Magazine* article on which this tribute was based – doubtless that story will be expanded elsewhere here. That debut was a chastening taste of the punishment that Briers was to endure from Saints over the next 14 summers, as the Wolves conceded 60 points, and he failed to convert any of their four tries. He therefore opened his Warrington account the following weekend in a home win against Paris – in which he kicked a first drop goal.

There was a narrow home defeat by Saints later in the season, and the Red V stayed on top, barring one memorable and misleading night at Wilderspool the week before the 2001 Challenge Cup Final, until 2011. 'The better we got, the worse it got, because they kept doing us in the last minute,' Briers reflected with the monkey finally off his back. 'For the first five or six years it was a no contest really. But from about 2005 or 2006, we started getting pretty close – but never close enough. That was heartbreaking, and it did become a burden, if I'm honest. It affected all of us, and definitely me.'

All that changed in 2011, but by that stage Briers had found fulfilment with two Wembley wins against Huddersfield and Leeds, and the Lance Todd Trophy in the second of them. It meant that by the time he finally tasted victory against Saints for the first time in a decade, on neutral territory in Widnes early in the season, he felt strangely underwhelmed. 'In olden days it would have been "This is it, let's go and celebrate",' he added. 'But the way we've come on as a team and a squad, it was a bit sombre really. Just another two points, we've done that now, who's next?'

The masterplan was for the Wolves to convert their cup success into Super League domination, and for most of last year they were on track. They finished top of the table, sealing the League Leaders Shield with a home win against Wigan in which Briers provided one of the highlights of the season with his long, slow walk to accept a ticking off from the referee Richard Silverwood with comically exaggerated respect. 'Oh yes, sir, of course, sir.'

I've always thought there's something vaguely lupine about Briers, certainly in later years, without ever quite working out exactly which character he reminded me of. It finally twigged in thinking about that *Forty20* piece – Wile E. Coyote, with all manner of unlikely Acme devices failing to secure victory over St Helens, before Super League's Roadrunners finally copped it in 2011.

There are a couple more points I think are worth noting here about Briers. The first is the influence of another Australian on his reinvention in recent years – Andrew Johns, with whom he struck up an immediate rapport when he arrived at Warrington for that memorable cameo late in 2005. 'The other lads thought I was stalking him, behaving like a fan who was after his autograph, but I wanted to take the chance to learn all I could,' reflected Lee.

He also stresses the importance of other high-pedigree team-mates such as Adrian Morley, Matt King, Michael Monaghan and many more in helping him to shine in recent years, but it is the Odd Couple he has formed with Smith that has provided one of the more surprising and uplifting Super League stories.

'I dare say I've been rejuvenated under him,' Briers said in a *Guardian* interview before that Lance Todd winning performance against Leeds in 2010. 'He's an astute coach and he knows how to handle his players. I know the general view was that him coming in would mean me going out. But we had a good, honest meeting, put our thoughts across. I think we've been good for each other.'

'Lee's got a bit more about him than your average half-back,' Smith responded. 'He's that bit more canny, that bit more scheming. Sometimes you've got to tell him to wind his neck in, because he does like a chat. But he can talk sense – I trust his judgement.'

Smith has also consistently refused to wonder, as so many others have done, about how many more Great Britain caps Briers could and should have earned. 'People live their lives as they see fit at the time,' he told me before Wembley 2010. 'You ask Lee and he's had a great life, and a terrific career. I wouldn't disagree when people say if he'd gone down a different track he'd have been a far better player. But it's really down to him whether he thinks he could have been the Great Britain half-back.'

'What's the point?' was the Briers response – at least until this autobiography appeared. 'I've not done bad.'

Nobby (Brian Noble)

'Surely it should be Lee Briers for Great Britain!' – I remember vividly the campaign that Sky Sports commentator Eddie Hemmings championed when Lee was in a particular vein of form for Warrington in 2004/2005 and I was the national coach!

Let me say right from the onset I am a Lee Briers fan. In an era when we tend to be dominated by sports scientists and technical and tactical prowess, I can easily champion Lee as one of the artists of our game. Erm ... probably not the kind of artists some of you were thinking of; I am talking about the art of rugby league, and giving Lee the credit he deserves as being one of the most influential players of our time. A player that can change a game on a whim of a kick or 'breeze' on the subtlety of a deft pass. He truly is a game breaker and vital to success of his beloved Warrington. I suppose one of the question marks against Lee would be his temperament and his professionalism. He's certainly answered that question over the past few years, culminating in both his and Warrington's successes. His leadership qualities have come to the fore and his obvious importance to the Warrington 'team' ethic is there for all to see.

Now Lee, I can hear you asking the question, 'What about the GB spot?' Well if I were coaching now, I would surely be tempted, I think your sublime kicking game is a must at the highest level, and I confess to loving the 'cheeky' side to your game. I know you're a good fella too; I remember 'fronting' up to a meeting with you and Paul Cullen, when the 'LB for GB' campaign was in full flow outlining agreed goals and challenges to get you into that team. And if I'm not mistaken a couple of injuries put paid to that.

You've been a thorn in any team I've coached. On your day, you can win a game single-handedly, not many players can claim that. Coaching and playing is as much an art as a science and you are a rugby artist!

Andrew Johns, Newcastle Knights, Warrington Wolves, Australia

Around the late 90s I'd watched Lee Briers play footy on the TV but hadn't seen him play live.

The first time I got the opportunity to do that was in the Rugby League World Cup in 2000 when Wales played Australia in the semi-final. Australia were expected to win the game by 50 points but that night Lee Briers played half a game of the purest and most talented rugby league I have ever seen. He played Brad Fittler off the park.

At one stage Wales were 20-8 up, and although Australia went on to win the game comfortably Wales really gave them a shock because of that superb performance from Lee Briers.

I was blown away by his talent and wondered why he never went on to play for Great Britain, especially when sometimes they lacked that little bit of polish in the halves. If Lee had gone on to play more games for GB he would have gone down as one of the all time great half-backs.

I don't know why he never played more games at the highest level, perhaps it was the larrikin streak in there, but I would have him right up there with the best players in Australia. He is up there with Laurie Daley, Brad Fittler and Darren Lockyer; with the elite half-backs because his skill and talent is so high.

It was always an ambition of mine to play in England and

when I came over to play a cameo for Warrington I had a great time. I got the chance to play in three matches and in those games I was blown away with how talented Lee was. One area of his game that stood out was his left to right pass and the combination he had Martin Gleeson. Both were unbelievable and his passing game was probably the best I had ever played with.

I enjoyed my time at Warrington and enjoyed his company too. He is a great man, strong leader, and good to be around. He has that natural trait too which means players will gravitate towards him and follow him. He is one of those players who has that gift for leading.

I know he is planning to coach the youngsters at Warrington when he has retired and I have no doubt his skill, talent and leadership will be passed on and he will have another successful career after his playing days.

Although we live in different parts of the world we still remain in touch and I hold him as a dear friend. Good luck mate.

Appendix: Lee Briers Record

Club and International Statistics

Team	Year	Apps	Subs	Tries	Goals	Drop	Points
St Helens	1997	6	-	1	24	-	52
Warrington	1997	22	-	4	45	6	112
	1998	22	-	4	49	5	119
	1999	32	1	6	83	6	196
	2000	23	9	17	93	1	255
	2001	25	2	12	86	4	224
	2002	28	-	9	75	11	197
	2003	15	-	7	64	4	160
	2004	23	-	7	83	2	196
	2005	23	-	6	28	2	82
	2006	30	-	10	114	9	277
	2007	26	-	12	93	5	239
	2008	26	-	9	26	1	89
	2009	23	1	10	2	4	48
	2010	23	-	10	35	4	114
	2011	25	-	21	35	4	158
	2012	27	-	4	29	3	77
	2013	18	1	6	8	3	43
Swinton	2013	1	-	1	-	-	4
GB (Test)	2001	1	-	1	1	-	6
Lancs	2001-02	1	1	-	-	-	-
GB (non-Test)	2006	1	-	-	5	-	10
Wales	1998-02, 2005-07, 2010-11	23	-	9	29	6	100
Rep Totals		*26*	*1*	*10*	*35*	*6*	*116*
Club Totals		*418*	*14*	*156*	*972*	*74*	*2642*
Grand Totals		*444*	*15*	*166*	*1007*	*80*	*2758*

Hat Tricks

27/02/2000	York	Wilderspool	Challenge Cup 4th Rd
11/03/2001	Villeneuve	Wilderspool	Challenge Cup Q/F
01/04/2001	Bradford	McAlpine Stadium	Challenge Cup S/F
27/07/2007	Hull KR	Craven Park	Super League
20/05/2011	Swinton	Halliwell Jones	Challenge Cup 5th Rd

Goals in a Match

16	20/05/2011	Swinton	Halliwell Jones	Challenge Cup 5th Rd
14	27/02/2000	York	Wilderspool	Challenge Cup 4th Rd
10	17/04/2006	Castleford Tigers	The Jungle	Super League
9	13/07/2003	London Broncos	Wilderspool	Super League
9	08/07/2007	Huddersfield	Galpharm	Super League
8	03/05/1999	Sheffield Eagles	Wilderspool	Super League
8	01/08/1999	Hull	Wilderspool	Super League
8	05/03/2000	London Broncos	Wilderspool	Super League
8	06/05/2006	Catalans Dragons	Perpignan	Super League
8	22/07/2007	Hull KR	Craven Park	Super League

Points in a Match

44	20/05/2011	Swinton	Halliwell Jones	Challenge Cup 5th Rd
40	27/02/2000	York Wasps	Wilderspool	Challenge Cup 4th Rd
24	17/04/2006	Castleford Tigers	The Jungle	Super League
28	22/07/2007	Hull KR	Craven Park	Super League
26	13/07/2003	London Broncos	Wilderspool	Super League
23	01/06/2001	Wigan	Wilderspool	Super League

Drop Goals in a Match

| 5 | 25/05/2002 | Halifax | The Shay | Super League |
| 4 | 10/03/2006 | Wigan | JJB Stadium | Super League |